DIMENSIONS OF MANPOWER POLICY: PROGRAMS AND RESEARCH

DIMENSIONS OF MANPOWER POLICY: PROGRAMS & RESEARCH

A VOLUME COMMEMORATING THE TWENTIETH ANNIVERSARY OF THE W. E. UPJOHN INSTITUTE FOR EMPLOYMENT RESEARCH

Edited by Sar A. Levitan & Irving H. Siegel

The Johns Hopkins Press, Baltimore, Maryland

INTRODUCTION

This volume commemorates completion of the first two decades of service of The W. E. Upjohn Institute for Employment Research. The seventeen papers presented here, by eighteen authors, are intended to reflect the character, scope, and variety of the work conducted by a research organization that is unique in its emphasis on both national and local employment and manpower problems.

From its earliest days, the Institute has tended to be problem-oriented. Its studies have always had a primarily empirical emphasis, underscoring a concern with rendering assistance to decision-makers who deal with policies and programs affecting employment and unemployment. While the Institute's work is expected to retain its predominantly empirical flavor in the future, this preference should not at all preclude increasing attention to theoretical and methodological topics in response to new challenges. Indeed, as this volume shows, such topics have hardly been neglected in the current and past research undertakings of the Institute.

Most of the authors are regular, full-time staff members, but four of the contributors are scholars not associated primarily or on a continuing basis with the Institute. In recent years, the Institute's own resources have been supplemented by Ford Foundation grants and federal agency contracts. The engagement of outside scholars and the availability of some outside special-purpose funds have helped the Institute to round out and strengthen its research program.

The contents of this volume convey the range and diversity of the Institute's research activity. To help the reader sample the contents and obtain a quick overview, a synopsis of each paper is provided here.

The first section, on "Manpower and Poverty," begins with a paper by Taylor, who draws upon experience in business organization to provide an insight into the structure of public institutions for the improvement of human resources and welfare. Appealing to a simple analogy, he shows that the same logic that dictates functional specialization, proliferation, coordination, and aggregation in the business world is also visibly at work in the public sphere.

The next paper, by Mangum, considers U.S. manpower policy of 1961–65 in a larger context. In the United States, as in Europe, policy has been primarily oriented to welfare rather than to human-resources development. In response to public concern about persistent unemployment, government policy in the early 1960's resumed a trend that first emerged in the 1930's and later led to the Employment Act of 1946. Training and other special manpower programs, operating at an experimental level, have not played a decisive role in the 1960's. However, strong fiscal action in 1964 has impressively reduced the volume of unemployment.

Levitan focuses on operations and policy issues under each major component of the anti-poverty program initiated by the Economic Opportunity Act. He notes that this new program involves only a relatively small addition to the funds previously allocated to aid the poor. At this stage, he believes it would be premature to conclude that the new approach represents a sharp break with the past or that we already know the most effective ways to fight poverty.

Next, Davidson examines the confrontation of novel manpower and poverty policies with established political institutions. He suggests that the conduct of a formal war on poverty may have the important incidental result of creating a new and politically potent clientele with which these institutions will have to reckon. Agency cultivation of special interest groups is hardly a new or unique phenomenon; and the poverty war, however innovative it may appear, illustrates the continual quest (now called "creative federalism") for workable arrangements among the various levels of government in order to reflect political realities.

The second section, "Income Maintenance for the Unemployed," opens with Haber's views on the development of the United States Employment Service as a central institution for the implementation of national manpower policy. He opposes federalization of the public employment offices, the compulsory listing of vacancies, and the complete physical separation of the unemployment insurance and job placement functions.

Income maintenance for the unemployed, which has long been a major interest of the Institute, is treated in the subsequent four papers. Murray's study deals with research needs for improving protection under the public unemployment insurance system. He regards benefit adequacy, benefit duration, and qualification criteria as three areas meriting further investigation. After nearly three decades of operation, and despite annual expenditures that have reached two to three billion dollars, some aspects of these fundamental elements of the unemployment insurance system still require comprehensive examination.

The paper by McKean considers factors determining the adequacy of unemployment insurance reserves of the various states. The high level of unemployment that continued into the first half of the present decade raised concern at the time about the solvency of the unemployment insurance system. The author examines interstate differences recorded in recent years in the light of tax rates, amount and duration of benefits, industry mix, and vulnerability to cyclical declines. He also weighs the implications of pending federal legislation for the adequacy of state reserve funds.

Mackin reviews salient characteristics of claimants aided under the 1961–62 federal program of temporary extended unemployment compensation benefits. His analysis indicates that, in the design of any future program for similar purposes, the record of labor force attachment should be considered a basic qualifying criterion for benefit eligibility.

Father Becker examines the variety and the roles of private programs that help to maintain the incomes of workers forced into idleness. During the past twenty-five years, numerous plans have been devised through collective bargaining and the unilateral action of management. The expanding scope of fringe benefits will encourage invention of additional schemes, as well as the spread of certain present arrangements that have proved useful. Continuing experimentation with private measures is favored by the author.

Joint authors, Smith and Thole, account for the first paper of the section on "Community Improvement." They review existing and needed educational and vocational programs and facilities in Kalamazoo County. The needs they see for additional programs and facilities in this community doubtless reflect similar gaps throughout the country in provisions for secondary and postsecondary education of youths and adults. They favor establishment of an intermediary organization (governed and supported by the schools, industry, and the community) that might offer work experience for school youths bound directly for employment.

Burt notes that citizen advisory groups can contribute decisively to the shaping of more effective vocational and technical education programs. He describes various formal and informal mechanisms and procedures for achieving constructive industry participation with educators toward the improvement of local schools and school systems.

A case study of the adaptation of Erie County, Pennsylvania, to changes in market demand and industrial location provide Belitsky with a basis for a more general view of the problems of local adjustment. While outmigration may improve the prospects for some individuals, it may also worsen the plight of those who stay. The author indicates the need for programs that reduce chance factors in occupational choice and could help an individual to modify his vocational development and prospects.

Holmquist describes a venture in which the Institute has sought to help a community improve its approach to problems of unemployment and job development. The Institute's role is primarily that of catalyst, of middleman—to generate interest, to involve key local individuals, to provide initial liaison between vital segments of the community, to assist communication and cooperation. The main ingredients of any successful community effort, however, are the motivated citizens themselves and the sustained leadership that they demonstrate.

The last section of the volume, on "Information Needs and Tools," begins with a paper by Striner, discussing various factors that will significantly influence manpower research in the years ahead. Among these are the application of systems analysis and other techniques to assist policy-shapers in determining program priorities and evaluating cost and effectiveness. He suggests that private research organizations and universities may play an increasingly vital role in helping government agencies design and apply objective criteria for program evaluation.

Morton's paper, which complements Striner's, examines emerging developments in the federal statistical system and program budgeting and their implications for manpower research. Interagency and interdisciplinary analysis of manpower information will be facilitated by "hardware" and institutional innovations at the federal level. Impressive difficulties will continue to impede the correlation and effective utilization of heterogeneous, though relevant, data compiled by state and local governments.

Sheppard stresses the need for an interdisciplinary approach to the study of manpower, an approach which has been used advantageously in the study of foreign economic development. No single discipline can presume to meet the analytical and prescriptive needs that are now generally recognized as important for the effective utilization of human resources. He illustrates his point with reference to his own studies of unemployment problems, particularly the matching of job seekers with job openings.

In the final paper of the volume, Siegel states that the more positive federal role asserted in economic affairs places new strains on the limited base of productivity information. Adoption of explicit wage-price and employment policies within the framework of the Employment Act of

1946 suggests a need for productivity forecasts in addition to historical series. Since the data base is not likely to develop in accord with requirements, a public information program regarding uses and limitations of the kinds of productivity statistics that are available might prove worthwhile. Recommendations are also made for the restatement of guidelines and for the use of productivity forecasts in their administration.

In addition to exhibiting some of the multiple "dimensions of manpower policy," the brief summaries above indicate that the Institute staff typically works close to the fire, where it is sometimes uncomfortably warm. The main emphasis is on subjects that may sometimes be "controversial." Such subjects are commonly charged with public interest or are, at least, within the current range of public vision. While it is highly tempting to select topics that permit retrospective or definitive study, the Institute's primary commitment is to contribute to the body of thought and opinion useful in shaping program proposals and in modifying established programs, including those that are relatively quiescent. This very emphasis has its risks, of course, as a fine balance is sought between timeliness and mature reflection.

HAROLD C. TAYLOR
Director
The Upjohn Institute

May 31, 1966
Kalamazoo, Michigan

CONTENTS

CONTENTS

PART IV: INFORMATION NEEDS AND TOOLS

I

MANPOWER AND POVERTY

1

PERSPECTIVE FOR
PUBLIC UNDERSTANDING OF FEDERAL
MANPOWER PROGRAMS

HAROLD C. TAYLOR

During the past few years, vast increases have occurred in the number and scope of federal government programs intended to help disadvantaged persons. Conspicuous among these programs are those implementing the Manpower Development and Training Act and the Economic Opportunity Act (the "war on poverty").

During the next few years, legislators and enlightened citizens will undertake sober appraisals of the new programs to arrive at conclusions as to which should be expanded, continued, modified, or terminated. Much public discussion is already underway, and, because of the number and complexity of the programs, a considerable amount of public confusion is evident. More confusion appears to exist, however, than is necessary.

The purpose of this paper is to identify some current sources of confusion which, once they are understood, can be avoided in the appraisal process. Recommendations as to which programs should be continued and which discarded are avoided. For the most part, such decisions require additional experience with the programs. The paper should help the reader to focus on pertinent questions, or at least to avoid asking some wrong questions about the new programs.

SCOPE OF PROGRAMS TO BE CONSIDERED

The programs to be considered in this paper all relate to the training or education of people. A common phrase used nowadays is "manpower development," and the training and educational activities now envisioned are much broader in scope than those traditionally encompassed. Much current emphasis is placed on the underprivileged and on the non-college-bound—groups generally believed to have received insufficient attention in our traditional system of public school education.

THE PUBLIC EDUCATION PATTERN OF THE FUTURE

Many new developments are shaping the future pattern of public education. It will help us greatly to keep this emerging pattern in mind as we look at the special manpower development programs that have been initiated in recent years.

With respect to the early elementary grades, it is recognized that the top half of the children adapt well and learn well and that no sweeping changes of curriculum or teaching methods are required. The situation with respect to the bottom half of the group, and especially the bottom quarter, is far different. These are the children who do not adapt well and do not learn well. They drift through the years of compulsory schooling, being promoted mostly according to age rather than achievement; and they tend to rank predictably among the eventual dropouts, and among the juvenile delinquents and clients of welfare agencies.

Special attention is required to see that the children in the bottom half or quarter keep up with their companions in the basic skills of reading, writing, and arithmetic. Equally important, and harder to overcome, are the factors of cultural deprivation by virtue of which these children lack the motivation to learn—the aspiration, the curiosity, the ability to pursue a task to completion, the ability to follow instructions, and even many of the daily routines of orderly living and personal appearance. To correct these deficiencies, it is necessary to reach back to the home, with the hope of favorably modifying parental attitudes and the home atmosphere. This concept is an integral part of the Office of Economic Opportunity's approach to Head Start programs, initiated in the summer of 1965.

Beginning with the high school years, a very considerable number of changes in our present practices are required. Throughout our history, almost the only well-defined and well-rounded high school curriculum has been the college preparatory course; with some notable exceptions, this largely remains the fact today. Yet, even in recent years, less than 10 percent of a given age group completed four or more years of college.

Much new thinking is now evident with respect to overhauling post-secondary school curricula. The well-informed citizen is familiar with such institutions as the comprehensive high school, the area-wide post-secondary technical-vocational institute, and the community college. The purpose guiding education in the future has been well stated by Harold T. Smith as follows:

> Vocational and technical education must be treated as an integral part of total education, which it is. Total education should introduce school

youth to the world of work along with the world of the professions and of culture. It should enable youth to move into their next role in life whether that be to attend college, the professional school, or the vocational-technical school; or to enter directly into employment. But there should be no dead end tracks.

The educational system should provide adults and out-of-school youth, wherever they may live, the opportunity for general and vocational-technical training or retraining while on the job.

The system should provide the facilities, the curricula, the teaching skills, and the organizational knowledge required for such special short courses and crash training programs as are constantly being required for the benefit of the unemployed and others needing them.[1]

This concept of the secondary and postsecondary education of the future, happily, is not an idle dream. It appears in the educational plans of many states; and in some states, notably California, considerable progress has been made toward implementation. On the other hand, progress toward the attainment of this goal in most states is likely to be slow, since all states have money difficulties, and they also have pressing problems other than educational ones. Even within education, they have problems of increasing enrollments (the baby boom) and of obsolete school buildings. To meet these two problems and at the same time to maintain the past quality and scope of education will require appropriations far beyond those of the past. Thus, even though there is considerable citizen awareness of, and considerable legislative sympathy for, the educational concept described above, the desired system is not likely to become a reality in less than fifteen years—and twenty-five years might be a more realistic figure.

To conclude: The kind of public educational system we need for preparing all young people for intelligent and productive citizenship is reasonably clear. We need greatly to have that system in effect right now, but we do not have it right now and we could not have it all right now, even if money were unlimited.

Against this backdrop, we now view the educational and training programs conducted under various federal acts. The Manpower Development and Training Act (MDTA) and the Economic Opportunity Act (EOA) deserve special attention, as already noted.

[1] Harold T. Smith, *Education and Training for the World of Work: A Vocational Education Program for the State of Michigan* (Kalamazoo, Mich.: Upjohn Institute for Employment Research, July, 1963), p. 3.

MANPOWER DEVELOPMENT PROGRAMS:
THE PROBLEM OF PRIORITIES

It seems fair to say that what the educational and training activities of the MDTA and EOA are trying to accomplish is to provide as quickly as possible and as effectively as possible some, but not all, of the programs that will some day be parts of our regular educational systems. The MDTA was set up to train the unemployed and the underemployed. It was established because of a national concern that, despite a general high level of prosperity, too many people are still unemployed. Many people not technically unemployed would still benefit from additional training, but they are not (for practical purposes) within the scope of MDTA, since the limited allocated resources are used almost exclusively to aid the unemployed and the underemployed. For example, many high school students not preparing for college are not now being trained for the world of work either. Many will eventually join the ranks of the unemployed and will then become eligible for special training programs. Some women not now in the labor force would like to work part-time or full-time if they could first get some vocational training or take refresher courses. Thus, MDTA cannot meet all the training deficiencies that will ultimately be remedied as we attain a full and well-rounded system of public education. It is set up to help the unemployed —that is, to alleviate some, but not all, of our present educational deficiencies.

The Economic Opportunity Act was established to help the poverty-stricken. Many intended beneficiaries—both Negroes and whites—are culturally deprived. Many—Negroes and whites—are illiterate, so that vocational training is impossible until basic educational deficiencies have been remedied. These persons are all eligible for help by special training or other educational assistance under EOA programs. But many persons who are not poverty-stricken, and some not even close to the poverty line, could also benefit greatly from programs offered to the poverty-stricken under EOA. Some self-supporting persons could improve their skill levels and their earning power greatly with special training; and they would take such training if the way could be made easier for them to do so, as it is for some of the poverty-stricken under EOA programs. But the restricted goal of the EOA programs is to help the poverty-stricken—that is, to provide rehabilitation, education, and training to some, but not all, of the persons who could benefit from such assistance.

If the nation could immediately have the well-rounded program of training and education envisioned for the future, such choices would not have to be made. The nation is still in process of working out the bases for these choices, but a few criteria are crystallizing. One is that a definite

6

historical wrong must be corrected; programs for the Negro are undertaken partly for this reason. A second is that society incurs a palpable and remediable economic loss if it does not do certain things; training programs for the most employable of the unemployed are justifiable on this ground. A third is that society faces a clear and present danger unless certain prompt and massive remedial efforts are pushed to a successful conclusion; a host of programs directed toward urban discontents are needed.

The problem is that only part of the total job can be done, at least in the immediate future. No matter how the choice of priorities is made, some persons barely excluded will need help nearly as much as some persons barely included. We may move the boundary lines, of course, so as to include more people; but then the same thing happens under the new rules. Resources are limited, even in an "affluent society," and the inclusion of too many potential beneficiaries under any single program may spread the aid too thinly to offer meaningful help.

Let us run through a typical sequence of proposals that might be made as we draw one line after another in devising special programs for manpower development.

1. We should have special programs to train and rehabilitate the Negro high school dropout. The plausibility of this as a starting point for meeting one of society's urgent problems hardly needs demonstrating.

2. We should extend such programs to give equal attention to the white high school dropout. The equitability of such an extension seems clear. We must observe, however, that this extension would require a program at least four or five times as large, and therefore four or five times as expensive, as one devoted solely to the Negro dropout.

3. The high school dropouts, though conspicuous, are not the only youngsters having trouble finding a place in society, especially in the world of work. With high school education largely emphasizing the college preparatory course, the non-college-bound are not getting an adequate education. That such youngsters as these need to be prepared better for life is not in doubt. But, if we accept this extension of our special programs to meet the most urgent problems of society, we include all non-high school graduates and the bottom one-fourth of all high school graduates. Our emergency program obviously is growing by leaps and bounds.

4. Our education system, furthermore, does not do justice to exceptionally gifted and creative youngsters. Courses are geared, inevitably, to the general level of the class as a whole, so the gifted student is not sufficiently stimulated and challenged. That we should do as well as we

7

can for our most talented young people seems undebatable, but these youngsters are already doing better than anyone else in our present education system. Do they really constitute an emergency group? Inasmuch as we must draw a line in developing crash programs, do we have to go this far?

5. Now we come in our sequence to everybody not already mentioned. Are not their needs worthy of notice, too, for achievement of a truly "Great Society"? A national magazine has made the point:

> All across the nation this fact is beginning to stand out: It is the average young American who is becoming the neglected and almost forgotten generation of today.
>
> Vast and growing sums of public and private funds are showering down on the dull youngster, the dropout, the delinquent—and those whom the sociologists call the "culturally deprived" young people of America.
>
> At the other extreme, children of the well-to-do, or youngsters with very high intelligence quotients, are getting access to well-staffed private schools, scholarships and other aids on their way to top colleges and choice careers.
>
> Left in the middle, without benefit of private privilege or of tax-supported bounties, is the great bulk of young persons of ordinary means and talent.[2]

As the above sequence illustrates, each item appears quite plausible in its own right, but the nation cannot do everything today, tomorrow, or next week. The inescapable problem is that of deciding where to draw the line, and the intelligent citizen should consider this matter thoughtfully and unemotionally. With this objective clearly in mind, a sound consensus for acceptable policies can surely be developed.

MAXIMUM UTILIZATION vs SPECIAL TREATMENT

We have talked in general terms about priorities in meeting the most urgent manpower needs on something like a crash basis, but each manpower program or project will meet a series of special problems concerning certain individuals or groups. These are related to the more general problem of priorities, but they require an intimate understanding on the part of the enlightened citizen. Let us trace through a typical sequence of operations, decisions, and problems.

The Manpower Development and Training Act administrators in Typicalburg have ascertained an acute shortage of qualified secretaries

[2] *U.S. News & World Report,* February 21, 1966, p. 52.

in the community. They decided to set up a program to train 100 secretaries. To whom shall this training be offered—to any woman who can qualify competitively to secure the training? Many excellent candidates now working on jobs below their potential would make fine secretaries, and would like to have the chance. But no! The MDTA is set up primarily to help the unemployed, so trainees will usually be selected from that group.

By advertising and by recruitment devices, the administrators seek the best applicants possible for this training course among the unemployed; they test and interview to find the best 100 candidates. Ninety complete the course in excellent fashion and in minimum time, and they find jobs as secretaries. Thus, ninety badly needed secretaries, formerly unemployed, are provided and become productive members of society. A fine achievement, many would say.

But some would not say so, because there is not a complete consensus that the mission of MDTA is simply to help the unemployed. Perhaps the mission is primarily to help the Negro unemployed, or the poverty-stricken unemployed, or some such hard-to-reach group rather than the most promising, easy-to-reach candidates whom the administrators in Typicalburg actually did train.

Let us look at the results in Typicalburg with respect to the choice of Negro candidates. (We must note first that there should be no discrimination against Negro applicants because of race. On both legal and moral grounds, such behavior is indefensible.) We find that, out of the 100 chosen candidates, only 10 were Negroes. Is this good or bad? Well, in Typicalburg, 10 percent of the total population are Negroes. If one were to choose the 100 most promising candidates for secretarial training (or for anything else), with neither positive nor negative discrimination concerning Negroes, it is not unlikely that about 10 percent would turn out to be Negroes.[3] Thus, the results in Typicalburg were fine, if the objective was to reduce unemployment as much as possible, with maximum speed and minimum cost. On the other hand, if the program was supposed to offer special help to Negroes, then probably many *more* than 10 of the trainees should have been Negroes!

The same line of reasoning may be pursued with respect to the poverty-stricken. In the Typicalburg program as described, the odds are that a good many of the trainees were married women with the husband

---

[3] Manifestly, the number to be expected is not really determined this simply. The Negro is overrepresented among the unemployed, but perhaps underrepresented with respect to the necessary educational attainment. We are trying in this report to present a perspective rather than to give a precise answer to a specific problem.

employed or single women living with parents in comfortable circumstances. If one thinks that the Typicalburg program should have been confined to persons in distress, these women should not have been selected for training.

A posture for the intelligent citizen now begins to emerge. If the Typicalburg program as actually carried out was devoted to a reasonably worthwhile objective, and if it accomplished that objective reasonably well, then the program deserves some merit points. Beyond that, the intelligent citizen must consider what other training needs he feels should be met in Typicalburg: whether there are, in fact, other training programs devoted to these additional objectives; whether, in total, these programs are well balanced or poorly balanced; whether the community is attempting too much for its resources or is not trying to do as much as it should.

SHOULD OBJECTIVES BE EXPLICIT OR IMPLICIT?

We have been reviewing the problem of priorities—the difficulties involved in drawing a line—in a situation where special programs of education and training are to be made available to some, but not all, of the individuals or groups in society. We must now emphasize that in the legislation for the special training programs now underway, these lines are not drawn with precision. The Manpower Development and Training Act, for example, was passed primarily to help the unemployed, but the first sentence of Section 202 (c) reads as follows: "Although priority in referral for training shall be extended to unemployed persons, the Secretary of Labor shall, to the maximum extent possible, also refer other persons qualified for training programs which will enable them to acquire needed skills."

At what point should the Secretary decide that he has given adequate priority to unemployed persons? Should 90 percent of the trainees in a course be from the ranks of the unemployed? Or 50 percent? Or what percent? And how shall he decide at what point he has offered training to other persons "to the maximum extent possible"?

In addition to the issue of priority for the unemployed over others, there are questions as to, say, priority of the poverty-stricken versus other low-income persons whose incomes are above an arbitrarily defined poverty line and questions as to priority of the Negro. On the last point, nowhere in any of the legislation is there a mention of special attention to the Negro, despite the fact that his plight, which has been emphatically brought to the attention of the nation during the past decade, was certainly a strong factor influencing the passage of both the Manpower Development and Training Act and the Economic Opportunity Act.

The vagueness of stated objectives in the legislation is pointed out here as a fact for the intelligent citizen to keep in mind, not necessarily as something that should be changed. Perhaps priority lines should be drawn more explicitly in the laws, or by the Secretary of Labor or others responsible for administration; but there are plausible reasons for not doing so. One reason is that many situations which would be hotly debated in principle cause remarkably little difficulty in practice. Two program administrators in Typicalburg, for example, might have sharp differences of opinion as to the extent to which their secretarial training course should concentrate on unemployed women versus others. Looking at the actual list of applicants, however, they might find themselves agreeing very closely as to which hundred women should be selected. Another reason for leaving objectives somewhat open-ended is that a priority proper for one program at one time in one place might not be very sensible for another program at another time in another place.

Inasmuch as priorities are not rigidly set forth in laws or administrative rules, the intelligent citizen has considerable leeway—and must recognize that he has—in forming a judgment as to what one program or another ought to try to accomplish. Furthermore, the citizen must remain alert to difficulties of interpreting the data that will be given to him purporting to show what a given program did in fact accomplish.

It is impossible to conclude this brief discussion of priorities without considering specifically the question of programs for Negroes. That the Negro has special problems, that his many problems are far out of proportion to his numbers, has been pointed out vigorously in recent years, and the facts are now widely appreciated. Indeed, these facts must have exerted strong influence in the establishment of MDTA, EOA, and some other special manpower programs.

At the same time, there seems to be a tacit but almost universal belief that to direct a program specifically or disproportionately toward helping the Negro dissatisfies both the white community and the Negro community. Thus, if a program is directed especially toward helping the Negro, the program must be so devised as to leave this intent obscure, and those in charge must not say that this is the intent. These built-in elements of fuzziness must increase considerably the difficulty of constructing and executing a program. We must recognize also that a program which discriminates against the white person is in violation of the Civil Rights Act, just as is a program that discriminates against the Negro. When it comes time to evaluate such a program, how can one say

11

whether the program accomplished its objective if one cannot discover what the objective was?

Whether targets can be made more explicit and whether they should be made more explicit are among the many related questions now troubling the nation. Meantime, the intelligent citizen must recognize this issue as a source of confusion concerning the new manpower programs.

FUNCTIONAL ORGANIZATIONS AND THE PROBLEMS OF SOCIETY

Many criticisms may properly be leveled at the new manpower programs. Governmental activities, like most private activities, are organized by functions; and functional organizations, although they have tremendous advantages, also have some inherent and inescapable limitations. With respect to these problems, there are devices and procedures for coping with them, but not for eliminating them. The thoughtful citizen should criticize, but he should also appreciate that a gap inevitably separates the attainable and the ideal.

Functional Organizations in Government

Let us note a few functional organizations in the public sphere as a background for indicating both their strengths and their problems. At the federal level, the Department of Health, Education, and Welfare includes the Office of Education, which is concerned with the federal role in education, regardless of what kind of education or for what persons. The Department of Labor has an organization concerned with running public employment offices; it performs that function (but no other) for anyone who comes to request it—youths, older persons, the handicapped, Negroes, or whites. The same Department has another organization concerned with the federal role in running the unemployment insurance system.

State governments also are organized around functions. Each state has: a state department of education; a state employment security department (concerned with employment offices and unemployment insurance); a state health department and, perhaps, a separate department of mental health; a state welfare department; and so on.

Communities, likewise, are organized around functions. At the community level, there is an added complication in that some important community functions are performed by agencies of the state, some by local governmental agencies—including school districts—and some by private organizations, operating usually under the umbrella of a community chest.

12

The advantages of functional organization are largely of two sorts. First, such an organization (for example, a public school system) can develop a high degree of know-how with respect to performance of its function—teaching. Second, it has great flexibility in responding to changes in the demand for various components of its particular service. It can adapt—better than any other type of organization—to a sudden increase in the number of kindergarten pupils, for instance, or to a change in the geographic distribution of pupils, or to a sudden increase in the number of shop students.

The great disadvantage of this form of organization is that no agency is responsible for the whole person or for a particular whole problem that may suddenly appear important to society. In more specific terms, no agency is responsible for a whole boy, who may not be moving smoothly through the schools, the recreational agencies, the employment services, and so on. No agency is responsible for a whole group, such as the elderly, the youth group, the Negro, the poverty-stricken, or the people on public welfare. Little wonder that we hear so much nowadays about integrated, multidisciplinary approaches—about "systems analysis," "operations research," and the like.

Business Organization

It is urgently necessary to recognize that we are dealing here with a fundamental issue of organizational schemes. We must organize in one way or another, and we cannot simultaneously organize in all ways. Even in management, the scarcities that affect an "affluent society" are all too evident. Since industrial organizations act in almost identical ways as those in the public sphere, it will be helpful to trace through the industrial problem briefly.

Let us assume a company with three major product lines: portable radios, police intercommunication systems, and hearing aids. Under a strictly functional organization, the engineering of all three lines will be located in one engineering department. In manufacturing, all wire-making will be done in one wiremill. All coilwinding will be in one department, all transistor circuit production in another department, and all plastics molding in still another. All marketing activities, as a rule, will be assigned to one marketing organization.

The advantages of know-how, flexibility, and supervision in this setup are tremendous. The difficulty is that nobody is necessarily responsible for total attention—total dedication to the hearing aid business, for example. There may come to the desk of the president all sorts of information suggesting that something is going wrong—here, there, or everywhere—with the hearing aid business. These troubles may become

13

too vexatious to ignore, and the president may feel they should not have reached him.

Why not put the whole activity in one place—from engineering through sales—and have one man responsible for making it work? This would be a product shop as distinct from the functional organization. What will happen if this change is made? It may be better in many ways, though it need not be.

Let us suppose that after the change is made the hearing aid business, for whatever reason, drops to half the expected volume. Now the company has some unutilized floor space, engineers, punch presses, molding equipment, salesmen, and so on. Meantime, the police intercommunication business may be booming. If all these unused facilities and people were not already committed, they could easily be utilized in the intercommunication business. Under the circumstances, these shifts are extremely difficult. If the company makes the shifts anyway, then what will it do if the hearing aid business picks up again? The point of all this is that the company is going to have problems either way. All it can do is to choose which kind of problem it prefers, which it would rather have.

Let us go back to the functional shop, within which the company was operating its hearing aid business. Even within that framework, there are some common procedures by which the company can cope with its problems, though no ways promise to eliminate the problems. One common way is to set up an *operating committee*. This committee, which will include the top men from engineering through sales, can look at all the problems of the hearing aid business and arrive at persuasive answers. This device is so obviously desirable that few companies fail to use it.

A second device, usually applicable within manufacturing alone, is the *expediter*. With no authority whatsoever over any operating unit, the expediter may start from the fact that 5,000 hearing aids are to be manufactured during February, and he may keep track of everything from the ordering of the steel and copper on through every processing phase to the warehousing of 5,000 units on March 1. He uses information and persuasion and, if necessary, seeks support from operating heads to assure that the job gets done.

A third device, newer and far broader than the expediter, is the *product manager*.[4] The company could appoint one man, reporting directly to the president, whose sole job it is to worry about the hearing

---

[4] National Industrial Conference Board, *The Product Manager System: A Symposium* ("Experiences in Marketing Management," No. 8; New York: National Industrial Conference Board, 1965).

aid business. Like the expediter, he has absolutely no authority over any operation. He uses information and persuasion to bring about changes, and he can call upon his boss, the president, to issue revised orders and directives as needed. His usefulness is generally regarded as great, but he has his special burdens. One is his total lack of authority to compel the engineers, or the wiremill personnel, or the sales force to do what he feels is necessary for the success of the hearing aid business. Another burden is that what he wants is bound to clash, on occasion, with what the product manager of the police intercommunication line wants. Each of them, for example, will think that the sales force should be devoting more time to plugging his product. Neither man can wind up getting all he would like.

We conclude our industrial analogy by saying: that most companies seem to prefer the functional structure, just as the functional structure has become almost universal in public activities; that operating committees are almost universal; that the product manager device is being viewed with increasing enthusiasm; and that, regardless of the organizational framework at the community, state, or national level, or in a company, the structure will carry its inherent and inescapable problems.

COORDINATION OF MANPOWER PROGRAMS

Let us return to the public functional organizations in the general field of manpower development to illustrate the organizational problems and some possible means of coping with them. This discussion is not expected to give federal or state officials brand-new ideas; the chances are that coordinational problems and possible solutions have been rather thoroughly canvassed by these people. Our purpose rather is to give the intelligent citizen a background for appraisal of both the problems he will read about and the solutions proposed.

Federal Level

At the federal level, it is certain that the need for coordination of manpower programs is recognized and that efforts to improve coordination will have a high priority. In these efforts, we can take for granted there will be, or there have been, interagency committees, corresponding reasonably well to the operating committee in the electronics firm used as an illustration. These will, however, be interagency committees on manpower programs, rather than one over-all operating committee.

In the light of our discussion of how to cope with the problems of functional organizations, it is natural to wonder whether there might be a federal "product manager" for manpower development programs.

15

Would he be in the Executive Office of the President, assigned full-time to worry about the various manpower programs, to act by information and persuasion, and, where necessary, to seek directives from the President or new legislation from the Congress? A presidential assistant could, of course, perform these functions without having any title designating him as the product manager, though there might be some advantage in his being acknowledged by all as the man assigned to these functions.

Some thoughts have been expressed that the Secretary of Labor has some mandate to assume this role. If so, the mandate seems hardly strong enough to enable him to do so. Moreover, his role as head of one of the operating departments does not seem compatible with the role of product manager.

Following the first Watts incident in Los Angeles, the federal government carried on an expediter operation that deserves serious consideration as a coordinating device. A high-level interagency team went to Los Angeles to determine what programs were needed to cope as effectively as possible with the adverse conditions that preceded the outbreak of violence. This team used information and persuasion to improve the program efforts of the state and local agencies involved in the Watts area. They determined also, in some detail, the financing efforts needed from all relevant federal agencies and returned to Washington with tangible recommendations. Program financing for the Watts area was made available very promptly. If these same programs had been developed solely by the Los Angeles people and had been sent to Washington through the usual channels, they would necessarily have been subject to a delay of several months or more.

The great potential of this type of expediter team approach is almost self-evident. The approach has been continued, but only within the Department of Labor itself, in a "selected cities" program, and is regarded as quite successful. One is forced to assume, however, that the device would be rated even more successful if it could be extended to include other federal agencies, especially the Department of Health, Education, and Welfare, and the Office of Economic Opportunity. At this moment of writing, such interagency coordinating teams are being established in a number of metropolitan areas.

In our discussion of functional structures at the federal level, we must observe that the Office of Economic Opportunity (OEO), in several respects, does not fit the usual mold. It is in part a product shop or problem-oriented organization. Thus, it operates Job Corps centers directly, with its own funds and under its own supervision, although most training and educational functions of the federal government are channeled through the Office of Education or through parts of the Labor Department. On the other hand, for the recruitment and referral of Job Corps applicants, the OEO relies substantially on existing public employment offices. There is nothing inherently irrational about this. For instance, the electronics firm could decide that, although its functional shops are good for most purposes, the whole hearing aid business is really something special and should be set up almost entirely as a separate business. Even so, a single employment office could refer applicants to all parts of the company, including the hearing aid division.

The Office of Economic Opportunity departs from the usual federal pattern also in that its activities cut directly from the federal level to the local level (thus essentially bypassing state governments). Furthermore, at the local level, it deals with private nongovernmental agencies as well as with public agencies.

Are these differences desirable or not? Perhaps the attitude of the electronics company will help us decide. Certainly, with an already established and generally excellent series of functional shops, the company would be very reluctant to jerk out the hearing aid business and set it up elsewhere. There would be duplication. For example, more punch presses would be needed, and more people to run them; and "duplication" is a bad word in business just as it is in government. Even so, if the company is forced to conclude that the hearing aid business is really something special, not readily meshed with the other parts of the business, it must set up this activity separately or give up the hearing aid business.

Thus, the structure of OEO is neither to be criticized nor to be lauded just because it is different. The issue is simply whether it works better this way. This point of view doesn't carry us far toward an answer, but at least it poses the right question.

Another observation should be made with regard to the separateness of the OEO from the departments previously carrying on the federal manpower programs. Being new, and having no long-standing commitments in terms of objectives and established procedures, the OEO might be expected to come up more readily with some fresh thinking and innovative ideas. Some observers believe that such new thinking is already evident and that it is beginning to permeate the thinking of the "old-line" and perhaps somewhat rigid agencies. If so, this is a plus mark of considerable importance.

State Level

Let us turn now from federal organizational problems and possible devices for coping with them to the state level. The multiplicity of functions being carried on at the state level seems even more confusing, if possible, than at the federal level. If, for example, an agency official in some community wants to understand everything going on in his state in the new field of manpower development, there will be a half-dozen to a dozen persons whom he will have to contact before his information is complete. These will include officers of the state government, state officers of federal agencies, regional officers of federal agencies, and, in some cases, persons in the Washington headquarters of agencies.

Manifestly, the sheer problem of ascertaining where to go and whom to see is very nearly insurmountable. A few devices for coping with this difficulty come easily to mind. First, in each state there could be a manpower programs information office. In this one office, an agency official from a community should be able to obtain all the information he needs to answer any specific question he may have in mind.

Second, the governor of each state could appoint a manpower coordinator or product manager to worry about the conduct and coordination of manpower programs in the state. This coordinator or manager, it must be noted, would have an even more troubled existence than his counterpart in industry because some of the matters with which he must concern himself (OEO programs, for example) are not under the management of his boss, the governor. The state manpower coordinator could, as a part of his job, operate the manpower programs information office referred to above.

An innovation now being tried in West Virginia and Hawaii is the manpower authority set up by statute and having defined powers. This legislative charter distinguishes it sharply from the product manager role. The "authority" device is too new to evaluate at this time.

All these devices illustrate, but surely do not exhaust, the list of possible procedures by which functionally diverse programs at the state level may be encompassed and coordinated. Let us turn now to local problems and instrumentalities for handling them.

Local Level

It is at the community level, of course, that all programs are actually being conducted. Federal and state roles are largely those of establishing requirements, of financing, and, to some degree, of monitoring performance.

The manifold character and complexity of functions performed therefore become most sharply apparent in the community. Some of these functions—notably in OEO programs—are based largely on directives from Washington. Some agencies are instruments of the state—the employment office, categorical aids, and others. Some functions are ad-

18

ministered by counties, some by municipal governments, some by independent school districts, and many by private nongovernmental agencies. The diversity is staggering. Let us note a number of community experiences and devices, largely to make clear how greatly the problems stem from the inescapable fact that organizational structures are mostly functional.

At the local level, the device of the product manager, a person designated to worry about all of the community's manpower problems, has some definite merits. However, the device does not seem promising, because there is no boss who has administrative control over any sizable proportion of the total range of programs.

There is in most communities a community services council, which, year in and year out, has the job of bringing about voluntary coordination among all the agencies, both public and private. On the other hand, citizens who have worked on council committees are painfully aware of the modest success that usually attends their efforts to direct "functional shops" toward the solution of multifunctional problems or multiproblem groups. A few of the community experiences may offer some useful insights into what works and what doesn't.

In St. Paul, Minnesota, a fairly large-scale project was initiated in 1948 to focus the efforts of the functional shops in that city on the problems of the hard-core poverty families. This followed the discovery that about 6 percent of the city's families "were suffering from such a compounding of serious problems that they were absorbing well over half of the combined services of the community's dependency, health, and adjustment agencies."[5] The procedure, basically, was that each of the major functional agencies loaned a staff member to a task force, which directed its attention entirely to the 6,600 hard-core poverty families. This cadre of workers thus represented in part a little product shop, devoted to the hard-core poverty family. In part, also, this cadre had some of the advantages of an operating committee, since each member of the cadre could carry back to his own functional shop some good ideas of other members.

The St. Paul voluntary cadre of functional agencies has long been regarded as a successful experiment and a useful pattern. Now, however, nearly two decades later, the procedure seems not to have inspired as much imitation as had been anticipated in 1950.

[5] Bradley Buell and Associates, *Community Planning for Human Services* (New York: Columbia University Press, 1952), p. 9.

19

In December, 1963, following the Studebaker shutdown in South Bend, Indiana, Dr. Harold L. Sheppard of the Upjohn Institute staff was asked by the Area Redevelopment Administration to go to South Bend to act as federal coordinator. The task was twofold: (1) to assist the people and agencies in South Bend to do all they could to cope with the emergency, and (2) to bring to bear quickly every pertinent federal aid program. This role of Dr. Sheppard's will be seen immediately as analogous to that of the expediter in dealing with a large group of functional shops in South Bend, in regional offices of federal agencies, and in Washington. Dr. Sheppard's report of his experiences displays considerable enthusiasm for the success of efforts within the South Bend community itself and considerable frustration and exasperation in moving the federal agencies to action.[6]

In view of our earlier observation that community coordinating efforts usually meet with only modest success, why was the South Bend community successful in banding together? It has long been observed that communities do respond well to a crisis. The closing of the Studebaker plant certainly posed a crisis. While the crisis situation itself is not difficult, what is difficult is the slogging, year-in and year-out effort of inducing functional organizations to devote coordinated attention to hard problems when these problems do not involve a clear and present danger.

Why did Dr. Sheppard meet with frustration in his efforts to get prompt action from the federal agencies? There are many reasons, no doubt. The process of getting things done in vast and ramified agencies is slow and tortuous at best. But, in terms of our analysis of organizational characteristics, we must note that a considerable amount of frustration is the inescapable lot of the expediter. In the electronics firm, the expediter of an order for hearing aids may have to go to the plastics molding department and try to persuade that department to drop whatever it is doing and put through a run of hearing aid cases. He believes that this is more important than the products being worked on at the moment; and, as we listen to the tribulations of the hearing aid expediter, we are inclined to sympathize with his point of view. But, if we could know the whole story, we might be forced to conclude that the order for hearing aid cases will just have to take its turn in the schedule. It is the expediter's job to push his order, but he will not always get what he wants.

[6] Harold L. Sheppard, *Closing of the Studebaker Plant, South Bend, Indiana*, U.S. Department of Commerce, Area Redevelopment Administration, ARA Case Book No. 5 (Washington: U.S. Government Printing Office, June, 1964).

FEDERAL MANPOWER PROGRAMS

THE NEIGHBORHOOD CENTER APPROACH

A coordinating device that offers perhaps more hope than any other at the community level is the neighborhood center. In the new manpower development and anti-poverty programs, which express our present national concern for the seriously disadvantaged members of the population, such a center would be located in a geographic area characterized by high unemployment, poor housing, low incomes, low education, and so on. Its basic purpose is to consider all the problems of any particular client, and then to refer that client to whatever community service may exist to help him with each and every one of his problems. The client may, for example, need welfare payments, legal aid, medical attention, vocational counseling, vocational or other training, a job, or whatnot. Whatever his problem, the neighborhood center can "expedite" directing the client to the proper place for help.

The culturally deprived, and often suspicious, persons who compose the clientele of this neighborhood center require the expediter's duties to extend far beyond his physical office. He must seek out the clientele in "the field," often by ringing doorbells in the neighborhood. And he must go beyond referring the client to, for example, the public employment service. He may need to take the client to the employment office, take him to a job interview in a company, and take him to and from work for a few days. To return to our industrial analogy for a moment: this expediter is not dealing with the hearing aids that go through the factory in fine shape and come out as salable products. He is concerned with the ones that don't go routinely through the line—the ones that, except for his efforts, would wind up in the scrap pile and the reject bin.

The neighborhood center can operate exactly as just described—that is, as a fully client-centered agency, performing nothing but the expediter function we have set forth. On the other hand, it can go, step by step, beyond that minimum function if local attitudes permit such extensions. Let us illustrate. The public employment office can voluntarily send one or more of its own counselors or placement people to work in the neighborhood center one day a week, or oftener if the load requires. The welfare department can do the same, and so can the marital counseling bureau, the legal aid bureau, and other agencies too. The basic neighborhood center—the expediter service—can gratefully utilize whatever functional services are brought to it, and it can get along too when functional services are not or can't be brought close to the disadvantaged clientele in that neighborhood.

The important word characterizing these extensions, of course, is "voluntary." If the public employment service voluntarily assigns a man to work in the office of the neighborhood center and at the same time maintains its full complement of employees, its full budget, its flexibility, and its responsibility for the uniform conduct of public employment functions, its public image is undiluted and unconfused. Performance of all these is important not only to the manager of the public employment office but also to the community as a whole. Where community attitudes and agency interrelationships are favorable, the voluntary assembly of services operating in conjunction with a neighborhood expediter service has much to commend it.

Let us consider now a markedly different pattern for a local neighborhood center. This is one in which all the necessary functional services are under the management of the neighborhood center. The center runs its own employment service, its own family counseling, legal aid, and child guidance services, its own medical clinic, and so on. It is a little product shop. Perhaps this procedure is better than letting the whole job go undone; but, clearly, such a pattern would encourage much local criticism. It involves duplication, certainly. It breeds confusion since, for example, two local outfits would be running employment offices. It would stimulate interagency conflict since the two employment offices (or the two family counseling services) would have somewhat different viewpoints and even engage in competition for clientele. The two sets of services would also be in competition for some of their funds, whether from federal or from local sources.

Syracuse, New York, has had experience that may offer useful lessons to other communities.[7] Among many efforts in that city to give attention to the problems of youth, one was an organization called Crusade for Opportunity. This organization was set up to provide expediter services to youth (intake, counseling, and referral) but also to initiate and administer training programs, both institutional and on-the-job, for disadvantaged youth. The Crusade for Opportunity was, therefore, to some degree a product shop—that is, an operating organization devoted to the specific service of helping disadvantaged youth through the performance of various functions. Without detailing the woes of the Crusade for Opportunity directly, let us consider them in the context of our illustrative electronics company.

[7] Sar A. Levitan, "Syracuse Faces Its Youth Unemployment Problems," in U.S. Congress, *1965 Manpower Report of the President; Joint Hearings before Senate Committee on Labor and Public Welfare and House Committee on Education and Labor,* 89th Cong., 1st Sess., pp. 381–93. Conclusions drawn in the present report are based on Dr. Levitan's description of conditions in early 1965, and do not take account of any developments that may have occurred in Syracuse since then.

This company, largely organized as a series of functional shops, has concluded reluctantly through its leadership that the hearing aid business is so special as to require a separate establishment as a product shop; moreover, it has effectuated that decision. Within the hearing aid division, there is a training department devoted to selection, training, and placement of employees for that division. The head of the training department is responsible for carrying out these functions for the division. Down the street, however, is the big factory making everything else but hearing aids, and it has a big training department that is selecting, training, and placing people for every part of the business except the hearing aid division. The training department head in the hearing aid division now finds his ability to carry out his own plans severely limited. He cannot even get any money to run his programs without the approval of the big training department. He cannot select his own trainees: the management of the big training department thinks that it can do the job better. He cannot set his own personnel policies: for example, he cannot decide to dock his trainees for absenteeism unless the big training department agrees—and for several months it doesn't agree. He cannot pay his own trainees: the big training department insists that it must pay his trainees, that his trainees must even go to the office of the big department to get their money.

The above list of tribulations is, of course, derived entirely from experience of the Syracuse Crusade for Opportunity. But let us continue for a moment with the electronics company. The big decision for the company, obviously, was the decision to set up a separate hearing aid division. We have already noted that the company would arrive at that decision only with great reluctance. The company would prefer to cope with the hearing aid problems simply with such devices as expediter services and a product manager. But if the company should decide to set up a hearing aid division, then it would certainly have to give that division autonomous decision-making powers and explicit funds.

We must go one step farther. A hearing aid company, or division, could operate successfully if it possessed nothing but its own decision-making powers and its own money. It could contract to an engineering firm the design of its hearing aid device. It could contract all of its production to a job shop, all of its transportation to a trucking organization, and all of its selling to a commercial merchandising organization. Similarly, a disadvantaged-youth-oriented product shop (such as the Crusade for Opportunity was, in part) could operate successfully with not much else but its own decision-making powers and its own money. It could contract, for example, with a local school administration to provide desired courses for disadvantaged youth. The important point is that the youth agency would make such contracts on its own terms (that is, without divided decision-making powers) and would pay the school for services rendered. The youth agency would not have to own school buildings or hire teachers on its own payroll. Similarly, it could contract for family counseling services, or testing and vocational guidance services, or on-the-job training courses in industry.

The disadvantaged-youth agency, as a product shop, would have to run its own client-centered expediter service, search for its hard-to-reach clientele, ascertain what help the clients needed, persuade them to accept help, and lead them through the process of getting help. The actual help —psychiatric counseling, vocational counseling, medical aid, vocational training, basic education, job finding, and so on—would be provided by existing agencies either as part of their already available services or by special contract, as requested, and paid for, by the youth agency.

One more qualification is needed before our discussion of organizational schemes and their inescapable problems is concluded. In discussing why some programs don't work very well, we have said nothing about government red tape, bureaucratic hardening of the arteries, and interagency jealousies. We have no thought of denying that such things exist. When programs run into difficulties, such explanations as these are always forthcoming, and often with the implication that they are sufficient to explain the trouble. Our point in this discourse is that these factors are not sufficient to explain the problems of running programs expeditiously. Organizational frameworks and their inescapable difficulties are in the picture too; and one might even make a case that these difficulties are more important sources of trouble than are the frailties of human nature.

AN INTEGRATED APPROACH TO ORGANIZATION FOR MANPOWER DEVELOPMENT

Let us summarize now the coordinational devices we have been discussing. Most of these are based on the premise that most of society's work will continue to be done by functional shops—employment offices, schools, family counseling services, welfare departments, recreational and character-building agencies, and so on. The difficulty to be faced is that in the functional setup nobody is concerned with the whole person, just as in a functionally organized factory nobody is concerned with a whole product, such as hearing aids.

The whole persons to whom the present spate of manpower programs is directed are, in general, the disadvantaged ones—the uneducated, the culturally disadvantaged, the poor, the victims of discrimination, the inadequately housed, and the unemployed. It is essential to keep in mind that we are talking about how to coordinate efforts directed toward some relatively small and clearly definable portion of the entire population of whole persons. Otherwise, we shall just be talking about how to co-ordinate the whole thing. That is a useful topic, too, but a quite different one.

Let us illustrate. If a coordinator of emergency manpower programs (a product-manager type of job) were set up in the Executive Office of the President, his area of concern would have to be defined carefully as relating, for example, to disadvantaged persons. Otherwise, if he is supposed to be concerned with everybody's cultural orientation, school-ing, physical and mental health, vocational training, income, housing, and employment, he will have to become involved in practically every-thing that is going on in the Department of Labor and in the Department of Health, Education, and Welfare, and in numerous activities in many other departments. With too much to worry about, such a man could hardly worry enough about the problems of disadvantaged persons.

Here, then, is a list of possible coordinational devices.

1. A federal coordinator of emergency manpower programs for the disadvantaged. This function is envisioned as a completely nonauthorita-tive one, analogous to the function of the product manager in industry.

2. An interagency team of expediters, operating as did the team in Los Angeles following the first Watts incident. This approach, practically speaking, would have to be confined to the largest cities and to those smaller ones in which the danger of conflict appears to be especially high.

3. An interagency manpower programs information center in each state.

4. A manpower programs coordinator appointed by, and reporting to, the governor. This function is envisioned as that of a product man-ager, and is limited in scope to emergency programs for the disadvan-taged.

5. A manpower-programs-oriented product-manager-type coordina-tor in each sizable community. Where this function might best be lodged in a community does not seem obvious. It could be in the community services council or community chest office. It could be a part of the city government. Depending on how the organizational pattern of OEO develops, it could be a function of the local community action program.

6. A client-oriented neighborhood center operation, presumably located in the target area or areas containing large proportions of dis-advantaged persons. This is basically a search-persuade-and-refer opera-tion for disadvantaged persons who need help. It would ascertain what

help they need and shepherd them to existing agencies and services that can provide such help. If a certain kind of needed help is not available in the community or is not provided readily to this disadvantaged clientele, the neighborhood center can expedite such services by informing, by persuading, and, if necessary, by badgering existing agencies.

Incidentally, the general usefulness of such a neighborhood center appears increasingly to be recognized. Indeed, there seems to be a danger that everybody will "get into the act" of setting up neighborhood centers. If that happens, there might have to be a super-referral center to decide to which center a given client should be sent. One neighborhood center in each neighborhood should be enough.

7. The neighborhood center's usefulness can be greatly augmented if some of the regular services of the community can be lodged voluntarily in the neighborhood center's building. The public employment office can assign a man to work in the neighborhood center at no increase in cost for his services. The welfare department, the family counseling center, and others can do the same. The capacity of agencies to make such assignments and their willingness to do so will vary, of course; but, in many communities, the effort will likely meet with considerable success.

The devices so far enumerated assume that all actual services to persons, with the exception of expediter services of various sorts, will be performed by existing functional organizations. As we have noted, a particular product (the hearing aid) or a particular group (the seriously disadvantaged group) may move through the functional shops at a pace which is less than the situation seems to require—even after all possible expediting devices have been brought to bear. The decision can then be made to set this business up as a separate operation (a product shop). If that decision is made, these criteria for the successful operation of a disadvantaged persons product shop seem to merit consideration:

1. Its product or its clientele must be as limited as possible and as well defined as possible. The agency must feel neither the temptation, nor the obligation, to do more and more things for more and more people until finally it is trying to do everything for everybody.

2. Within its rigorously defined sphere, the agency should have maximum power to make its own decisions.

3. Again within its rigorously defined sphere, the agency should have unilateral control over funds required to implement its own decisions.

4. The agency should be as severely limited as possible in its capacity to set up operating facilities of sorts already available in existing functional shops. Thus, if it wants courses in remedial reading to be carried on for its own clientele (the seriously disadvantaged persons in society), it should contract with a local school system to provide such courses on a reimbursable basis. It should not rent its own buildings and hire its own teachers. If it wants on-the-job training courses conducted for young men of its choosing, it should contract with industry to provide that training on a reimbursable basis. Where such common services as family casework counseling and employment counseling cannot be provided adequately to the agency's clientele on a voluntary basis, the agency should contract for these as well.

In presenting this review of organizational frameworks, problems, and remedies, we have not mentioned all the issues involved in the new special manpower programs. Since organizational issues are seldom made a specific point of reference, we hope that our so doing may provide useful insights that might not otherwise be encouraged.

REALISTIC EXPECTATIONS

The nation is now undertaking a job it has not until recently even attempted: to bring massive and multifunctional programs to bear on the problems of the seriously disadvantaged persons in our society. The moral and humanitarian reasons for such efforts are apparent. A compelling further reason is that the safety, even the continued functioning, of the entire society may be jeopardized unless the present efforts prove successful.

This job was never thought to be easy, but it is proving to be even harder than expected. Because of historically understandable resentments and suspicions, even well-oriented and well-directed programs often meet with resistance rather than with eager acceptance on the part of the target clientele. On the heartening side of the picture, some programs have met with a response successful beyond all reasonable expectation. These successes give much reason to hope that the future can be bright.

The combined wisdom and knowledge of our society are not yet fully commensurate with the challenge of this present task. To a troublesome extent, we do not know just what to do or just how to do it. The intelligent citizen must keep this limitation in mind. He is not expected, of course, to condone actual wastes of time and money or demonstrable blunders in objectives or in the administration of programs. But he must recognize that most programs are going to succeed only in part. He must school himself to be grateful that there is some success, instead of becoming irritated because the success is less than total. The viability and safety of his world and his children's world demand that the effort be pursued. And not only does he have a stake in the outcome, he also has a responsibility for participation and encouragement.

2

THE DEVELOPMENT OF MANPOWER
POLICY, 1961–65

GARTH L. MANGUM

Neither advocates nor critics of recent developments would deny that the period 1961–65 was characterized by a spirit of social and economic experimentation unmatched since the 1930's. Not the least of these experiments is the emergence of an "active manpower policy." The term has become a familiar one, particularly with the appearance of the annual *Manpower Report of the President,* but its meaning is not always clear. The purposes of this paper are to define manpower policy, provide both an international and a historical perspective to its development, assess its present status in the United States, and speculate upon its future direction.

THE GOALS OF MANPOWER POLICY

Manpower policy is concerned with the development and use of human labor as an economic resource and as a source of individual and family income. The relative priorities given these two aspects of manpower policy depend upon the economic and political circumstances. In the United States and Western Europe, manpower policy tends to depart from the economist's traditional preoccupation with efficiency. Efficient allocation of resources is considered important but secondary to the welfare of the workers themselves.

A clear definition of manpower policy is made difficult by its overlap with employment and education policies, among others. But precise lines of demarcation are important only when jurisdictional issues are at stake. It is more useful to define manpower policy in terms of its goals and the tools with which it pursues those goals, rejoicing that those same goals are pursued simultaneously with other policy tools. The goals of manpower policy are:

1. Employment opportunities for all who want them in jobs which balance free occupational choice and adequate income with society's relative preferences for alternative goods and services.

2. Education and training capable of fully developing each individual's productive potential.

3. The matching of men and jobs with a minimum of lost income and production.

To distinguish it from other policy tools, at least for purposes of this paper, employment policy involves the use of the federal government's fiscal and monetary powers to affect the general levels of employment, while education policy is concerned primarily with general education as opposed to training in specific skills. Manpower policy embraces the demand side of the economic equation in the creation of jobs for specific individuals, groups, and locations. It covers the supply side in the development of skills. It bridges the two in the matching process. In its concern for the welfare of workers it inevitably becomes involved in income distribution and wage issues. Manpower policies involve individuals, employers, labor organizations, and state and local governments, but the most significant developments of the past five years have been those occurring within the federal government.

INTERNATIONAL PERSPECTIVES ON MANPOWER POLICY

The growth of manpower policy in the postwar period has been an almost universal phenomenon, and it is worthwhile asking why. The process of industrialization with its consequent specialization of labor is the key, though differences in emphasis involve stages of political development as well as economic development. The similarity of both goals and policies among countries at vastly different stages of industrialization is surprising.

The manpower policies of developing nations emphasize education planning. In the classic case of a completely primitive society, no unemployment exists. Nearly the entire population is engaged in an inefficient subsistence agriculture. Health is poor; starvation is always near; illiteracy is general; underemployment, compared with the productivity of a truly efficient agriculture, is complete.

The economy is trapped. An efficient agriculture must await skilled agriculturists who can wean the population from primitive practices. There can be no industrialization with its higher income potential without entrepreneurs, managers, and skilled workers. There is no educational system to produce them. If the trained cadre existed, there would be no employment for them until some takeoff point had been reached. Yet the demand for high-level manpower cannot be created until the nucleus of such manpower is present.

30

Manpower policy in this situation, which is only an extreme case of what exists to some extent in two-thirds of the world, must consist primarily of a manpower and educational element in economic planning. The initial nucleus of highly trained manpower must be borrowed or created. It must be supported by taxation or foreign assistance. The manpower requirements of the economic development plan must be charted in terms of educational levels and an educational system capable of achieving those levels must be created. A careful balance between agriculture and industry must be maintained both to provide the necessary calorie base and to prevent the flooding of urban areas with as yet unemployable migrants in search of higher industrial incomes. The alternative to manpower planning is chaos.

But added to the economic complications is a political one. At least in those developing nations where political leaders, whether democratic or totalitarian in orientation, depend upon the support of the masses for survival, the demands for social welfare provisions impose burdens that the economy is not prepared to support.

The Western European nations from which the term "active manpower policy" has been appropriated have maintained unemployment rates below 2 percent of the labor force throughout the postwar period. The postwar "baby boom," which became a permanent part of the U.S. scene, subsided quickly in Europe. Labor shortages have been endemic there and inflationary pressures persistent. Yet social welfare provisions have played an even larger role in manpower policy in Western Europe than in the unemployment-prone developing nations and in the United States. Full employment has been the supreme economic goal. The unemployment levels generally equated with full employment in the United States would topple governments throughout most of Western Europe and Japan. Though several job vacancies exist for every worker who loses a job, prevention of displacement, whether from economic or technological causes, and the easing of adjustment when it occurs are the focus of European manpower policy.

The use of increased labor market efficiency as a restraint upon inflationary pressures has received considerable attention. The importance of technological advancement as the only dependable road to economic growth with static labor forces is just beginning to be recognized. International competition from more complex technologies has increased interest in the development of scientific, engineering, and technical skills. As potent as any forces in the recent drives toward higher output per man-hour in many Western European nations have been the social and political pressures to eliminate imported laborers who comprise as much as one-third of the labor force in some countries. In Sweden, confidence in the continuance of full employment and trust in the government commitment to ease the adjustment to change are sufficient for fears of displacement to recede into secondary importance. But in the rest of Western Europe, despite full-employment labor shortages, protection against displacement is still the public concern of highest priority.

U.S. MANPOWER POLICY IN HISTORICAL PERSPECTIVE

Manpower policy in the United States has a long history, which, lacking present national coherence, is difficult to trace. The dual threads of concern for manpower as an economic resource and concern for the welfare of workers have always been present—the former paramount in slavery, immigration, the Morrill Act, and the Smith-Hughes Act, the latter predominating in abolition of slavery and child labor and in wage and hour legislation. But, though both concerns have coexisted historically, dominance of the social welfare orientation is a development of recent decades.

The overwhelming influence on U.S. manpower policy at its present stage has been persistent unemployment. The depression of the 1930's provides a "continental divide" not only in the history of the U.S. economic policies, but in that of most liberal democracies. The success of the policies of the time was meager, but so in retrospect was the effort relative to the magnitude of the problem. But both the insecurities of industrial society and the political power of the insecure were amply demonstrated. The Second World War turned attention temporarily to allocation of scarce manpower, but the fear of resumption of serious unemployment was a constant policy goad.

The Employment Act of 1946, which recognized the new political reality—that the level of employment was subject to, and the responsibility of, public policy—had its correlates abroad. But, while Western European nations moved ahead aggressively into full employment policy and then into manpower policy, public policy in the United States took a temporary detour. The postwar boom quieted fears of unemployment, while the frustrations of the Korean conflict, following hard upon global war, brought demands for recess from public exertion. There followed seven years during which private enterprise, budget balance, international balance of payments equilibrium, and price stability took priority over economic growth, and inflation, mild though it was, appeared a greater threat than unemployment.

32

THE DEVELOPMENT OF MANPOWER POLICY

The peculiarities of the recess in U.S. employment policy produced an aberration in the development of manpower policy in this country in contrast to others. Western Europeans followed their declarations of employment policy with aggressive fiscal actions. Then, when these proved inadequate to eliminate the insecurities of industrial life, and when labor shortages exerted heavy pressures on price levels, they developed manpower policies designed to ease adjustment and increase labor market efficiency. Only now, as labor shortages and the demands of more sophisticated technologies threaten to throttle economic growth for lack of highly educated and trained manpower, is the development of labor as an economic resource receiving attention in those countries.

In this country, competition with communism became the focus of international policy at the same time anti-inflation was dominating domestic policy. The success of the Soviet Union in the development of nuclear weapons and the launching of the first space satellite plunged us into a race to produce scientific and technical manpower, three years before we returned to welfare-oriented manpower policies.

When the path charted during the depression was resumed, we again pursued manpower policy in reverse order to European developments. The demand to "get America moving again" was a slogan of the 1960 presidential campaign and the decision was an extraordinarily close one. The major domestic issue was unemployment and its elimination was the first order of business. Yet several years of experimentation, education, and political realignment were required before substantial gains were made.

In retrospect, the explanation of the unemployment which rose persistently following the Korean conflict is readily apparent. The gross national product, which grew an average of 4.9 percent per year between 1947 and 1953, grew only 2.4 percent per year during 1953–60. The fiscal exertions that would have been necessary to prevent unemployment from rising above its 1953 level of 2.9 percent of the labor force would have been slight.[1] Lacking this narrow margin, labor force growth and productivity increases exceeded economic growth, and unemployment rose to an average of 5 percent during the post-Korean decade and 6 percent from 1958 to 1963.

[1] Assuming that the rates of labor force growth and productivity increase which actually occurred would have been no greater, an addition to GNP growth rates of another 0.4 percent per year would have been adequate to prevent the rise of unemployment between 1953 and 1960. Given faster economic growth, however, both the labor force and productivity would have probably experienced somewhat more rapid increases. It is doubtful that more than the postwar average growth rate of 3.5 percent would have been necessary to restrain unemployment.

33

With inadequate economic growth the primary source of unemployment, the economically rational solution would have been immediate adoption of aggressive fiscal policies. Politically, the nation was not prepared to step so far so fast. The location and characteristics of the unemployed were readily observable, but the solutions to general unemployment required more flexibility and courage among the populace and their representatives than was available. Therefore the first experimental efforts were directed at the structural impacts rather than the basic causes of unemployment, and manpower policy took precedence over employment policy.

With the legislature structured along geographical lines, the attack upon unemployment began with federal aid to depressed areas. The next consensus reached was upon the need for a training program. The concentration of unemployment among the unskilled and uneducated was noted and accepted by many as an explanation of unemployment. The fiscally conservative blamed lack of salable skills rather than the lack of jobs. Others, noting the unabsorbed victims of technological change, and overly impressed by a few early examples of automation, hypothesized that a new technological revolution was twisting the demand for labor, eliminating jobs for the unskilled, and creating unfillable demands for workers with higher education and skills. Those who would have given first priority to aggressive fiscal policies advocated education, training, and expenditure increases as good, in and of themselves. Accordingly, the Manpower Development and Training Act of 1962 (MDTA) and the Vocational Education Act of 1963 received overwhelming bipartisan support. When experience demonstrated that many unemployed lacked the basic literacy skills required for successful retraining, MDTA was amended in 1963 to add basic education to skill training for the unemployed. With continued unemployment, relocation allowances, once political anathema, were written into the law on an experimental basis. Each of these amendments and other more minor ones enjoyed bipartisan endorsement and minimal opposition.

Just as unemployment was concentrated according to education, skill, and location, it was also concentrated according to age and race. The youth unemployment rate, persisting at nearly three times the high general unemployment rate, was described as "social dynamite," and a Youth Employment Act was passed by the Senate in 1963 as a rescue operation. Essentially, the Act was modeled upon the Civilian Conservation Corps legislation of the 1930's and provided for: (1) a conservation corps to employ youth in rural conservation camps, and (2) a hometown youth corps to employ youth in socially desirable activities in their home environments. Once again, the proposal appeared to have prevailing support but it foundered in the House Rules Committee upon the integration issue. Negro unemployment, persistently double the over-all rate, was an important element in the civil rights struggles occurring at the same time.

Concern for the two related issues, youth and Negro unemployment, was a primary impetus to the Economic Opportunity Act passed in 1964. The Act was an enlargement and a repackaging of several existing and proposed programs but still marked a new departure in manpower programs. The Area Redevelopment Administration, the Manpower Development and Training Act and the Vocational Education Act were all directed at the mainstream of employment in the private, profit-making sector of the economy. In contrast the Youth Employment Bill had proposed public and nonprofit employment for youth. Under the 1962 Social Security Amendments, a $2 million per year pittance had been earmarked to match state expenditures to allow parents of dependent children to work for benefits they would have received without working. The Juvenile Delinquency and Youth Offenses Control Act had underwritten local experiments with an emphasis upon employment. All of these were picked up, enlarged, and repackaged as the heart of the new "war on poverty." They are now respectively the Job Corps, the Neighborhood Youth Corps, the Work Experience Program and the Community Action Program. For the first time since the experimental 1930's, direct public employment was provided upon a substantial scale to the unemployed.

Also inspired by concern for youth and Negro unemployment was a new look at the schools from which, along with home environments, the disadvantages of many stemmed. The fruits of this recognition came the following year with the Primary and Secondary Education Act and Operation Head Start.

But all of these dramatic legislative developments were largely of long-run significance. Though they were aimed primarily at unemployment, they had relatively little to offer in the short run. At the end of 1963, unemployment still stood at 5.6 percent. A year later it had dropped to 5 percent and the following year to 4 percent. But the reason was not the accumulated impact of the impressive package of manpower tools which had been developed. The solution to unemployment came through aggressive fiscal policies, first through the deliberate act of cutting taxes in February, 1964—while maintaining expenditures, despite an already large deficit in the federal budget—and then through the unfortunate coincidence of international conflict.

35

EVALUATING MANPOWER POLICY DEVELOPMENTS

In the development of manpower policy, the United States put the cart before the horse. But, since horsepower was soon furnished, the ordering of priorities is now of more academic than practical interest. A more rational approach would have supplied jobs through fiscal policies, provided skills through education and training, and matched them through labor market programs. But the experimentation was necessary for public education. Some element of mythology is probably inherent in the policy-making process and policy-makers are often more concerned with the practicality of results than the rationality of approach.

Despite the haphazardness of approach, the United States now has all of the basic elements of an active manpower policy. The 1946 commitment to "maximum" employment was given under duress—the fear of resumption of the depression. A new commitment may have been made based upon understanding of the effectiveness of the tools and the implications of their use. The tax cut of 1964 is likely to stand out as the most important economic act of a generation. Its precision of impact was remarkable. It fell short of its 4 percent unemployment goal only because the federal budget failed to rise along unexpected trends. Its economic impetus has now faded but the educational value remains.

However, the success of fiscal policy does not diminish the importance of the manpower programs. Rather, it has only created the environment within which the manpower tools can be worked effectively. The Area Redevelopment Administration made little imprint, but the Appalachian Commission and the Economic Development Administration hope to learn from its experience. Training the unemployed under MDTA did not create jobs but the experimental size of the program reduced the significance of that fact. The 188,000 persons who had completed MDTA retraining programs by the end of 1965 did not exhaust the inevitable mismatches in a 75 million person labor force. Seventy percent of the trainees found training-related jobs, but the extent to which they did so in preference to others who would have filled the same jobs cannot be known. The implementation of the relocation experiments was at first blocked by the absence of labor shortage areas to which the unemployed could be relocated. With the resumption of rapid growth, 1,200 persons—also a relatively small number—were assisted by relocation grants and loans between late 1964 and the close of 1965.

The manpower elements of the Economic Opportunity Act were more rationally related to their targets. The Neighborhood Youth Corps (NYC) was employing 150,000 a month in early 1966 but three-fourths were in school and employed part-time on NYC projects; approximately

20,000 were enlisted in the Job Corps; 66,000 adults had been aided by the Work Experience Program. But these totals are small compared to the 3½ million unemployed at the beginning of 1965 and the 2½ million jobs created by the ordinary workings of the economy during the same year.

However, inability to solve unemployment does not imply criticism of any of the programs. The mating of strange bedfellows and the dramatization of the prosaic are central to the art of politics. In 1961, 1962, or 1963, aggressive fiscal policies were not yet politically salable, but manpower programs were. Prosaic appeals, for instance, that manpower training would enable the unskilled to compete more effectively for the few existing jobs, or that it might be wise to tool up for possible future periods of labor shortage, would have attracted little support. Combining the carrot and the stick—the suggestion of any easy solution to unemployment through matching a supposedly near equal number of unemployed and job vacancies and the fears of automation gobbling up unskilled jobs and spawning only skilled ones—was highly effective.

Each of the programs, though limited in over-all impact, was helpful to thousands of individuals. The benefits no doubt justified the limited amounts spent. The whole period has been one of social experimentation, the results of which will probably reverberate favorably into the future. Yet, after all of the arguments concerning the relative merits of aggregate demand and structural cures of unemployment, only the aggregative measures—first the tax cut, then the Vietnam escalation—have as yet made a significant impact.

THE UNFINISHED BUSINESS OF MANPOWER POLICY

The task of creating adequate numbers of job opportunities is nearing accomplishment. By early 1966, unemployment had dropped below 4 percent and the average for the year was expected to be 3.5 percent or below. It is unfortunate that the required stimulus had to come from military involvement. But had the Vietnam escalation not occurred, fiscal action would likely have been taken to reduce or restrain unemployment, though at a more relaxed pace. The faith in fiscal policy is high, and the disposition to use it is strong. Arguments will continue over the relative threats of unemployment and inflation, but these involve the timing and use of tools, not their appropriateness or effectiveness. And those with a vested interest in continuing prosperity and growth are increasingly vocal.

Western European nations have demonstrated ability to maintain unemployment levels below 2 percent. But their labor forces are more homogeneous, their people less mobile and their inflation tolerances higher than ours. We have yet to prove our ability to sustain unemployment levels below 4 percent without substantial pressures on price levels. To do so will increase rather than decrease the importance of manpower policy. Despite the rapid progress of the past five years, there is much unfinished business, administrative and conceptual, before our manpower programs and policies are equal to the task.

The United States now has an extensive kit of manpower tools. The primary challenge is to learn to use them effectively. We are discovering that it is a long way from the halls of Congress or the desk of the federal administrator to the home, the workplace, the classroom, and the local community. The federal manpower programs were put together piecemeal. They often function more as competitors for the privilege of serving the unemployed or the unsatisfactorily employed than as a carefully honed and polished set of tools available to the social and economic mechanic for application in the appropriate combination. Instead, each tool tends to belong to a separate mechanic who has only that tool and insists on applying it regardless of fit. Federal, state, and local officials are both aware of and working at the problem of improved coordination at the Washington and local levels but solutions are elusive. Similarly, only the most sophisticated communities are aware of the availability and the nuances of every federal manpower program; only such communities have the ingenuity to design a combination applicable to local circumstances and the political astuteness to know where and how to obtain assistance. This, too, comes with experience, but the channels should be more apparent and readily accessible.

Conceptually, all three aspects of manpower policy—job creation, manpower development, and the matching of men and jobs—will face continued challenges. In the creation of employment opportunities, the unfinished business is (1) to supply jobs for those unable to compete effectively in the labor market, (2) to raise the quality of the jobs provided, and (3) to assume a satisfactory relationship of jobs to income.

In concept, sufficient demand could be created to provide a job for everyone available for work, and more. In actuality, the price in inflation would be unacceptable. If one conceives of the entire labor force as being queued in order of their relative attractiveness to employers, employers could be forced to dig more deeply down the line through increased demand. But the differences between those at the front and those at the rear of the line are probably greater in the United States than anywhere else. Rapidly rising educational attainment inevitably puts age at a disadvantage. High educational attainment puts the school dropout further behind. Race, accompanied by prejudice, adds an additional competitive burden. And employers do have alternatives. They can bid with their fellow employers for the more attractive workers at the front of the line. They can increase their substitution of machines for labor, thus raising even higher the aggregate demand required for full employment.

But the problem is not insoluble and experimentation is already under way. For youths in the Neighborhood Youth Corps and the Job Corps, and for parents of dependent children under Title V of the Economic Opportunity Act, public service jobs are being provided tailored to the abilities and limitations of the unemployed. The experience has been favorable. There is enough productive work to be done outside the usual market system to justify the federal government's constituting itself as an "employer of last resort" for all but the short-term frictionally unemployed. Development of a full-scale program will not be easy, but we have the experimental base upon which to start. But the full use and, more importantly, the welfare of the people who make up our human resources will require more than the availability of employment opportunities. Experimental door-to-door contacting in labor-short Chicago has discovered numerous people involuntarily out of the labor force for reasons ranging from lack of transportation to lack of false teeth. Ferreting out and aiding them is an expensive but humanitarianly appropriate task. It includes as well individual identification of jobs appropriate to their often limited capabilities.

As long as the problem has been to create enough jobs to go around, the quality of the jobs created has been of little concern. Various levels of government have prescribed certain minimum conditions of employment in terms of wages, working hours, and safety. As time goes on, these minimum requirements may be raised and others added, but the potential contribution of government regulation to quality is always limited. Public policy, however, need not rest only on government fiat. Positive incentives can be provided and social norms can be favorably modified. The most potent factors in the quality of employment are technological progress and educational attainment. Despite recent fears of "automation," technology has been the factor primarily responsible for gradually freeing man from slavery to his own physical needs. The trick is not to prevent technological change from displacing man from the strain, dangers, and tedium of the farms, the mines, and the factories, but to see that he is prepared for more "human" work and that more human work is available.

Wage and income policies have been almost totally absent from the manpower policy developments of the past few years. As far as policies of wage restraint are concerned, the neglect, in a period of slack demand, stable prices, and concentration upon welfare-oriented manpower programs, has been wise. In the long run, low wages might encourage the employment of labor relative to the employment of machines. However, the effect would become apparent only in the long run, and the price would be lower levels of productivity and lower standards of living. Fortunately, better alternatives are available. Higher levels of demand, fostered by appropriate fiscal policies, can generate employment for both men and machines at higher levels of productivity and income.

However, this is true only in maintaining wage levels in periods of unemployment and relatively stable prices. Full employment creates product and labor market environments which all participants, if not restrained, will exploit to their advantage. It may also include shortages of labor and capacity, which ratchet costs and prices upward. Theoretically, such pressures should be reduced by more widespread and better education and training and improvements in labor market efficiency, but this has yet to be proven. The advantages, both economic and philosophical, of free markets make us reluctant to adopt wage and price controls. So far there is no apparent alternative to some considered compromise among full employment, stable prices, and economic freedom. Whether it be called manpower policy, wage-price policy, or economic policy, achievement of the "best" wage-price-employment relationship remains an open challenge.

However, income policy is not only a matter of price stability. Increased sensitivity to the injustices of poverty has been one of the great social accomplishments of this impressive half-decade. The war on poverty has merely defined poverty incomes. None of the programs has really launched an attack. Minimum wages, wage-related social insurance benefits, and public assistance have not met the need. The degree of consensus that some form of a guaranteed minimum family income is needed is remarkable. But the methods of providing it have yet to receive serious legislative study.

The heart of manpower policy is on the supply side, however. The solutions to unemployment will allow us to turn our attention more appropriately to preparing the labor force for employment and matching available manpower with vacant jobs.

We really know little about the relative effectiveness of alternative ways of preparing people for employment. In reaction to the concentration of unemployment among the uneducated, there have been demands for more specific occupational preparation within the schools. In a calmer atmosphere there now appears to be a drawing back from this position. Education as a major answer to general unemployment, it is generally conceded, can guarantee only better-educated unemployed.

Education can affect who becomes employed and who unemployed, but not, at least in the short run, how many. But education is for more than employment; it is for life, of which employment is only a part, if an important one. The optimum combination of general education and occupational training, the appropriate locus of each within the educational system, the relative responsibility of the schools and the employers, the extent of adaptability, and the transferability of skills—these are all questions which can best be researched and answered in a climate of adequate employment opportunity. Problems of motivation and social and psychological handicaps are also relatively unplumbed. As manpower policy continues to traverse uncharted seas, the research and experimentation capability of MDTA Title I and the allocation of 10 percent of Vocational Education Act funds to research could and should become important contributions to success.

The matching of men and jobs has primarily geographical and occupational dimensions. Throughout the five years of active assault on unemployment, a few students have continued to maintain that skill shortage rather than job shortage is the problem. As they appear right in 1966, and hopefully in 1967 and beyond, they seem likely to claim retroactive confirmation for 1961–65 as well. But the problem is nevertheless real. The gap between the "hard-core" unemployed in a central city slum—or in an Appalachian hollow—and the vacant tool and die job in the suburb of another city is a wide one. Having to bridge this gap is a relatively pleasant, though challenging, task.

The Area Redevelopment Act, the Accelerated Public Works Act, the Public Works and Economic Development Act, and the Appalachian Regional Development Act all had as their assignment the attraction of jobs to areas of surplus labor. The desirability of protecting investments in private and public facilities and maintaining the stable values of homes and communities is clear. The effective means for reversing long-term regional economic decline are still elusive. Unassisted outmigration has historically been the most effective answer but it weakens communities even further. In the relatively small and immobile societies of Western Europe relocation assistance has proven its value as one of a kit of manpower tools. Only further experience can determine its effectiveness here.

Throughout all of the manpower policy developments of the past five years, the United States Employment Service, despite constant criticism, has neither enjoyed nor suffered legislative attention. With nearly 1,900 affiliated State Employment Service offices scattered throughout the country, the federally financed but state-administered public employment service is inevitably the front-line arm of any locally oriented manpower policy. Each new manpower program has increased the workload of the employment service offices without corresponding increases in budgets. National economic developments have buffeted them, despite their local-orientation. State salary structures have prevented the recruitment of sufficient competent personnel to handle the involved problems of the unemployed. The public employment service has been simultaneously criticized for weakness and inability to aid the unemployed and for attempting to monopolize the labor markets of the nation. Only now, as unemployment is declining as a general problem, is Congress turning its attention to strengthening this vital arm of manpower policy. The results of current legislative efforts remain to be seen.

MANPOWER POLICY IN PERSPECTIVE: A SUMMARY STATEMENT

Manpower policy has developed dramatically in the United States in the last five years. Though impressive in its concepts, the impact upon the world of employment has been small. While general economic measures have achieved great success, specialized structural policies remain in the experimental stage.

Unemployment is not the sum and substance of manpower problems. In fact, only as unemployment ends, can a rounded manpower policy demonstrate its true effectiveness. Once before, after a decade of progress, the apathy and ennui following the exertions of war overcame employment policy. The Employment Act of 1946 and the G.I. Bill expressed intent, but a decade and a half was lost before the battle was rejoined. It is to be hoped that employment and manpower policies are now more deeply embedded in our institutions. We have the tools and the environment for effective manpower policy. The challenge is to make them work on other than experimental levels.

3

IS THIS POVERTY WAR "DIFFERENT"?[1]

SAR A. LEVITAN

In 1964, when President Lyndon B. Johnson exhorted the nation to commit its resources to a "total war on poverty," the United States was already spending about $15 billion to aid the poor. Congress responded by appropriating nearly $800 million during the first year and $1.5 billion the next year for the new Office of Economic Opportunity (OEO). Related Great Society programs approved by Congress in 1965 —the 1965 amendments to the Social Security Act, as well as education, housing and aid to depressed areas—will, when they become fully effective, add another $1.5 billion annually in aid of the poor.

It may therefore be estimated that about $3 billion in additional funds to combat poverty were allocated under the Great Society programs during 1965. Roughly, this means that since the President declared total war on poverty our government has committed itself for new expenditures of about $90 a year per poor person in the country. If Congress approves the Administration's proposals for fiscal 1967, expenditures under the Economic Opportunity Act will be raised by another $9 per poor person. Obviously, these amounts fall far short of the Great Society's "unconditional war on poverty."

Granted that the additional resources allocated under the Economic Opportunity Act do not mean a total war against poverty, the new programs might have an economic and social significance not suggested by the dollar amounts. Do the programs inaugurated under the new legislation really differ radically, in substance and administration, from past efforts to aid the poor? Is the Economic Opportunity Act the harbinger of a new approach to dealing with the impoverished? And what is the appropriate role of the poor in this war?

This paper focuses on these questions, dealing *only* with the program inaugurated under the Economic Opportunity Act as implemented during the first year of operations through the end of 1965.[2] It is ob-

[1] This paper is a preliminary statement of a study dealing with the Economic Opportunity Act supported by a grant from the Ford Foundation.

[2] The Economic Opportunity Act was signed into law on August 20, 1964, but no funds were disbursed for more than three months. Calendar 1965 roughly coincides, therefore, with the first year of operations under the legislation.

viously premature at this stage to attempt an evaluation of the effects of the fledgling programs. However, an examination of major past developments and stated objectives should yield some tentative conclusions as to whether the Great Society's war on poverty differs from traditional assistance laws.

THE 1964 ANTI-POVERTY ACT

The Economic Opportunity Act provides for four major groups of programs:

1. *Work training for youth from impoverished homes and for adults, primarily parents whose families are on relief.* These programs (the Neighborhood Youth Corps and the Work Experience Program, respectively) provide relatively unskilled public jobs for unemployed youths and parents.[3]

2. *Special rehabilitation and training for youth from impoverished homes.* This program, the Job Corps, emphasizes training rather than job creation. It removes youths from their home environment and places them in special centers where the training is provided.

3. *Expansion of services to the poor, including education and various welfare services.* The Community Action Program stresses coordinated welfare services to the poor, attempting wherever feasible to employ persons from impoverished homes in providing services to their indigent neighbors and to involve the poor in the planning and administration of the programs.

4. *Loans to impoverished rural residents and to small businessmen.* These programs aim at fostering self-employment of poor people.

The relative importance of these programs, measured in terms of funds allocated during fiscal 1966 and proposed by the Administration for fiscal 1967, can be gleaned from Table 1.

[3] A subsidiary program providing for employment of youth, in order to permit them to continue with their college education, was included in the 1965 Higher Education Act and is no longer part of the Economic Opportunity Act. This change itself indicates the eclectic character of the programs included in the 1964 anti-poverty package.

TABLE 1.
Economic Opportunity Act Programs, Fiscal 1966 and 1967.

Program	Millions of Dollars		Percent	
	Fiscal 1966 Allocations	Fiscal 1967 Proposals	1966	1967
Total	1,512[a]	1,800	100.0	100.0
Work training	439	490	29.1	27.4
Neighborhood Youth Corps	259	300	17.2	16.8
Adult work experience	150[b]	160	10.0	8.9
Adult basic education	30	30	2.0	1.7
Job Corps	310	228[c]	20.6	12.7
Community Action Program	637	914	42.3	51.1
Self-employment	63	83	4.2	4.6
Small business	28	55[d]	1.9	3.1
Rural loans	35	28	2.3	1.6
Administration and other[e]	63	85	3.8	4.2

[a] Congress appropriated a lump-sum, and the allocation of funds for each of the programs was determined administratively within constraints indicated by the enabling legislation. Funds allocated to college work-study are not included since this program is no longer part of EOA.

[b] Includes $25 million, unused in fiscal 1965.

[c] Despite the apparent cut, this does not represent an actual reduction in Job Corps activity due to advance funding of urban centers from 1966 appropriation.

[d] Includes $5 million to be allocated for the establishment of Small Business Development Centers financed in 1966 from Community Action Program funds. The loan funds are appropriated directly to the Small Business Administration and earmarked for this program.

[e] Includes domestic peace corps (VISTA) volunteers and Migrant Labor — $41 million in 1966 and $63 million in 1967.

Work Training Programs

The Neighborhood Youth Corps (NYC) is geared to provide employment opportunities and income for youths from impoverished homes by providing conventional work relief with few, if any, "frills." The bulk of the funds (85 percent) was spent in 1965 to pay wages of $1.25 an hour to youths selected for employment on Neighborhood Youth Corps projects sponsored by government agencies or nonprofit organizations. The jobs performed by Neighborhood Youth Corps enrollees normally require minimum skills. To the extent that funds have been available, NYC has accomplished its task efficiently and effectively. During the summer of 1965, eight months after the program was put into effect, 278,000 youths were on NYC payrolls.

Some knowledgeable observers have claimed that, in addition to providing income to impoverished youths and their families, the program might well have prevented disturbances and possibly even riots during the summer of 1965. Indeed, aside from complaints from some quarters that the rate of pay is too high, the program has generated little controversy. The $1.25 hourly pay rate has caused some problems in low-wage areas; a number of communities have failed to participate in NYC projects because the pay was in excess of the prevailing wage rate for unskilled labor.

The Neighborhood Youth Corps has been criticized on the basis that the work it provides does not equip the enrollees with salable skills and therefore accomplishes little toward increasing his chances for regular employment. This criticism hardly applies, however, to nearly three of every four NYC enrollees, who are attending school. NYC supplies the in-school enrollees with much-needed pocket money and family income support, aside from some work experience, and thus should help them continue their schooling. Precise estimates of the extent to which NYC programs have prevented school dropouts are not known.

Criticism of the meager fare offered by NYC projects to out-of-school enrollees is more pertinent. NYC's critics have urged that the program be "enriched" by offering enrollees more counseling, guidance, remedial education, and training. In view of the limited resources of NYC and the great numbers wishing to qualify for the program, it is not at all clear that allocating a larger proportion of funds for supportive services would be justified, even if qualified personnel—teachers, counselors, social workers—could be secured. The fact is that the incidence of unemployment decreases as the youths mature. It may therefore be a wiser public policy to provide as many unemployed youths as possible with jobs to tide them over the critical years when they find it most difficult to secure employment in the marketplace, and to supply them with some income while they continue their education.

While the Neighborhood Youth Corps focuses on providing stopgap employment and income to youth from impoverished families, the goal of the program for adults is to raise the "level of employability" of un-employed parents and other needy persons through a comprehensive program of work experience and training. This new approach to work relief entails vocational training, counseling, guidance, work motivation, remedial health care, rudimentary education and placement.

It is not yet evident whether the program will live up to its promise. During the first year Department of Health, Education, and Welfare (HEW) officials in charge of the program and their state and local counterparts concentrated on developing projects. Statistics are not yet available concerning the characteristics of the trainees, the extent and quality of supportive services which are built into the program, or the impact of the training upon the enrollees. Nor is it clear whether welfare officials who are in charge of local projects will be able to change their orientation from relief services to developing effective training programs.

The precise extent to which the projects in the Work Experience Program provide additional income to participants is not known. Under the provisions of the program, trainees receive the full amount for basic needs as determined by the appropriate state welfare agencies. Therefore, in those states or localities where the relief recipient receives benefits adequate to cover his basic needs, a person selected to participate in a work-experience project is not provided extra pay except for those expenses connected with working (e.g., carfare). But in a majority of states payments to relief recipients are insufficient to meet basic needs. In these states participants in the Work Experience Program receive the full amount needed to cover basic needs. The program is of additional value because about four of every ten participants have not qualified for relief in their states.

The work performed by the trainees was limited almost exclusively to government agencies and nonprofit organizations. Unlike the Secretary of Labor in the case of NYC, the Secretary of HEW is authorized to place selectees for training with profit-making establishments, but he exercised this authority most sparingly during the first year of operations. Rough estimates indicate that during 1965 about four of every ten trainees worked in service occupations, predominantly as nurses' aides or as janitors. A similar proportion performed clerical work or such semi-skilled duties as highway beautification, landscaping, and ground maintenance. The balance, two of every ten, worked in skilled and sub-professional occupations—though the extent of skill required of the trainees is not known.

Many of the persons accepted for training are unemployed because of deficient education, while others may have personal and family difficulties which are handicaps to employment. Preliminary data indicate that nearly a third of the participants' time was spent in training and education, as distinguished from actual "work." Since the components for education, training, and other supportive services involve the use of professional workers, a significant proportion of the total funds for the Work Experience Program—almost as much as half (excluding assistance payments)—is allocated to supportive services. Given the limited funds available under the program, an emphasis on supportive services necessarily limits the number of participants. Since demand for work experience far exceeds currently available funds, it may again be asked whether it would not be wiser to maximize work relief rather than stress supportive professional services already in short supply. Emphasis on work relief would not only increase the income of some relief recipients and other needy persons, but also provide them opportunities for performing useful work which would otherwise not be undertaken.

Moreover, some expert observers suggest that the mere provision of opportunities for relief recipients to "work off" the aid they receive has considerable rehabilitative value and eventually helps them secure gainful employment in the competitive market. HEW officials estimated that in 1965 between 200,000 and 300,000 recipients of aid to families with dependent children (AFDC) alone would be available to participate in work-experience projects, provided adequate funds could be allocated to expand the program. Other needy persons who have not qualified for AFDC—including impoverished marginal farmers who became eligible under a 1965 amendment to the Economic Opportunity Act—might increase the number of potential work-experience participants to a million or more, far in excess of the funds available under the program.

Job Corps

The Job Corps differs radically from the Neighborhood Youth Corps in that it seeks to equip selectees with salable skills and offers them an opportunity to acquire a basic education, which many trainees failed to obtain in school. The cost per trainee is substantial, but it cannot be measured precisely since a large proportion of the funds expended during the first year of the Job Corps was allocated to the construction and renovation of camp sites. Even when the programs become fully operative, however, the average annual cost will exceed appreciably $6,600 per enrollee, the latest available official estimate made by OEO officials.

The underlying theory of the Job Corps is that a youth from an impoverished home must sometimes be removed from his (or her) environment to undergo an effective training program. The Job Corps enrollee receives a monthly allowance of $30 and is also provided room, board, clothing, and medical care while in training. Upon discharge from the Job Corps, the enrollee receives a readjustment allowance of $50 for each month spent in the Job Corps. The trainee may allocate as much as half of this allowance to support his family, and when he elects to make such a monthly allotment, the government matches the contribution. Six of every ten enrollees have selected to aid their families with an average monthly contribution of $45, including the government share.

The Job Corps sponsors conservation and urban centers. The Economic Opportunity Act requires that 40 percent of all male Job Corps enrollees be assigned to conservation centers, which are located in national parks, forests, and other public facilities. Enrollment in these camps, averaging about 100 in some 75 centers, is limited to males. Training is focused on basic education and, as the title indicates, on conservation work and related activity, which may include fire control, timber management, improvement in recreation sites, wildlife management, operation of heavy equipment, and maintenance of conservation facilities.

The urban training centers, with a planned enrollment of 800 to 3,000 in the eight male centers and 250 to 1,000 for three female centers, are operated under contract by private corporations or educational institutions. In addition to training enrollees for various skilled and service occupations, the urban centers offer enrollees an opportunity to acquire the basic education which most of them missed in elementary and secondary schools. Centers for men are normally located in renovated federal facilities, such as former military camps, while projects for women are located in former residential facilities, such as hotels.

The Job Corps has been the subject of considerable controversy. Opponents of the program are fond of pointing out, though with questionable validity (if opportunity costs are to be considered), that it costs more to maintain a boy in the Job Corps than at Harvard College. This in itself is not sufficient cause to raise criticism against the program. It should hardly be surprising, moreover, that when several hundred boys or girls from slum neighborhoods and impoverished homes are brought together, cases of antisocial behavior will arise. The news media and others have been diligent in exploiting unfavorable publicity about the Job Corps. The wide publicity given such incidents has impaired the public image of the Job Corps.

Some social workers and educators have also questioned the wisdom of the Job Corps practice of uprooting of slum youths. These critics have suggested that the resources allocated to the Job Corps would have greater social returns if the trainee were left in the "natural" environment. They argue that a rustic environment under "paramilitary" conditions is not the most efficient way of preparing youths for urban life. The high rate of dropouts—about 30 percent of the enrollees have left the program before completing their course of training—does indicate that many youths find it difficult to adjust to the camp environment and discipline. Defenders of the Job Corps reply that these criticisms are based on a naïve and romantic idea about slum life: many of the youths who enroll in the Job Corps do not, in fact, have any permanent homes. For example, the Job Corps offered an all-expenses-paid trip home to its 17,500 trainees for the 1965 Christmas holidays. More than one in five trainees chose to remain at camp. And 95 percent of the enrollees returned to their camps when their leaves expired.

Advocates of the Job Corps have argued that it may be the most innovative program inaugurated under the Economic Opportunity Act. The Job Corps is often compared to the Civilian Conservation Corps (CCC) of the 1930's, but this comparison is misleading. While the CCC did offer basic education to illiterate and poorly educated enrollees, the emphasis was mainly on providing sustenance and some employment opportunities during a period when mass unemployment prevailed throughout the United States. The Job Corps has much broader goals. In addition to training youths for the world of work by equipping them with skills salable in the free market, it encourages enrollees to continue with their education after completion of the course and tries to motivate them to enter the mainstream of American economic and social life. To accomplish these goals, the Office of Economic Opportunity has enlisted the aid not only of the traditional educational and welfare institutions, but also the active participation of major American business organizations. This is perhaps the first instance in which the American business community has taken a direct role in the rehabilitation of the poor. And some major corporations are sufficiently involved in the operations of the Job Corps to have identified their public image with the success of this venture.

There is already some evidence that business involvement in training Job Corps enrollees has brought new dimensions to the training and rehabilitation of disadvantaged youth. No claim is made that corporate involvement so far has brought new techniques or fresh insights to the rehabilitation process. But the limited available data suggest that business know-how and approach are not encumbered by the usual red tape and abhorrence of change associated with our educational system. Still, there is no guarantee that the participation of the business community will insure success in achieving the Job Corps' goals. The history of American business is replete with instances of huge investments which failed to develop successful new products. In the case of the Job Corps, private firms have undertaken no financial risks since all the operations are administered under a cost-plus-fixed-fee basis.

At this early stage, any evaluation of the Job Corps must be speculative. The program may have important benefits which transcend the rehabilitation of a limited number of selectees. Ample evidence shows that our educational system has failed to provide even a basic education for millions of youngsters. The reference here is not only to "dropouts" who leave school to accept remunerative employment, but to millions who go through years of unproductive schooling, in many cases even achieving a "graduation" diploma. A disproportionate number of those who fail in school—or, as some would say, for whom the school has been a failure—come from impoverished homes.

The Job Corps is attempting to develop new techniques and approaches to educate and train youngsters who have not succeeded in the traditional educational system. Job Corps centers may therefore be

50

viewed as laboratories, albeit expensive laboratories, to develop techniques to educate and train vast numbers who failed to get a rudimentary education in school. If the Job Corps succeeds with the limited number of enrollees, it will offer a striking challenge to our educational system and perhaps stimulate the adoption of new techniques and approaches that may be transferable to school systems and adult basic education programs throughout the country.

At this stage, however, such impacts of the Job Corps remain to be seen. Whether the highest potentials of the Job Corps will materialize can hardly be guessed.

Community Action Programs

The OEO-sponsored Community Action Program (CAP) has thus far attracted the greatest public interest and controversy. CAP is a catchall effort to aid the poor. Practically any project that aims at reducing poverty in a community may be funded by OEO provided the poor or their spokesmen participate in the planning and execution of the project and provided racial discrimination is barred. Approved projects have included remedial and preschool education, employment and job training, health services, birth control clinics, vocational rehabilitation, housing and home management, consumer education, legal aid, social services including day-care services, recreation, and the establishment of neighborhood centers aimed at providing "one-stop" services to the poor in the area. The list is not exhaustive, but it indicates the broad scope of activities that CAP may support.

The presumed innovations of the CAP consist of three major and related components:

1. Community Action Programs provide for comprehensive approaches to community welfare problems;

2. Community Action Programs may establish new federal-local relations; and

3. Community Action Programs require that the programs be developed and implemented with "maximum feasible participation" of the residents.

The emphasis that the agency places on broadly based community programs is more rhetoric than reality. Most of the OEO projects have been of the common garden variety and have differed little from traditional welfare programs. Coordination with established programs has thus far been minimal; and even some of the programs inaugurated under the Economic Opportunity Act have been administered independently by separate federal agencies and by the communities which received OEO grants. The emphasis placed upon preschool education does not necessarily indicate a new type of program, but rather a recognition that publicly supported education should start before age six and is in fact an extension of the kindergarten and nursery school. It is true that such facilities are normally not available to poor children, but there is little evidence that the hastily improvised Head Start Program has fostered new techniques or educational practices. Neighborhood centers, the core of comprehensive programs (representing a tenth of CAP funds), are an extension of old settlement houses which had their origin at the turn of the century. One area in which OEO could have had a noticeable impact, within its resources, is family planning. However, OEO has so far muffed this opportunity and has supported only a few birth control projects, which are obliged to operate under strict and binding regulations imposed by OEO guidelines.

While OEO spokesmen might acknowledge that little innovation has been evidenced during the short life of the program, they suggest that this is hardly germane to an evaluation of the anti-poverty program. A more valid issue is whether the program provides the poor with needed services and aid which were otherwise unavailable to them. It is of little consequence that the concept of community centers has existed for decades; what is significant for the purposes of appraising the effectiveness of the anti-poverty program is that these one-stop services to the poor have been made available on a broader basis. Similarly, it is quite irrelevant that the need for preschool facilities has been known for many years. The fact that these facilities, including medical services, have been made available to slum children before they are universally provided in more affluent neighborhoods is by itself a significant innovation.

Partisans of the anti-poverty program also insist that the return on every OEO dollar is greater than under traditional welfare programs. By stressing coordinated community anti-poverty programs, CAP-funded projects allegedly have an impact which is greater than the sum of their parts. This claim is difficult to substantiate, and again there is really no evidence that the "comprehensive community action program" differs radically from old-fashioned welfare programs. While not generally acknowledged, the traditional fractionalized welfare programs are subject to a review under the normal budgetary process. Since city officials must consider all welfare needs before funds are allocated, a definite element of review is introduced into decisions for support of specific programs. Similarly, there is strong competition for the funds allocated by private philanthropic institutions, such as the United Givers

Fund, and the officials of these organizations must review total resources and the claims of individual programs in order to determine rationally the amounts to be allocated for each project.

It is, in short, difficult to discern substantive differences between the allocation of funds under multipurpose CAP projects and traditional welfare programs. It might be suspected that differences in procedures of allocating funds under CAP as opposed to established programs are more apparent than real and may well reflect the relative newness of the CAP. By allocating additional funds, CAP in its formative stages is still reviewing the many competing claims upon its resources while the allocation of funds under established welfare programs has already been determined.

Nevertheless, it would be a mistake to dismiss the contribution made by the CAP comprehensive approach and to assume that it is merely an addition of resources to existing welfare programs. There is no denying the fact that the allocation of funds for established welfare programs is mostly based on long-established claims and that each welfare program is normally operated independently. By stressing comprehensive approaches to welfare needs, OEO presumably requires the administrators of independent programs to review their operations in relation to over-all welfare needs. But the impact of CAP in most communities is rather insignificant and accounts for a small increment in total welfare expenditures. Originally conceived as model pilot programs in a score of areas, CAP has already spread its limited resources thinly over some 700 communities and new CAP's are being funded almost daily.

The Community Action Program also has important implications for federal relations with state and local governments. It establishes direct relations between federal and local governments, largely ignoring state and, occasionally, local governments. Students of public administration may not agree that this is a wholesome development. Precedents for direct federal-local relations exist in the juvenile delinquency program, urban renewal program, and, to a lesser extent, in federal aid to depressed areas, and in other programs; but these are exceptions. Federal grants for welfare, education, and related programs are as a rule, allocated to the states, which in turn distribute funds among political subdivisions. Those who favor the CAP approach argue that OEO is in a better position than states to allocate funds efficiently, and that direct federal-local relationships bring the federal government closer to the people, eliminating the layer of state bureaucracy. Others argue that most communities do not have the necessary expertise to handle welfare programs, and that allocation of federal aid through state channels provides for an orderly distribution of funds with technical assistance not otherwise available to communities.[4]

Perhaps the most troublesome (and, according to some, potentially the most innovative) feature of the Economic Opportunity Act is Section 203(a)(3)—the provision that Community Action Programs must be "developed, conducted, and administered with maximum feasible participation of residents of the areas and members of the groups served." Few question the desirability of involving the poor in Community Action Programs, or dispute the advantages of employing the poor on community action projects. But the legislation goes beyond this, requiring that they or their representatives participate also in planning and administering these programs. This provision has raised serious difficulties. Two related questions are involved: Who is to represent the poor? How are the representatives to be selected?

Underlying the controversy on participation of the poor is a disagreement over the causes of poverty. Asserting that the causes of poverty are basically institutional, such as discrimination and lack of opportunity, some argue that the poor are in the best position to determine needed changes in institutions and thus eliminate the causes of poverty. Proponents of this view suggest that the very title of the anti-poverty program, the Economic Opportunity Act, supports their thesis. This position has been widely challenged on the ground that poor people who have failed in their own personal war on poverty can hardly be expected to plan a successful attack on poverty for others. Implied in this view is the belief that the causes of poverty are basically due to individual shortcomings.

Obviously, the causes of poverty are much more complex than the above views would suggest, although each position contains some elements of truth. The recognition of institutional impediments to economic opportunity does not support the claim that only the poor are knowledgeable enough to plan an effective war on poverty. Nor is the fact that some people are poor because of low intelligence adequate reason for rejecting the desirability of getting other poor involved in the administration and execution of anti-poverty programs. The planning and execution of effective anti-poverty programs are complicated tasks requiring expert knowledge and appropriate participation by all those involved. No single group or discipline has a monopoly of the wisdom and know-how for waging this type of war.

[4] This "new federalism" is discussed in greater detail in Roger H. Davidson, "Poverty and the New Federalism," this volume.

The case for the desirability of involving the poor in the war on poverty is clear. Not only is this in line with traditional democratic processes, but there is general consensus that self-help is the most effective form of aid. This necessarily implies that the poor should participate in shaping and directing projects on their behalf. One of the most serious weaknesses of our welfare institutions is that officials of established programs have normally assumed that they know what is best for the poor and have consequently treated the poor only as passive recipients.

Granted the desirability of obtaining representation of the poor in the planning and execution of anti-poverty programs, the question arises as to how the representatives are to be selected. The usual practice in selecting governing or advisory boards to administer government programs is for the established political authority (governor, mayor, or county supervisor) to designate representatives from the groups involved along with prominent citizens interested in a given program. However, the poor have few if any recognized spokesmen, because they lack the organizations from which appropriate representatives could be drawn.

OEO has frowned upon the exercise of arbitrary authority by City Hall or the County Courthouse in selecting spokesmen for the poor. Obviously, such appointments do not constitute involvement of the poor. Since the establishment of the Economic Opportunity Act and its Community Action Programs, a number of techniques have been established to select representatives of the poor for governing bodies that would plan and execute these projects.

The Philadelphia experience indicates the problems faced by city officials in designating the representatives of the poor. When Philadelphia embarked on a Community Action Program in 1965, the mayor appointed a nineteen-member CAP committee consisting of city officials, delegates from welfare agencies and representatives from labor and civil rights groups, including the National Association for the Advancement of Colored People, the Congress of Racial Equality, and the Urban League. Indicating that these groups did not necessarily represent the poor, OEO insisted that the mayor add to the committee twelve persons selected by the poor. After considerable wrangling it was decided that the representatives should be elected from those neighborhoods in the city where families with low incomes were concentrated. About half a million people were eligible to vote in this election, but only 13,493 votes were cast, less than 3 percent of all those eligible to vote. Similar elections were held in Cleveland, Ohio, Kansas City, Missouri, and Los Angeles, California, where the participation rate ranged from 1 to 5 percent. Since these elections were widely publicized, particularly in the low-income neighborhoods, it was apparent that the vast majority of the poor did not participate in the election to designate representatives for the local community action programs. Whether this low participation rate was due to apathy or to the inherent difficulties of reaching many of the poor is unclear. A Bureau of the Census survey in a Washington, D.C., slum area disclosed that more than half of the residents were unaware of the anti-poverty war six months after the legislation was enacted.

Few cities have followed Philadelphia's example. In some cities the representatives of the poor were elected by neighborhood groups in low-income (slum) areas. In most, however, the representatives continued to be selected by the mayor, city council, or county supervisors. Despite some displeasure on the part of OEO officials in Washington, these CAP committees have normally been declared eligible to receive federal funds.

But even direct election of representatives of the poor or selection by neighborhood groups does not assure meaningful involvement of the poor in the planning of CAP projects. CAP boards normally consist of several dozen persons, and sometimes the membership may exceed a hundred. The usual procedure is to select a small executive committee which actually makes the decisions. Inclusion of the poor representatives on the full board does not therefore guarantee that they actually participate in the formulation of CAP policy or in planning projects.

The controversy concerning participation of the poor is more than a tempest in a teapot. It is not necessary to accept the hysterical thesis advanced by a nationally syndicated columnist, who equated participation of the poor on CAP boards with the soviets established by Lenin, to recognize that involving the poor does mean organizing them for expression of social protest. Organization of the poor in low-income areas tends to focus on specific grievances, real or imagined, which are directed against established institutions. Local opposition to OEO becomes especially pronounced when paid officials of CAP projects take active roles or leadership in the organizations of the poor which attack established institutions. The grievances may be directed at the school system, welfare agencies, or related activities. Such protest actions do represent challenges to established institutions when they are buttressed and supported by broader civil rights groups. And although the activities of civil rights groups frequently become intertwined with the actual implementation and prosecution of the war on poverty, just as often the two may be only remotely related.

The political implications of combining civil rights activities with anti-poverty programs are obvious, especially in large cities where minority groups have been a mainstay of the city machines, usually Democratic.

To develop political muscle, some civil rights groups have tried to use protest action and organization of the poor to help establish new political alignments or coalitions, thus threatening the established political structure in their communities.

This situation is somewhat reminiscent of the 1930's, when the Congress of Industrial Organizations organized workers in mass industries. The newly organized labor groups then proceeded to form a potent political force within their communities and nationally. Frequently, these political activities had little or nothing to do with bread-and-butter issues. Yet, the political activities of unions have continued to remain a major political factor over the past three decades. Whether the coalition of the anti-poverty groups with the civil rights movement can become a viable political force for an extended period of time remains to be seen and predictions at this stage would be premature. But it is clear that the war on poverty, and specifically community action programs, may have deeper implication than that of merely providing an improvement of welfare services. On the other hand, concentration on broad social and political issues tends to de-emphasize the more immediate services needed by the poor. If the experience of the labor movement has any relevance at all to the poverty program, it is worthy to note that labor unions which placed greater emphasis on the "big picture" largely dissipated their energies and resources without visibly improving the immediate economic conditions of their members.

Self-Employment

The Economic Opportunity Act provides for two separate loan programs: to small businessmen and to low-income rural families. Loans to small businessmen are an extension of a program inaugurated in 1963 by the Small Business Administration (SBA). This was the "six by six" program—maximum $6,000 loans to be repaid over a period of six years. The Economic Opportunity Act raised the credit limitation to $25,000 and the duration of repayment to 15 years, though since November, 1965, loans have been restricted to $15,000.

It was not surprising that the federal lenders found a scarcity of entrepreneurs among the intended beneficiaries of the anti-poverty program. The Small Business Administration, which administers the loan program under the Economic Opportunity Act, therefore liberalized income criteria, qualifying individuals whose annual income was as much as double or more the OEO poverty criteria to receive loans. For example, while under OEO criteria an annual income of less than $3,130 for a family of four denotes poverty, the SBA qualified a borrower with three dependents if his income exceeded even $6,260 a year. Few if any poor people benefited from these loans. After one year of activity, the SBA (in November, 1965) imposed more stringent limitations on borrowers and qualified only persons whose income did not exceed the poverty income by more than 50 percent. This change reduced sharply the number of eligible applicants.

Based on the experience acquired during the first year, serious doubts may be raised about the effectiveness of a business loan program, even with "very small" loans, as a tool to fight poverty. This experience does not negate the general usefulness of such a program, but the scarcity of credit available to small businessmen is hardly a justification for including the program as an anti-poverty weapon.

The scarcity of qualified applicants certainly does not extend to credit extended to the low-income rural poor. This program is administered by the Farmers Home Administration in the Department of Agriculture, whose lending experience to farmers (under predecessor agencies) dates back to the New Deal days. But until the passage of the Economic Opportunity Act, some 500,000 poor farm families did not qualify for loans because they could not meet the stringent credit qualifications and nonfarm rural poor were completely excluded.

Under the program, loans of up to $2,500 per family were made for farm improvements which might lead to raising the income level of marginal farmers, or for small nonfarm family-operated enterprises, such as purchasing equipment for cutting and hauling timber, digging wells or operating farm equipment repair services. About a third of the loans made to individuals during the first year was to nonfarm rural poor, and more than four of every ten loans were extended for nonfarming activities. Other loans, averaging $17,000, were made to farm cooperatives whose membership is largely limited to low-income rural families.

THE DIFFICULT TERRAIN

The first year's experience clearly indicates the inherent difficulties involved in waging an effective war on poverty. Scarcity of funds was only one impediment, though apparently not the most pressing one for the purpose of implementing the programs inaugurated under the Economic Opportunity Act. This is not to say that providing income to the poor is not an essential ingredient in the war on poverty. But the waging of war on poverty through income maintenance is beyond the scope of the present discussion, since the emphasis of the Economic Opportunity Act is the rehabilitation of the impoverished to make them economically independent in the long run.

During the first year, administrative and bureaucratic difficulties abounded. The poverty program was superimposed upon an extensive though far from adequate welfare system. To conduct a successful campaign, the new anti-poverty warriors were obliged to coordinate their resources and new activities with long-established programs. For example, the planning of a new neighborhood center attempting to provide coordinated services in one place has to take into consideration the existence in the area of available family services, legal aid and other facilities. This proved at best a difficult task. Established welfare institutions were less than delighted with the intrusion of the new anti-poverty warriors upon their vested domains. Similarly, state officials generally did not welcome federal grants which bypass established political jurisdictions. Time, energy, and resources were wasted during the first year of the program in attempts to accommodate the various conflicting groups supposedly working toward aiding the poor.

Also distressing was the unwillingness of many southern communities to participate in the anti-poverty program because OEO insisted, as required by law, that all federally financed projects must be racially integrated. But racial segregation was only one factor discouraging communities from participating in the anti-poverty program. Many communities ignored the anti-poverty war because they regarded the requirement of participation by the poor as alien, or at least novel—even under the relatively undemanding criteria established by the OEO. Los Angeles, for example, delayed participation in OEO programs until the Watts riots broke out in August, 1965.

OEO officials have found it difficult even to coordinate the programs inaugurated under the Act which established the agency. Work-experience projects were initiated and administered by the Department of Health, Education, and Welfare with little reference to other community action activities. Similarly, Neighborhood Youth Corps projects, which should logically have been an integral part of comprehensive community programs, were administered independently by the Department of Labor; and a majority of these projects were conducted in communities which failed to organize other CAP projects. At the same time the Job Corps, which had little relation to community action programs, was an integral part of OEO.

Administrative, bureaucratic, and ideological impediments accounted for only part of the difficulties. The first year of experience under the Economic Opportunity Act yielded little insight or circumstantial evidence to permit a winnowing out of the most promising weapons in the anti-poverty arsenal. Is it wise to continue to invest four times as much, or more, in a Job Corps enrollee than in an out-of-school Neighborhood

Youth Corps participant? Is a dollar invested in birth control more effective in fighting poverty than a dollar spent on Head Start or legal aid? Is a dollar spent on AFDC—old-fashioned relief—a less potent tool in combating poverty than a dollar spent on neighborhood centers? These are just a few representative basic issues which remain as yet unanswered.

OEO officials are fully cognizant of the need for deeper insights regarding these issues and their significance in gaining direction for future program development. OEO has placed major emphasis on obtaining meaningful evaluation of its programs, and its staff includes outstanding authorities and technicians in system analysis and related techniques. Whether the questions are susceptible to helpful answers is not yet known.[5]

The fact that OEO has not yet come up with even tentative answers to these basic questions is no reflection on the agency, but serves to reemphasize that the road to the millennium of a poorless society is not clearly charted. And the first year of activities under the Economic Opportunity Act has not provided us with adequate insights for future action. Combating poverty remains a matter of faith and good works.

The response to the Great Society's clarion call for an all-out war on poverty, sounded in 1964, has been most gratifying. The establishment of a federal agency with considerable resources devoted exclusively to waging war on poverty has helped to stimulate interest in the problem and to provide a focal point for persons dedicated to the battle. Persons from all walks of life have rallied behind the federal banner, and many state and local governments have also mobilized to combat the economic and social ills of poverty. But actual accomplishments thus far have fallen far short of the communiqués issued from headquarters and the various command posts. The promises of eventual victory have been widely heralded, though the battle has hardly been joined. The struggle will surely be protracted, and the issue is certainly still in doubt. It seems clear, however, that an effective total war on poverty will require considerably greater expenditures than those expended during the first year of the Economic Opportunity Act.

---

[5] An optimistic view about the potential of applying system analysis techniques to anti-poverty programs is presented in Herbert E. Striner, "Research Strategy for Manpower Policies," in Part IV of this volume.

4

POVERTY AND THE NEW FEDERALISM

ROGER H. DAVIDSON

The ultimate outcome of the nation's war on poverty will depend in large measure upon harnessing the complex set of institutions and relationships embodied in the American federal system. These multiple levels of public agencies, with their attendant access points for private individuals and interests, often act as a severe constraint upon the enactment and implementation of nationwide manpower and employment programs. It would be tempting to look upon such programs in terms of the national economic picture. But political decision-making processes almost inevitably place the stamp of the federal system upon such policies, and established local power structures will work to condition the implementation of the programs. Indeed, a prime reason why the war on poverty has been almost constantly in the public headlines since 1964 is the threat which it poses to established state and local political institutions.

In this paper I propose to undertake a brief discussion of the relationships between the poverty programs and the federal system. The purpose, it must be stressed, is not to praise or condemn the federal system, but merely to explain its impact upon the formulation and implementation of manpower policies. First, it will be useful to summarize the contemporary federal system and the changes which are being wrought in it. We will then discuss several points of cleavage between the poverty programs and federalism—considering both the impact of federalism upon the programs and the potentialities inherent in the war on poverty for modifying established federal relationships.

THE NETWORK OF FEDERAL RELATIONSHIPS

Federalism is traditionally thought of as a device for dividing decisions and functions among various levels of government.[1] The federal structure is an artifact of historical necessity, simply because the con-

---

[1] See, for example, Morton Grodzins, "The Federal System," in *Goals for Americans* (Englewood Cliffs, N.J.: Prentice-Hall, 1960), p. 265.

stituent parts of the union—states and, for that matter, localities—existed prior to the union itself. For economic and defense purposes it became imperative to extend the reach of government across existing colonial lines, an end which could not be attained by conquest.[2] Thus in the federal bargain which was struck at the Philadelphia Convention of 1787, the price of union was the retention of the sovereign states and of institutional devices designed to perpetuate their powers. In the words of Chief Justice Chase, "the Constitution, in all its provisions, looks to an indestructible Union, composed of indestructible states."[3]

Until relatively recently, the Supreme Court served as the chief arbiter of the federal system, attempting to rationalize distinctions between the powers of federal and state agencies. These litigations were hardly academic: they were manifestations not only of clashes between locally articulated and nationally articulated interests, but also of the larger controversy over the absolute dimensions of governmental power. The court system could not invariably contain these conflicts, as the Civil War tragically showed. After the 1930's, authority for determining the scope of the central government's powers passed from the courts to Congress and the Executive Branch. This was one effect of the Supreme Court's liberalized interpretations of constitutional grants of power for the central government.[4] Hence, "the policy-making authorities of the national government are for most purposes the arbiters of the federal system."[5] In a sense, therefore, the contemporary revisions in relationships between governmental units represent an ongoing process of constitution-making.

The federal bargain has never produced a neat delineation of functions among levels of government. So-called cooperative federalism—"the patterned sharing of governmental activities by all levels of government"—has characterized the federal system since its inception.[6] Participation by the central government has traditionally been in the form of the grant-in-aid—intergovernmental transfer to states and localities

[2] William Riker, *Federalism* (Boston: Little, Brown & Co., 1964).

[3] *Texas* v. *White,* 7 Wallace 700 (1869).

[4] The words of a federal circuit court of appeals in defining the reach of the National Labor Relations Act under the commerce clause serve to indicate the extent to which these decisions have passed from judicial determination: "Perhaps the cackle of the farmer's hen as she announces completion of her daily chore, or the squeal of the pig in its struggle to become a porker, are not beyond this boundary line [between intra- and interstate commerce], but in this we give no assurance." *Polish National Alliance* v. *NLRB,* 136 F. 2nd 180 (1943).

[5] U.S. Commission on Intergovernmental Relations, *A Report to the President for Transmittal to the Congress* (1955), p. 59.

[6] Daniel J. Elazar, *The American Partnership* (Chicago: University of Chicago Press, 1962).

for specified purposes. During the nineteenth century, the grants were typically in the form of land from the plentiful public domain. With the close of the frontier, the federal government sought other forms of revenue, of which the personal and corporate income tax became the most important. The central government so exploited the income tax, in fact, as to place real limitations on the states' utilization of this source of revenue. Since the New Deal, therefore, grants-in-aid have usually assumed the form of cash transfers appropriated by Congress and administered by state agencies under federally set standards.

Despite the inherently cooperative nature of governmental activities, the relative inactivity of the central government in certain fields was for a long period assumed to vindicate the theory that governmental powers were indeed "separate." The Constitution says nothing, for example, about maintaining full employment or providing minimum income for the unemployed, the aged, dependent children, or other handicapped classes. Congress, to be sure, enjoyed the constitutional power to tax (and spend) to provide for "the general welfare"; but this authority remained vague and largely untapped during the first 150 years of our national life. Congress did provide veterans' pensions and, upon occasion, funds for disaster relief.[7] But in the main, public assistance for the needy was assumed to be the province of state governments. For their part, the states disposed of their responsibility by allowing (and sometimes requiring) counties, towns, villages, and cities to levy taxes for poor relief and to provide such relief through their own officials. (Some states, however, established state institutions for the needy disabled.) In turn, the localities relied heavily on churches and other private groups to provide relief and welfare services.

The depression of the 1930's occurred with such force and swiftness that state and local governments, not to mention private organizations, were unable to meet even the most pressing welfare needs. Though constitutional disputes over the role of the federal government were not immediately resolved, Congress experimented with a series of emergency relief programs—providing grants-in-aid to state and local governments for direct relief, work relief, loans and grants to farmers, aids to students, and other purposes. The basic enactment of the depression was the Social Security Act of 1935, which remains the cornerstone of federal public assistance policy. The Act's public assistance provisions are clearly grant-in-aid programs in the traditional pattern. The employment security program, though implemented through state agencies, is not a

[7] William Anderson, *The Nation and the States, Rivals or Partners?* (Minneapolis: University of Minnesota Press, 1955), pp. 29ff.

grant-in-aid. And the Old Age, Survivors, and Disability Insurance (OASDI) program—as well as the more recent "Medicare"—conformed to the earlier veterans' pension pattern in bypassing the states entirely to deal directly with individual citizens.

This sudden and cataclysmic involvement of the federal government in social welfare programs has been paralleled by a slower but nonetheless steady increase in federal activity in other fields—construction of airports, highways, public housing, and so forth. This growth has taken place almost wholly in this century. In 1902 the federal government had only five grant-in-aid programs to the states, totaling $3 million; by fiscal 1966 there were seventy-eight separate programs to state and local governments, administered by thirteen different agencies. The total expenditures for grants-in-aid, $13.3 billion, represented 10 percent of the federal expenditures and approximately 15 percent of the total revenue of states and localities.[8] Intergovernmental financial transfers more than tripled in volume during the decade following 1955.

A further development has been the federal government's increasing willingness to bypass the states and deal directly with local governments and even quasi-public agencies. In absolute terms, federal aid to cities and localities has not been great—about 12 percent of all federal payments to states and localities in 1963. But federal agencies exert some influence in assuring that grants to states are equitably distributed among localities. And direct aid to localities is increasing at a faster pace than aid to states.

Two factors have been instrumental in this change of emphasis. First, the society which has emerged in this century is a predominantly urban one, which is beset with problems of unprecedented magnitude and complexity. Second, urban officials typically found that states, limited in fund-raising capacities and influenced by rural-dominated legislatures, were unwilling or unable to deal effectively with urban problems. The U.S. Conference of Mayors, for example, was founded partly under the assumptions that the problems of the large cities were national in scope and that state legislatures weren't going to do much about them. This view has not abated in the intervening years. The 1964 House hearings on the poverty bill, for example, found Republican Representative Albert Quie (Minnesota) trying to persuade William F. Walsh of Syracuse, a Republican mayor from a state with a Republican administration, to admit the desirability of state participation:

[8] U.S. Bureau of the Budget, *Special Analyses, Budget of the United States, 1967* (Washington, 1966), pp. 36–37.

QUIE: [D]o you think there ought to be any state relation in Title II that is not provided in the bill right now?

WALSH: My own inclination is that the money should come directly to the locality and not go through the state.

* * * * *

QUIE: [D]o you think that each community ought to go to the federal government as opposed to going to the states, which would set priorities?

WALSH: I think each community should go to the federal government, just the way we did on [the juvenile delinquency program]. Then the federal government decides which are more worthwhile.

* * * * *

QUIE: I was wondering if the state should not be involved in some way. . . . I may be wrong on this, but I always had the feeling that [in] programs that were inaugurated to be on-going . . . the state did share a portion of the responsibility.

WALSH: The problem when we get the state in, . . . is that you again get too much control. If you get state control or if you get federal control there isn't much left for the locality to decide.[9]

Many of the newer federal aid programs have therefore dealt with services in which the interest of the big cities is especially strong—urban renewal, public housing, airports, and urban highways, for example.

State officials have not generally welcomed these direct federal-local relationships. At first intimidated by the depression, state legislators saw no objection to such relationships as emerged from the emergency programs of the 1930's. After World War II, however, state officialdom—including the Governors' Conference—began to voice concern over these alleged intrusions. Their contentions were supported by states' rights political groups. The governors pointed out that many federal aid programs tended to compound the problems of state administration. For one thing, because it is often politically unfeasible to turn down federal grants, state budgets may be warped in the direction of interests embodied in the federal programs. In addition, the equalization features of federal programs mean that wealthier states are taxed to support poorer ones. Finally, there are inevitable conflicts over administration of the funds, and state officials complain about duplication, delays, and federal inspection procedures.

[9] U.S., Congress, House, Committee on Education and Labor, *Hearings on the Economic Opportunity Act of 1964* (Washington: U.S. Government Printing Office, 1964), II, 825.

These reactions against federal activity have not typically been shared by local officials. Yet the inability of many local governments to cope with broad functional problems suggested that local officials too might soon face the threat of obsolescence. Coordinated action was often difficult in the face of the welter of local, county, and special-purpose governments—no less than 1,400 in the New York City area, for example. At the same time, the dispersion of population into the suburbs typically eroded the tax base of the core city and rendered its governmental structure anomalous. Should the federal government decide to deal increasingly with private agencies, or even directly with individual clients in programs traditionally administered by the localities, the local officials might find themselves added to the ranks of the disaffected. Something approaching this actually occurred among community officials during the early implementation of the poverty programs, and will be discussed presently.

Analyses of increased central government activity have often proceeded from two fallacious assumptions. The first is the contention, in the words of the Kestnbaum report, that "the main tradition of American federalism [is] the tradition of separateness."[10] We have seen that this premise is not justified historically. The second fallacy is the assumption that any addition of activities at one level of government necessarily results in a corresponding loss at other levels. As William Anderson has concluded, "this is not in accordance with American experience or with reason."[11] Indeed, the figures in Table 1 indicate that expenditures of state and local governments have grown faster than those of the central government, in proportion to gross national product and in absolute dollar terms. Governmental payrolls reveal a similar picture—while state

TABLE 1.
Governmental Expenditures as Percentage of Gross National Product,
1946 and 1964

Expenditure	1946	1964
Total federal expenditures	17.6%	18.8%
Federal payments to states, localities	.4%	1.7%
State and local expenditures	5.2%	11.0%
Gross national product (billions of dollars)	210.7	628.7

SOURCE: *Economic Report of the President, 1966* (Washington: U.S. Government Printing Office, January, 1966).
NOTE: Expenditures are for fiscal years, GNP for calendar years.

[10] U.S. Commission on Intergovernmental Relations, *A Report to the President for Transmittal to Congress,* House Doc. 198, 84th Congress, 1st session (Washington: Government Printing Office, 1955).
[11] Anderson, *The Nation and the States,* p. 139.

and local government employment doubled between 1947 and 1963, nondefense employment in the federal government was the same proportion of the total civilian labor force (1.9 percent) in 1963 as in 1948. Much of this growth is no doubt due to the vast increases in educational expenditures, where states and localities have enjoyed a virtual monopoly. Nevertheless, the figures strongly suggest that, contrary to the thinking of both the states' righters and the centralizers, the reports of the imminent demise of local and state functions are grossly exaggerated.

Nor are the states and localities likely soon, if indeed ever, to be erased as significant factors in public policy-making and implementation. The continued functioning of the peripheral governments is assured for at least two reasons. First, among the myriads of interests which mark the American political system, many have developed their most effective political access at local or state levels. The most conspicuous example— that of local segregationist majorities in the South—is also an invidious one; but many others could be cited. As long as the central government remains unable to satisfy all the political demands made upon it (an unlikely status in any event), local and state-based interests will continue to give life to local governments. The most important of these interests, of course, are the political parties, which retain continuing localized bases of support.[12]

A second reason we may expect local and state governments to retain their position is the sheer impossibility of the central government's administering directly all of the programs it is likely to undertake in the coming generation. Even in the unlikely event that all the governmental programs now advocated by activist-centrists were to be adopted, the limited capacities of the central government to absorb the administrative burden and account for local variations in needs would undoubtedly preclude direct administration. Thus, many federal programs—ranging from scientific research to community welfare—take the form of grants to public and private agencies possessing the capability for implementing them. The central government can meet more demands without commensurate increases in its own staff, as indicated by the fact that while the federal budget has grown 1.2 percent as a proportion of GNP in the postwar years, federal employment has remained steady in relation to the total civilian labor force. In this sense, the central government becomes an allocator, supervisor, coordinator, and reviewer for funds administered by other people for "the public welfare."

[12] David B. Truman, "Federalism and the Party System," in Arthur W. Macmahon (ed.), *Federalism Mature and Emergent* (Garden City: Doubleday, 1955), pp. 115–36.

This suggests some final refinements of our concept of federalism. The distribution of the functions we would label "governmental" involves not merely the relationships among different levels of public agencies. It also involves relationships, vertical as well as horizontal, among various types of public officials at these different levels. We are dealing not only with a question of horizontal loyalties among all officials at a single level vis-à-vis all officials at other levels but additionally with vertical relationships among, for example, technicians, administrators, or politicians from *all* levels of government. The relationships generated within local, state, and national federations of teachers or social workers, for instance, may produce a professionalism which operates independently of levels of governmental agencies themselves. Or, alternatively, these federations may look to one or another level of government as their chief spokesman in public policy matters.

A second complicating factor is the increasing presence of private agencies—civic or professional groups, social service organizations, and even private entrepreneurial firms—in the direction of implementation and even direction of public programs. These nongovernmental agencies are typically found as contractors or subcontractors for programs supervised by governmental agencies; but the so-called community action agencies of the war on poverty actually play a role in planning and directing local programs. Consequently, it is impossible to limit a discussion of the federal network of relationships merely to those actors which are commonly called governmental. The Economic Opportunity Act of 1964 has served to engage many of these nongovernmental interests in social welfare policy-making, and promises to call many of these relationships into play during the years ahead. The "war on poverty" is therefore an instructive point of departure for analyzing the contemporary operation of the American federal system.

THE STATES AND THE POVERTY WAR

The Johnson Administration's 1964 draft bill for the war on poverty (H.R. 10440) contained scant reference to state agencies. Rather, the bill was designed to give the new Office of Economic Opportunity (OEO) maximum flexibility in choosing to deal with state, local, or private organizations. OEO's director was authorized, for example, to contract with state agencies for technical assistance to localities in developing community action programs and, generally, to utilize services and facilities of the states or their subdivisions. There was additionally a very mild equalization feature for three of the programs—work training, work study, and community action—in the guarantee that no more than 12½ percent of the funds could be allocated to a single state. Since it would appear politically unfeasible to direct that much to a single state, this guarantee could hardly be considered a major instrument for equalizing distribution of poverty funds. The draft bill included two provisions for gubernatorial participation: domestic peace corps (VISTA) volunteers could not be dispatched to a state without the governor's consent, and for the important community action programs (Title II), the OEO director was directed to "facilitate effective participation of the states" and to refer project applications to the state's governor for "comment."

This flexibility in dealing with the states (except for VISTA) was provided deliberately. Some of the Administration officials who drafted the measure foresaw that certain governors, for policy or political reasons, might sabotage the objectives of the war on poverty. (One member of the task force which drafted the bill recalls that whenever the role of the states was discussed, the name of Alabama's Governor George C. Wallace would be mentioned and the discussion would immediately terminate.) And the community action programs, which many saw as the heart of the new legislation, implied that state participation in other than an advisory or supportive role was simply not relevant.

The concept of recasting the community's structure and social services is essential to understanding the war on poverty, and especially the new community action programs. The U.S. Conference of Mayors had warned President Johnson that "the major battlefields in the war against poverty lie in the cities and towns." And the President himself indicated that the problems of the urban environment, a major item on the Great Society's agenda, would "require us to create new concepts of cooperation—a creative federalism—between the National Capital and the leaders of local communities."[13] Local officials echoed this sentiment during congressional hearings on the Economic Opportunity Act in their refusal to acknowledge the utility of state participation.

When congressional Republicans countered that the bill gave inadequate recognition to the states, moreover, they got scant help from those governors recruited by the Administration to testify in favor of the bill. The governors (all Democrats) displayed almost unmitigated optimism concerning the poverty program; and, whatever the vagueness of the guarantees, all seemed confident of their ability to deal with the federal government. However, there was more to the states' position than met the eye. Under questioning, Governor Matthew Welsh (D-Ind.) admitted that the states should control the Job Corps program, and

[13] Commencement address at the University of Michigan, Ann Arbor, May 22, 1964.

Governor Edmund Brown (D-Calif.) agreed with Representative Peter Frelinghuysen (R-N.J.) that "it might be well to spell out certain safeguards to preserve and define an appropriate role for state governments."[14]

Congress did, in fact, devise "certain safeguards" during its deliberations. The Republican substitute bill (H.R. 11050), sponsored by Frelinghuysen as the ranking Republican of the House Committee on Education and Labor, included many of the Administration's program proposals but envisioned a more active role for the states in decision-making, implementation, and financing. But beyond creating a more complex and restrictive formula for allocating funds among the states, Administration Democrats on the House Committee made few concessions to this approach. It was during the Senate floor debate that a concerted effort was launched to revise the bill. In a series of close roll-call votes, Administration Democrats turned back various attempts to require gubernatorial approval for all poverty programs in each state. Finally, however, two compromise amendments sponsored by Senator George Smathers (D-Fla.) were accepted by the bill's floor managers in order to win southern votes. These amendments provided for a governor's veto of Job Corps contracts and all contracts with nongovernmental agencies (including community action agencies). Later accepted by the House, the amendments were included in the final version of Public Law 88–452.

Governors of both parties viewed the veto power as an important weapon for coordinating poverty programs and for insuring that their own political position would not be jeopardized by the policies and "patronage" personnel associated with the program. It was this latter objective that precipitated the most bitter disputes between the Office of Economic Opportunity and state officials in the first year and a half of OEO's existence, provoking many threats of gubernatorial veto and its actual use on five occasions. In all five cases—involving three southern Democrats and two northern Republicans—the political ingredient, in which the governors' positions were at stake, seemed to be predominant.

The most controversial veto came from Governor Wallace of Alabama. He had long been feuding with the biracial Birmingham Area Committee for Development of Economic Opportunity, Inc., a group created in the fall of 1964 and headed by C. H. Erskine Smith, a Birmingham attorney and political enemy of the Governor. In an effort to head off the Birmingham group, "lily-white" Wallace-sponsored

[14] U.S., Congress, House, Committee on Education and Labor, *Hearings on the Economic Opportunity Act,* III, 1390.

70

poverty councils were established at the county level throughout the state. The Birmingham county organization was headed by Major Jess Lanier, a close political ally of the Governor. The power struggle continued for several months, until in April OEO granted funds for the Smith group and three other biracial poverty groups in Alabama. Wallace's veto of the Birmingham grant on May 12, 1965, therefore set off a storm of protest because of its racial implications. It was ironic indeed that Wallace's action had much to do with the demise of the gubernatorial veto, for Congress was then considering amendments to the Economic Opportunity Act.

The Administration's 1965 amendments to the Act contained no mention of the governors' veto, but the Wallace incident provoked immediate action from Representative Adam Clayton Powell's (D-N.Y.) Education and Labor Committee, which first decided to delete the veto entirely, and then under Republican pressure provided for vetoes which could be overriden by OEO's Director. This version of the bill (H.R. 8283) passed the House, but the Senate dropped the veto entirely after a lively floor debate and several close votes. House-Senate conferees accepted the Senate action (House Report 1001), but the House sent the bill back to conference by a 209–180 roll-call vote. Adoption of the recommittal was a victory for House Republicans, who voted unanimously for it (along with 65 Southern Democrats and 17 Northern Democrats). The second conference accepted the House version (House Report 1061). The amended Act therefore retained the governors' veto over Neighborhood Youth Corps, community action, and adult basic education programs; but the OEO Director was authorized to reverse the veto within thirty days.

States' rights groups fought determinedly for retention of the original veto provisions. The Governors' Conference lobbied openly for retention of the veto, with Governor William Scranton (R-Pa.) heading a special subcommittee on the subject. Governor John Connally (D-Texas), onetime political ally of the President, was especially forceful in arguing for the veto. Outwardly, the Administration maintained a bland attitude, Shriver testifying merely that he would stand by the provisions of the original 1964 draft bill (veto for VISTA projects, consultation on community action programs). But Administration lobbyists worked behind the scenes to delete the veto, and the President reportedly gave assurances to several Democratic governors that in the future their opinions on poverty programs would be solicited if they dropped their opposition to the amendment. While congressional Republicans were pleased with their victory, they were hardly complacent. Senator Peter H. Dominick (R-Colo.) termed the final compromise "a completely anomalous situation" in which "an executive appointed official can overrule the elected governor of a state on activities within that governor's state."[15]

While the issue of the governors' veto generated considerable publicity and was no doubt symptomatic of very real frustrations on the part of state officials, its significance can be overemphasized. The formal veto, to be sure, has been eliminated for most practical purposes; but there is every evidence that informal vetoes by state officials are widely employed. Moreover, the states play a wide variety of positive functions in the war against poverty. Even in the vaunted community action programs, OEO funds have enabled almost every state to create technical assistance agencies (TAA's) to help localities organize and apply for OEO grants. This service has proved especially valuable to rural communities, which often lack the indigenous leadership and expertise to develop community action programs and have consequently fallen behind the better-organized urban areas in procuring federal funds.[16] After generations of complaints that state governments have favored rural areas at the expense of the cities, one of the larger ironies of the war on poverty is the rescue operation which the states have had to perform for nonurban areas which are ill-prepared to engage in planning and implementation of federally backed programs.

The states are involved in other ways. State TAA's perform a variety of supportive and coordinating functions, sometimes even administering their own anti-poverty programs; and when they enjoy the active support of the governor, they have become effective lobbyists for human resources policies in the state legislature and among state departments. In the HEW-administered programs of Title V—work experience and adult basic education—grants are made through state boards of education for local distribution, in the traditional grant-in-aid pattern. In other programs, the states (as well as localities) are eligible to become contractors—as, for example, in work projects performed for improving state facilities. And where standards for professional personnel such as teachers or social workers are involved, state licensing practices inevitably come into play. The problems of interlevel cooperation are complex in the extreme, and are marked not so much by permanent state-federal conflicts as by the complicated adjustments required to mesh programs to the many and differing state laws, practices, and personnel. It would

---

[15] U.S., *Congressional Record* 89th Cong., 1st Sess., August 19, 1965, p. 20335.
[16] Although there are no reliable statistics, it is beyond dispute that OEO funds have disproportionately benefited urban areas. For example, the National Association for Community Development (NACD), a Title II clientele group, charged in early 1966 that rural areas, which contain approximately 47 percent of the nation's poor, had received only 6.4 percent of OEO's grant funds.

be easy to conclude that the states are ignored in the war on poverty; but, as we have suggested, such a conclusion would be superficial and misleading.

REVOLT AGAINST CITY HALL?

One of the most important, if not unique, features of the Economic Opportunity Act is its unabashedly innovative approach to federal-local relations. Title II—which many view as the only really new weapon in the war on poverty—authorizes comprehensive community-wide planning and implementation of poverty-related programs. The institutional vehicle for this purpose is the umbrella-type "Community Action Agency" (CAA), a public or private nonprofit agency which can pull together the locality's existing institutional resources for combatting poverty. The "Community Action Program" (CAP) evolved by such an umbrella organization constitutes a functional agenda for the community's needs in fighting poverty.

The community action concept has the capacity to restructure social services in several ways. First, from the standpoint of the federal government, the multipurpose CAP's represent an alternative to the traditional special-purpose grant-in-aid, and approach the concept of the block grant. Local planning will presumably account for unique local needs in a way not achieved when numerous federal agencies sponsor specialized grant programs in a single locality. It was understandable, therefore, that very early in the evolution of the Act the Bureau of the Budget became interested in Title II as a new method of coordinating federal programs and bypassing traditional agency jurisdictional lines.

Second, and more fundamentally, the concept envisions coordination at the local level, since the CAP's are to be broadly representative of community opinion. This feature of the Act was a direct outgrowth of theoretical and practical work on juvenile delinquency in the 1950's and early 1960's, in which the need for "restructuring the community" became as important as reorienting the juvenile offender himself. Thus, it was with considerable casualness (surprising only in retrospect) that the drafters of the Act specified that CAP's be "developed, conducted and administered with the maximum feasible participation of residents of the areas and members of the groups served."[17]

A third and related aspect of the CAP concept is its functional approach to geographic and political boundaries. The Act speaks of "communities" and not of cities, towns, counties, or even metropolitan areas.

[17] Section 202(a)(3).

Though CAP's frequently parallel existing political boundaries, the concept is open-ended in permitting these boundaries to be crossed for functional purposes of planning or implementing poverty-related programs. This development is significant for both urban and rural areas: for the former, because governmental and political jurisdictions have often proliferated beyond control; for the latter, because many counties lack the people or the resources to support effective welfare services.

At the outset, a few local officials recognized the potential threat of the CAP's to their authority. The U.S. Conference of Mayors, for example, endorsed the bill with only one exception—that Title II funds be channeled through official agencies, such as local human development corporations. The spokesman for the National Association of Counties took a similar position, and Syracuse (New York) Mayor Walsh went so far as to observe that "if we could not have direct control of the program we would not want it."[18] But when congressional Republicans tried to frighten the mayors by pointing to the absence of guarantees, the response was, if anything, more bland than the response from the governors. At one point the bill's House sponsor, Representative Phil Landrum (D-Ga.), promised to "draft language" to assure inclusion of local governments, but for some unexplained reason the bill was never altered in this respect. The community action concept thus remains functional, comprehensive, and free of formal requirements for the involvement of local politicians and elected officials.

The vast majority of the 600 community action agencies funded during OEO's initial year of operation enjoyed at least the tacit cooperation of City Hall. In urban areas, a mayor's task force typically set the process in motion, although a coalition of civil rights groups sometimes served the same function. Rural areas, lacking the institutional richness of their urban counterparts, typically relied on private organizations— church agencies, 4-H groups, or professional societies—to mobilize the community, sometimes under prodding from state TAA's. From OEO's point of view, City Hall cooperation is valuable because it provides access to local governmental funds and facilities.[19] From the vantage point of City Hall, too, cooperation has its payoffs. Most mayors prefer to exercise some control over the CAP's, although some find it con-

---

[18] U.S., Congress, House, Committee on Education and Labor, *Hearings on the Economic Opportunity Act*, II, 822; also pp. 790ff.

[19] Under the Act, at least 10 percent of the CAP funding must come from the locality—although this may be in the form of "in kind" contributions, such as staff time. OEO guidelines, moreover, specify that CAA's must be capable of mobilizing existing local "service systems," such as the schools and welfare agencies.

venient to pursue a policy of calculated indifference—exercising informal direction while appearing to grant independence to the CAA's.

The "maximum feasible participation" clause, however, has become a rallying cry in many localities throughout the country. The language of the Act is vague, not only because "feasible" is susceptible to diverse interpretations, but because the poor themselves are not mentioned. OEO has tended to interpret the phrase narrowly, and in most cases local community action agencies are recognized if they can simply show that some persons from the area to be served—social service professionals, or even self-appointed spokesmen—are on the community action agency's governing board. Some community action agencies have experimented with elaborate representational schemes, including neighborhood councils or area elections. During the first year of the war on poverty, about ten major cities held elections for membership on CAA boards, neighborhood planning councils, or both. The elections produced, in the words of one OEO official, "a mixed bag of results": in most cases turnout was disappointing, though in Hartford, Connecticut, the vote was heavier than in the previous general election.

By requiring involvement of those with a stake in the welfare programs—whether or not they are actually "poor"—the local poverty programs represent a new development in participatory democracy. In some instances, however, local activists have interpreted the war on poverty as a war on City Hall itself. These forces distrust both the local politicians and the welfare professionals, holding that these "establishment" groups are reactionary, unconcerned, or even corrupt. The solution is to tear down the local power structures by mobilizing militant neighborhood protests—"rubbing raw the sores of discontent," in the language of Saul D. Alinsky. Some of the more revolutionary spirits within OEO initially encouraged this sort of action, and indeed the agency's guidelines for prospective applicants seem to equate the poor with the "participation" requirement.[20] Moreover, many CAP grants have included programs for generalized political education and involvement of the poor.

Though an extreme example, Syracuse, New York, provided an illustration of the forces at work. The Crusade for Opportunity (CFO), the local CAA, was the creature of City Hall. Where CFO's activities would have been considered radical a year or so earlier, by 1965 it had alienated local militants because, as they charged, it relied too much on traditional institutions and local industry, and was reluctant to offend these forces. Meanwhile, OEO funded an experimental political action

[20] U.S., Office of Economic Opportunity, *Community Action Program Guide,* October, 1965, I, 16.

training program run by Syracuse University's Community Action Training Center (CATC). The grant, made in February, 1965, was designed to train political organizers and initiate field work in three local "target areas" (current terminology for "slums"), in order to test the feasibility of organizing the poor into a politically assertive element of the community. The spin-off group from the University project, the Syracuse Community Development Association (SCDA), established nine neighborhood groups and helped register 2,500 new voters—mostly Democrats. (Alinsky was meanwhile hired by the University as a CATC consultant.) The affair was not calculated to please Mayor Walsh, a popular Republican who was reelected overwhelmingly in November, 1965.[21]

Walsh's unhappiness was echoed by other mayors who were having their own troubles with militant poverty warriors. In June, 1965, the executive committee of the U.S. Conference of Mayors urged OEO to recognize City Hall-endorsed CAA's as the appropriate channels for community action. The mayors appointed a special poverty subcommittee including Mayor Walsh and headed by Chicago's Mayor Richard J. Daley (whose poverty effort had been characterized by Representative Powell as having "minimum feasible participation of the poor and maximum participation of the politicians"). Daley's group conferred with Vice-President Humphrey, who later described himself as the mayors' "built-in special agent" and assured the complainants that the Administration had no intention of bypassing City Hall.

Humphrey and certain pragmatists within OEO apparently succeeded in blunting the earlier anti-City Hall attitude. In Syracuse, the grant to the University's CATC was terminated and the militants instructed to work through the Mayor's CFO agency—causing a delegation to camp on Shriver's doorstep in Washington in protest of the "sellout." Meanwhile, at least temporarily acceptable compromises were worked out in Chicago, Newark, and other cities, and in early 1966 it was revealed that OEO had granted at least 15 cities and counties the right of formal veto over CAP projects. Shriver, who had earlier seemed unconcerned about the social service professionals, found himself "humbly" asking the American Public Welfare Association for "your help in creating new programs." The *détente* seemed complete when the U.S. Conference of Mayors issued a highly enthusiastic guidebook on the poverty pro-

---

[21] Of the many published accounts of the Syracuse situation, see Jules Witcover and Erwin Knoll, "Politics and the Poor: Shriver's Second Thoughts," *The Reporter*, December 30, 1965, pp. 23–25.

gram, which urged local officialdom to allow "some actual *sharing* of planning and decision-making power. . . ."[22]

Like the gubernatorial reaction, the revolt of the mayors was more apparent than real. It is hardly conceivable that a program of such magnitude and innovation could proceed without political conflicts, and such conflicts are likely to recur. Indeed, if one concedes the validity of at least some of what the militants are trying to say, a certain level of friction will continue to be a desirable feature of the war on poverty. On the other hand, City Halls have not been completely obdurate: the vast majority of CAP's have gotten underway with at least the tacit acceptance of local officials. Even the archetypical Mayor Daley has not been wholly insensitive to the new forces at work; and, while involvement of the poor has perhaps not been "maximum," at least it is more than had been attempted previously.

It is hard to ascertain what kind of involvement is now "feasible," or will be "feasible" in the future. Patterns of influence will no doubt vary among localities, as they always have. The poverty constituency will not be an easy one to mobilize. By any accepted measure, the poor tend to be nonparticipants in political life. Most coalitions which purport to speak for the poor are synthetic in the sense that they are composed mainly of middle-class political activists, whether professional social workers or amateurs. And this is as true of Alinsky as of, say, Mayor Daley. Whether the poor themselves will someday assume leadership of their cause is quite another matter: in a sense, such an eventuality would be a contradiction in terms, since many of the attitudes associated with the so-called "culture of poverty" would have to be supplanted by an essentially middle-class sense of political efficacy and reinforced by acquired political skills. But regardless of the actual midwifery of this political development, something quite significant is happening in American communities: political mobilization of disadvantaged citizens is the more or less explicit object of a significant piece of public policy. A new constituency is being heard from. Local power structures (however constituted or defined) are being challenged to absorb the demands of the poor, or coopt their leaders, or both—under threat of electoral challenge by as-yet-inchoate reformist coalitions.

Indeed, the war on poverty may very well be judged ultimately for its role in mobilizing the poor as an effective political force, rather than for the number of dollars it puts in their pockets. Governmental sponsorship of political clienteles, it should be remembered, is hardly

[22] U.S. Conference of Mayors, *Economic Opportunity in Cities* (Washington, January, 1966), p. 26. (Italics in original.)

a new phenomenon. The county agricultural extension system, for example, fostered the creation of a stable, politically oriented farm movement: for many years the county extension agents served as organizers of the American Farm Bureau Federation, restricting the system's services to Federation members. Other federal programs have resulted in the creation of clientele groups. The labor movement, too, is sustained by federal recognition of the unions' right to organize, and in many cases compulsory membership arrangements are enforced by state or federal regulations. The attention being given to the poor as a potential clientele is important because of the apparent difficulties of organizing this grouping, and the new wrinkles which this governmental sponsorship promises for the federal structure of relationships.

FEDERALISM, COMPLEX AND CREATIVE

Standing behind the early controversies surrounding the war on poverty, therefore, is the larger phenomenon which has provided the theme for this discussion: the proliferation of governmental and quasi-governmental relations within the framework of the institutions of federalism. We have seen that it is incorrect, even within the policy context of the war on poverty, to speak of the demise of the formal institutions of city or state government. But it is equally true that contemporary American federalism extends far beyond governmental institutions and involves complex interrelationships of local and national, public and private entities. In late 1965, a single application for a New York City area Project Head Start (preschool) program for 20,000 youngsters involved coordination of no less than fifty-four community agencies, was as bulky as the telephone directories of the 5 New York boroughs put together, and required 4,000 man-hours merely to review.

Such complexities are not likely to be reduced in coming years. Nor is the Plimsoll line between public and private sectors of the common enterprise likely to become more clearly defined. Not to eradicate this complexity, but rather to make some sense out of it, should be the goal of President Johnson's proposed investigation into the dimensions of "creative federalism."

II

JOB ASSISTANCE AND UNEMPLOYMENT AIDS

5

THE PUBLIC EMPLOYMENT SERVICE

WILLIAM HABER

Public concern with manpower policy and problems has been increasing for over three decades. The Great Depression of the 1930's, spelling joblessness for millions of men and women, made this nation exceedingly sensitive to the level of unemployment. Traditional ideas that deflations and depressions had to "take their course" were set aside, and public programs to aid the jobless were adopted and vigorously pursued. New temporary agencies for providing work became widely known by their initials—CWA, WPA, CCC, NYA, PWA, and FERA. For the first time in our history the federal government became directly involved in what President Roosevelt referred to as "this business of relief." But since "relief," essential though it was, was hardly a solution, emergency work programs on public projects for adults and schools and camps for youth were also developed under the New Deal.

At the same time it was recognized that neither relief nor emergency programs offered an acceptable approach to the job problem. Three legislative enactments reflecting public concern with employment levels and fluctuations were adopted. The first, the Wagner-Peyser Act, was passed in 1933. It set up the United States Employment Service, a joint federal-state system operated with federal matching grants. Thus, after many years of agitation and discussion, a formal or organized market mechanism to bring the jobless man and the manless job together came into existence. A bill, somewhat similar to the one eventually adopted in 1933 was passed by the Congress and vetoed by President Hoover in 1931.

Opposition to involvement of the federal government in supporting employment offices and in the organization of the labor market was based on the theory that the federal government had no more justification for establishing or aiding in the creation of such offices than "for the establishment of grocery stores or government dry goods shops." These were areas for private enterprise. A distinguished student of the labor market, William M. Leiserson, writing on "the theory of public employment offices," observed that to compare employment offices with dry goods and grocery stores is to fail to understand the nature of "the employment business." A more appropriate comparison, he suggested, "should be with the Post Office, the school system, and weather and crop reports."[1]

Basic economic changes in American society as well as the clarification of public interest and policy concerning the level of employment were bound to enlarge support for a strong public employment service. A pertinent companion development was the passage in 1935 of the Social Security Act. Among other provisions, this Act established a federal-state system of unemployment insurance for jobless workers. To qualify for weekly insurance payments, the unemployed wage earner was required to register at a public employment office, which was responsible for the administration of the availability-for-work test. As coverage expanded and a larger proportion of the work force came under the protection of this job-insurance legislation, an increasing number of employees came in contact with the local employment service when changes in job status entitling them to benefits took place.

The Employment Act of 1946 represented another major development in the trend toward federal support of high levels of employment. The memory of the Great Depression was still fresh. Experience with full employment and "overemployment" from 1943 to 1945 did not assure a continuation with the war's end. Rapid demobilization of nearly 12 million from the armed forces and the required shift from military production to civilian goods could still have meant the return of economic depression and an unemployment problem of staggering proportions. While this prospect was disputed by some economists, there was nevertheless strong sentiment in the Administration and the Congress for legislation of a public commitment to "full employment."

As it finally emerged from the Congress in 1946, the Employment Act did not guarantee jobs. It did, however, declare a federal policy of promoting maximum employment. The Council of Economic Advisers, created by the Act, provides an annual report on the economic state of the nation, with special analysis reference to the national objective of maximum employment.

TOWARD A NATIONAL MANPOWER POLICY

A fully developed program for organization of the labor market on

[1] "The Theory of Public Employment Offices," *Political Science Quarterly,* March, 1914, p. 30.

a national, regional, and local basis must await the formulation of a national manpower policy. The United States has not engaged in "manpower planning" on a national scale except in emergency, as in World War II to 1945. National requirements in that war compelled assignment of priority to labor recruitment, training and retraining, and referral of new and displaced workers to unfilled jobs. A regional and national "clearinghouse" had to be established for transferring "surplus" workers from one area to another where shortages existed, often with provisions for the cost of transportation. Techniques of interviewing, testing, and counseling were sharpened. Interest in manpower utilization was enlarged, and the role of the labor market was recognized as an integral part in manpower planning.

Surprisingly, perhaps, public interest in manpower utilization and the organization of the labor market has continued to increase since World War II. This is striking because even the postwar period, the 1950's, and the 1960's have been generally affluent. Of course, the whole interval has not been truly peaceful; Korea, Vietnam, and the "cold war" should not be overlooked.

One other factor in the continuing and enlarged interest in manpower utilization has been the experience of recurring recessions. Although the economy has been growing, definite setbacks nevertheless occurred in 1949, 1954, 1958, and again in 1961. A depression of the 1930 variety has indeed been avoided, but we have not escaped serious fluctuations in business conditions.

Persistent unemployment has remained a matter of dominant concern during the whole postwar period. Unemployment rates of about 5 percent of the labor force during "good" times have threatened to become normal. Moreover, some groups in the population have had rates of unemployment twice or even three times the national average—young people, the unskilled, Negro workers, and older people.

Two principal explanations have been offered for unemployment in the midst of general prosperity. One relates to the level of demand. Idle manpower and resources, according to the Council of Economic Advisers, could be reduced substantially by a significant acceleration of the annual rate of economic growth beyond, say, the 2.4 percent average for the late 1950's. Consequently, fiscal and monetary policies were urged by the Council to stimulate more rapid growth.

The second principal explanation for sticky unemployment has focused upon structural phenomena. Among these are technological advance, change in the composition of the labor force, increasing educational requirements for jobs, secular decline in employment in certain segments of the economy (e.g., agriculture), changing patterns of consumer demand, and the distress of areas experiencing exhaustion of natural resources or the outmigration of industry.

These adverse elements were considered especially difficult to overcome in the face of rapid growth of the labor force. During the 1960's the labor force has experienced a net annual growth in the work force of about 1.1 million—substantially above the net annual increase for the decade earlier.

Technological change, including automation, was supposed to be a special culprit, according to the structuralists. Its impact upon skills, materials, products, and techniques has been widely dramatized. The computer's entry into the office as well as the factory was deemed important.

Employment in some industries, furthermore, declined steadily and sharply in the postwar years, and the losses were often attributed to automation. Railroad employment fell by more than 50 percent, from 1.4 million to less than 700,000 in twenty years. The soft coal industry suffered an even more drastic decline. The demand for agricultural labor has also been decreasing steadily. The automation of longshoring and newspaper publishing, to cite two more instances, suggests further curtailments in labor demand in these industries.

Higher levels of education were required for many new jobs, while openings in the less skilled and the unskilled jobs have been diminishing for a long time. Indeed, jobs with "bright futures" called for more years of schooling than the dropouts or even high school graduates possessed. These changes suggested a severe test for manpower institutions.

The problems of the past two or more decades encourage emergence of a national manpower program. Definite steps have been taken in the direction of formulating a manpower policy. Measures adopted by the Congress involve enlargement and strengthening of public programs for education at all levels. The Area Redevelopment Act (adopted in 1961 and revised in 1965), the Manpower Development and Training Act (1962), the Vocational Education Act (1963), and the Economic Opportunity Act (1964) have added new responsibilities and dimensions to the Employment Service. The Service is required to make labor surveys, certify training needs, provide testing and counseling, expand job placement for persons trained, and provide information and guidance on occupational needs. Unemployment insurance and the Employment Service were among the topics covered in legislative proposals during 1966.

THE PUBLIC EMPLOYMENT SERVICE

ROLE OF UNITED STATES EMPLOYMENT SERVICE

The United States Employment Service (USES) is the central instrument for any future public program for manpower development. It has been tested and refined in every manpower crisis of our recent history. An improvised national Employment Service was found essential in the mobilization of the nation's manpower during World War I in 1917–18. Nearly a half a century ago, the local Employment Offices which functioned in a score of cities were brought together in a makeshift national plan for the duration of the emergency. With the return to "normalcy" in the 1920's, the national system of public employment exchanges was neglected and all but abolished. It was revived again at the beginning of the Great Depression, and permanent legislation was enacted in 1933. During the 1930's, the Employment Service and the National Re-employment Service (created while the new agency was being established) had a major role in the administration of the large number of emergency public programs for relief and work projects. In 1941–45, the Employment Service made an invaluable contribution to the mobilization of the nation's manpower, to recruiting and placement, and to provision of job information for labor mobility. Many millions of new workers were drawn into the labor force to fill wartime jobs, in factories, in shipyards, logging camps, and construction projects.

In 1945, in contrast with 1919, there was public recognition of the role an employment service must play in "normal" times. Permanent legislation provided a "national network" that includes now about 2,000 public employment offices, to aid in the administration of the unemployment insurance programs, as well as to deal with the special and urgent problems of recession. In the prosperous 1960's, a new set of problems has reaffirmed dependence and reliance upon the public Employment Service as the core of a comprehensive program. It is fitting, therefore, that the role of the public Employment Service and its place in a manpower program has in recent years been subjected to fresh analysis by the Congress and by independent scholars.[2]

[2] In *A Positive Labor Market Policy* (Columbus, Ohio: Charles E. Merrill, Inc., 1963), E. W. Bakke explores the critical issues involved in the operation and development of the Employment and Manpower Services. In *Unemployment and the American Economy* (New York: John Wiley & Sons, 1964), edited by Arthur M. Ross, a group of experts on employment and unemployment explore the persistence of unemployment in the midst of prosperity and the role of training and labor market organization in dealing with the problem. The Upjohn Institute's report on *The Role of the Employment Service in a Changing Economy* (Kalamazoo, Mich., 1964) describes the historical evolution from a labor exchange to an employment service and analyzes the emerging problems and issues. In *Manpower Planning in a Free Society* (Princeton, N.J.: Princeton University Press, 1966), Richard A. Lester provides a provocative discussion of the importance of man-

Much of this analysis and many of the ensuing recommendations have been incorporated in the proposed Employment Service Act of 1966. In view of the enlarged tasks which Congress has from time to time over a thirty-year period "imposed" upon the USES, there is a strong case for a new "mandate," one that goes beyond the Wagner-Peyser Act of 1933. The reappraisal of the objectives, areas of service, structure, and performance of the Employment Service contained in recent studies and in the reports of the manpower committees of the Congress suggest the advisability of comprehensive legislation to give the Employment Service the necessary status, as well as a charter, for developing a national manpower program. The issues involved in redefinition of the role of a new USES are not without controversy. Several of these are noted in the following paragraphs.

Should the Employment Service be federalized? Considerable support exists for such a proposal. Much of it originates with organized labor, which favors uniform compensation for personnel under U.S. Civil Service standards, and the removal of state control (which in certain areas has led to discrimination on the basis of race, notwithstanding national regulations to the contrary). National control and direction would, it is urged, permit unification of policy, better administration, and a reorganization of operations to reflect the increasingly national character of the U.S. economy. Local and regional labor markets do exist, of course, but employment service operations are influenced to a substantial degree by national decisions.

Federalization, as might be expected, is strongly opposed by the states, employer groups in general, and some students of the labor market. The case for a national or federal employment service is, in this writer's view, unassailable for times of emergency but less persuasive for normal periods. Much progress has been made, particularly during the past decade, in the administration and financing of the Employment Service and in federal-state relations. Some local markets differ in important respects from others. While other sound reasons may be offered for maintaining the present system, many important functions of the Employment Service could more efficiently be performed on a national or regional, rather than on a state or local, basis.

---

power policy and of the place of a good public employment service in the organization of the labor market. *In Aid of the Unemployed* (Baltimore: The Johns Hopkins Press, 1965), by Joseph M. Becker and others, surveys the problems of unemployment and analyzes the public and private programs of assistance, including training, insurance, work, welfare, and employment services. The Employment Service Task Force, in its report to the Secertary of Labor in December, 1965, examined "the role and mission" of the USES and proposed several drastic changes in the organization and administration.

THE PUBLIC EMPLOYMENT SERVICE

Should the Employment Service be given more "power"? Should all unfilled vacancies be listed with the local and state offices? The affirmative argument is in part influenced by the fact that the public Employment Service accounts for a relatively small fraction of total job placements—about 15 percent. Most workers secure their jobs by direct application to the employer; others rely upon the information supplied by relatives, friends, or employees; still others rely upon newspaper advertising or private fee-charging agencies. Consequently, the Employment Service offices do not attract most workers who wish to change jobs. Required listing of all vacancies would result in a more general use of the Employment Service and lead to a higher "penetration rate" in job placements.

It has been suggested that, as a sanction, employers who do not list their vacancies with the local Employment Service should not be permitted to use the experience-rating features of the unemployment insurance legislation. In the writer's view, compulsory listing of vacancies and the use of sanctions should be avoided. In times of national manpower stringency, when loss of time between jobs and waste in utilization can endanger the country, a strong case for compulsion exists. In peacetime, the free labor market should be preserved. A "good" Employment Service, efficiently administered and able to aid the wage earner and employers alike, ought to attract "orders" and applicants. Compulsory listing alone is not likely to improve the quality of USES and should be avoided.

To whom should the public Employment Service be available? Should its work be limited to aiding the jobless, or should it also be available to the employed who wish to change jobs? Private fee-charging employment agencies, of course, prefer that a public agency should not compete with private business, that public operations be confined to aid to the unemployed. Fee-charging agencies can and do perform important functions in establishing job contacts for many job seekers. Such agencies, however, cannot contribute to the organization of the labor market—an essential development if the nation's manpower objectives are to be served. The Employment Service has been expanding its volume of placements for managerial, professional, skilled, clerical, and sales personnel. It is becoming less and less an agency for the placement of unskilled and domestic workers.

To limit the activity of USES to the unemployed would prevent proper future development. In the author's view, USES should pursue an aggressive policy of calling attention to its "openings." It should strengthen its relations with colleges and universities; it should expand advertising in the press and on the radio; it should seek to make its listings available to all who can improve their job position.

Should the Employment Service be separated from responsibility for the administration of unemployment insurance? Such a proposal was recommended by the Secretary of Labor's Employment Service Task Force in December, 1965. Physical separation of all Employment Service offices from unemployment insurance was proposed to correct the impression that the Employment Service is an unemployment office and to permit concentration on the job placement function.

In the author's view, there are distinct disadvantages in functional separation, which may in any case be impracticable. Many local offices are too small for division; there are 544 local offices with five or fewer employees, 471 with six to ten employees, and 279 with eleven to fifteen employees. Separation of functions in the small offices would obviously be uneconomical and could also be unnecessary.

Finally, there is need for basic research in the manpower field, as other papers in this volume note. This area is a relatively new one for social science inquiry. It is complex and interdisciplinary. The major type of research heretofore undertaken by the Employment Service has involved operational data. This activity is important and needs to be expanded. Its major concern is with the characteristics of local labor supply and commuting patterns. We need also to know much more, however, about work attitudes, job requirements, occupational outlook, and labor mobility, especially to help the counselors who influence occupational choice. The labor market is in constant flux, and the dynamics of the economy prohibit assumptions about tomorrow's manpower needs. Social scientists in the universities and elsewhere must be involved in manpower analysis and planning as deeply as the physical scientists already are involved in making the "space age" a reality.

6

GAPS IN UNEMPLOYMENT INSURANCE
BENEFIT RESEARCH

MERRILL G. MURRAY

Major disagreements on almost every feature of the unemployment insurance program persist despite thirty years of experience. This paper focuses on research needs for policy formulation with respect to the qualifying requirement for entitlement to benefits, the weekly benefit amount, and the duration of benefits. The issues regarding these provisions mostly involve questions of adequacy: Is enough previous employment required as a qualifying requirement to assure adequate attachment to the labor force? Is the benefit amount large enough to be adequate? Is the duration of benefits long enough?

Considerable research has been undertaken on other aspects of the unemployment insurance program. Practically every state has made one or more studies of financial needs, but the research directed at the benefit features of the program has been surprisingly limited in view of the several billions of dollars paid out in benefits each year. This has been partly due to the inadequacy of available data. A great volume of statistics has been accumulated on the benefit *operations* of the state laws, but most of it has been of limited value for program research. Special studies are, therefore, necessary.

When the policy-maker attempts to use available research results, he often finds that they fall short of supplying precisely the information that is needed. Part of the difficulty is due to the great variation in the employment and unemployment experience of claimants, who do not fit into neat patterns. For example, there is no point at which the duration of unemployment is concentrated, so that one might say that the duration of benefits should extend to this point. Little is known, furthermore, concerning the "why" of the claimant's employment and unemployment experience. For example, why do some claimants have so little previous employment? Were they continuously in the labor force? If not, why not?

In this paper, major issues with respect to the benefit features of unemployment insurance are described, the nature of research conducted on these issues is indicated, and the need for additional research is outlined.[1] The author hopes to stimulate the policy-maker to ask for, and to use, more facts before he makes his decisions, and to stimulate fellow researchers to delve into areas badly in need of additional and more meaningful information.[2]

QUALIFYING REQUIREMENT

As one of the requirements for entitlement to unemployment compensation, all state laws specify a certain amount of employment or earnings in the "base period"[3] preceding an initial claim for benefits. While not the most controversial issue in unemployment insurance, the character of this qualifying requirement is most difficult to determine satisfactorily.

It may be asked why any qualifying requirement is necessary. Is it not sufficient that one has been in insured employment and has become unemployed? In workmen's compensation, a worker is qualified for benefits the moment that he is hired. If he walks out of the hiring office and slips and falls, he may claim workmen's compensation for any injury that occurs. On the other hand, it is thought necessary that a worker have a prescribed minimum amount of employment or wages in a recent period in order to qualify for unemployment compensation. Why? The answer lies in the fact that unemployment is an intangible condition that cannot be demonstrated in some objective manner as can a broken leg. Although it may not be the only test, a record of substantial prior employment or wages has been considered the best test that the unemployed worker has suffered an insurable wage loss. While there is general agreement on this, differences do arise as to the required amounts of previous employment or wages.

Much of the disagreement on qualifying requirements grows out of the absence of a well-defined norm for adequate attachment to employment. There should be "substantial" employment, but no one is prepared to say whether the employment must have been substantial enough to demonstrate the worker's availability for work on a full-time, year-round

[1] See U.S., Department of Labor, Bureau of Employment Security, *Selected Bibliography of Unemployment Insurance Benefit Studies and Related Topics, 1951–56,* BES No. U-170, May, 1957 (new bibliography is in preparation); also *Suggested Unemployment Insurance Program and Financial Research Subjects* (Attachment to UIPL Letter No. 656, April 1962).

[2] For a full discussion of the policy issues outlined in this paper, see William Haber and Merrill G. Murray, *Unemployment Insurance in the American Economy* (Homewood, Ill.: Richard D. Irwin, Inc., 1966).

[3] The base period is usually the first four of the last five calendar quarters, or the fifty-two weeks preceding the claim.

basis. Should a seasonal worker who has had a substantial amount of employment during the usual season qualify for benefits? Should a worker available the year-round on a part-time basis be able to qualify for benefits? Until such basic questions are answered, research on the qualifying requirement is not very fruitful. But the basic deficiency is the paucity of information on the employment experience of claimants prior to unemployment.

Types of Qualifying Requirements

The form of the qualifying requirements in most of the state laws has been largely dictated by the type of information secured in the tax reports from employers. Originally, the state laws were so written that the qualifying requirement was stated in terms of a minimum number of weeks of employment. Early in the program, however, it became evident that it would not be administratively feasible to secure and keep employment records on a weekly basis. Accordingly, most of the states, except Wisconsin, shifted to the gathering of quarterly dollar earnings for each worker from quarterly tax returns and based qualifying requirements and benefits on such earnings. A small number of states shifted to annual earnings for the determination of qualifying requirements and benefits. These states set a minimum amount of annual earnings as a qualifying requirement, and a few states that shifted to quarterly earnings did likewise.

Most states that adopted quarterly wage reporting did not require a fixed amount of earnings, but required annual earnings equal to a given multiple of the weekly benefit—usually thirty times this amount. Since the benefit formula was usually designed to produce a weekly benefit amount equal to 50 percent of average wages, it was assumed that this amount of annual earnings would be about the equivalent of a requirement of fifteen weeks of employment for a worker employed on a full-time basis.

A flat dollar qualifying requirement, such as $500 in earnings in the base year, is least satisfactory, since the length of required employment varies inversely with the wage rate. Dollar requirements also become obsolescent as wages increase. Alternative requirements based on quarterly or annual wages are criticized as making it possible for a worker to qualify for benefits on the basis of a very short period of employment if he earned very high wages. As an extreme example, if the qualifying requirement is thirty times the benefit amount and the benefit amount is $50, an entertainer earning $500 a performance could qualify for benefits in three days. Some states have sought to restrict this possibility by requiring earnings in at least two calendar quarters. Other states, on the recommendation of the Bureau of Employment Security, have gone a step further and set the qualifying wages at one and one-half (or some similar multiple) times the earnings in the highest quarter of the base year.

Following World War II, employer representatives in some industrial states began to seek legislation to determine both the qualifying requirement and benefits on the basis of weeks of employment. Wisconsin, which had retained a weekly basis, had demonstrated that weeks of employment could be secured from employers on a "request reporting" basis for workers who actually filed claims for benefits. Unfortunately, the proposal to use weeks of employment for determining the qualifying requirement and benefits was tied up in a "package plan" which included recommendations for much more stringent disqualification provisions. The proposal therefore encountered the opposition of organized labor and was adopted in only a few states.

The number of states that use a weekly basis for eligibility and benefit determination has gradually grown, however, and now totals nine states. In addition, five states that still use quarterly or annual earnings to determine the benefit amount now use weeks of employment for the qualifying requirement. The requirement in these states varies from fourteen to twenty-six weeks in the preceding year, with twenty weeks the most usual figure. A minimum amount of earnings, usually about $15, is required for any week to count as a week of employment.

How Much Employment or Wages Should Be Required?

Only a few states have completed any research studies to determine whether or not qualifying requirements were satisfactory, and if not, to determine what change should be made. More states are conducting such research, making analyses of quarterly wage record data for covered workers over a three-year period.[4]

In those states that depend on earnings data, it is possible to cross-tabulate annual earnings with the number of quarters during the year in which there were earnings, and to tabulate annual earnings as a multiple of high-quarter earnings. Studies of wage record data for a three-year period also provide some information on the degree of correspondence between one-year base period labor force attachment and longer term attachment. After such studies are completed, however, it still is not known how long—how many weeks—the workers have been employed in the high quarter or in other quarters. It is also not known

[4] These studies use the methodology and form of analysis provided in U.S., Department of Labor, Bureau of Employment Security, *Guide for the Conduct of Unemployment Benefit Entitlement Studies,* BES No. U-190, July, 1960.

whether high earnings reflect substantial employment or high wage rates. Using the extreme example of a high-paid entertainer again, annual earnings of one and one-half times high-quarter earnings could have been secured simply through two days of work in the high quarter and one day of work in another quarter.

States that base qualifying requirement on former earnings, therefore, tend to establish a statistical measure of the "best" qualifying requirements—e.g., that not more than a fourth of the workers should be ruled out by the requirement. When doing this, they must take care that low-paid workers who have been employed a considerable length of time are able to qualify for benefits. The problems involved can be illustrated by a study made by the West Virginia Department of Employment Security, which used the earnings of covered workers for the period 1961–63, with special emphasis on earnings in 1962.[5] The study discloses that in 1962, 16 percent of all covered workers had earnings in only one quarter, 13 percent in two quarters, 13 percent in three quarters, and 58 percent in four quarters. From the distribution of workers at different ratios of annual earnings to high-quarter earnings, it was found that at least one and one-half times high-quarter earnings would be necessary as a qualifying requirement if one-fourth of the covered workers were to be excluded. On the other hand, a minimum of $800 in annual earnings would eliminate about 6 percent of those who had had three or four quarters of earnings during the year. Accordingly a qualifying requirement in terms of a multiple of high-quarter earnings was recommended in addition to a flat annual earnings requirement, although the report avoided recommending any particular multiple.

In states using weeks of employment as a qualifying requirement, it is known how long the worker has been employed—at least in how many weeks he had the required amount of earnings. Two states, Oregon and New York, have secured weekly employment data and compared the relative merits of basing the qualifying requirements on quarterly and weekly wages. Both found that weeks of employment more effectively tested labor force attachment, and both have adopted a qualifying requirement of twenty weeks of employment.[6]

The first and basic need, then, is for the states now using quarterly or annual wages to gather information on the weeks of employment of

[5] West Virginia, Department of Employment Security, Research and Statistics Division, *Unemployment Benefit Entitlement Study, 1961–1963,* RS-No. 101 (Charleston, February, 1965).

[6] New York has an alternative requirement of fifteen weeks in one year and forty weeks in two years. Oregon requires a minimum of $700 in annual earnings in addition.

covered workers. This information will serve as a basis for evaluating the quarterly or annual wage requirements, and can provide a factual foundation for a shift to a qualifying requirement expressed in terms of weeks of employment. Florida, Missouri and Oregon required employers to report weeks of employment on quarterly tax returns before a shift to a weeks-of-employment qualifying requirement.

The studies thus far published indicate that not much more than twenty weeks of employment or its equivalent in earnings can be required without the exclusion of a large percentage of covered workers. These studies do not show why those who do not meet the qualifying requirement fail to do so. What are the characteristics of such workers as compared with the characteristics of workers who do meet the qualifying requirement? What proportions are out of the labor market part of the time and why? What proportion of those with low earnings were part-time workers but worked part-time throughout the year? These questions are important because millions of workers move in and out of the labor market each year. Much more intensive research needs to be done before we can really know what the qualifying requirements are doing.

The only types of information that the states have, if they depend on their records for studies, relate to wages and perhaps the weeks of employment, too, of covered workers, and the industry in which the wages are earned. With knowledge of industries in their states, researchers can form some judgment as to whether the qualifying requirement is including "too many" or "too few" according to some statistical norm. Also, analysis by industry makes possible the comparison of employment experience in seasonal and nonseasonal industries.

Analysis of employment experience by industry, however, is not enough. Research on the labor force attachment of covered workers over a period of time is needed.

In recognition of the need for information on the labor force experience and characteristics of workers and claimants covered by the unemployment insurance program, the Bureau of Employment Security has developed a *Guide for a Continuous Wage and Benefit History Program*.[7] About three-fourths of the states are in various stages of planning, developing, or conducting partial or total programs of this nature. In addition to the accumulation of data on wages and employment data and the industries in which covered workers have been employed, the Bureau recommends, and some states have secured, information on the

[7] U.S., Department of Labor, Bureau of Employment Security, BES No. U-251, January, 1966.

age, sex, and race of workers in the samples from worker data accumulated by the Social Security Administration. The data available from the continuous work history programs will be of great value in studies of the benefit amount, benefit duration, and especially of qualifying requirements.

Comprehensive information was secured on the labor market attachment and characteristics of claimants for extended benefits under the Temporary Extended Unemployment Compensation (TEUC) program of 1961.[8] Such information recently became available from thirteen states through sample studies of regular claimants made in 1961–62 at the same time information was secured on the characteristics of claimants for extended benefits under the TEUC program. The results were encouraging in that they showed strong labor force attachment on the part of most of the claimants. Three-fourths of the regular claimants had been in the labor force during all of the thirty-six months prior to filing for unemployment benefits. On the other hand, a larger proportion of men (82 percent) than of women (61 percent) showed this degree of attachment. Primary workers in families showed the strongest attachment (84 percent), and married secondary workers in families showed weakest attachment (58 percent).[9] The amount of employment and unemployment of these workers during the thirty-six-month period was also tabulated. Other states need to carry on such studies and make more intensive analysis of those groups that showed poor labor force attachment.

WEEKLY BENEFIT AMOUNT

One of the most controversial—if not the most controversial—issue in unemployment insurance is the adequacy of the weekly benefit amount. There are two elements in the weekly benefit amount—a given percentage of earnings (hereafter referred to as the basic benefit) and a maximum.

The original unemployment insurance laws, following the example of workmen's compensation, paid a weekly benefit equal to a percentage of full-time weekly wages. The usual percentage was 50 percent. The concept of providing benefits equal to a percentage of weekly wages has

[8] See, in this volume, Paul J. Mackin, *"Extended Unemployment Benefits: For Whom?"*

[9] U.S., Department of Labor, Bureau of Employment Security, in cooperation with Georgia, Department of Labor, Employment Security Agency, *The Long-Term Unemployed: Comparison with Regular Unemployment Insurance Claimants,* Special TEUC Report No. 3, BES No. 3, BES No. U-225-3, Tables 14A and 14D.

survived the shift in most states to benefits based on quarterly or annual wages. Most states that base their benefits on actual weekly wages average only weeks in which earnings are above a stated amount, such as $14 or $20.

The states that use quarterly wages seek an approximation to 50 percent of full-time weekly wages by paying weekly benefit amounts equal to 1/26 of wages earned in the calendar quarter during the base period in which wages are highest. To allow for some unemployment or under-employment during the quarter, or to pay a benefit equal to more than 50 percent of wages, some states use somewhat larger fractions, which may be large as 1/20. The states using annual wages pay weekly benefit amounts equal to a percentage of annual earnings. These percentages vary from 1.0 to 2.2. They are larger for the lower wage levels, presumably to allow for more unemployment and also to assure a higher fraction of wages as a benefit than in the case of higher paid workers.

There has been little or no research to determine whether the fractions of quarterly or annual wages are realistic. It would be very desirable to make sample studies of the weeks worked by claimants as well as the amount of underemployment. From such inquiries, the percentage of full-time weekly wages paid under the benefit formula of each state would be determined.

Adequacy of 50 Percent

The adequacy of a benefit equal to 50 percent of weekly wages has been generally taken for granted. In fact, "the *principle* of 50 percent of wages" is an expression frequently used. There has been some recognition that 50 percent of weekly earnings may be inadequate for low-paid workers and for workers with families to support. A few state laws weight their benefit schedules so that low-paid workers get a higher proportion of their weekly earnings, some formulas running as high as 66⅔ percent of earnings, at least for the lowest paid workers. Ten states now supplement the benefits of claimants with dependents' allowances for minor children and in some cases for nonworking wives. Nevertheless, the adequacy of 50 percent of weekly wages as the basic benefit amount has never been seriously challenged.

Research into how claimants get along on their benefits has been limited to seven sample surveys of beneficiaries in six states, made in the 1950's. In these studies, stratified samples were selected to represent single beneficiaries and beneficiaries in four-person families. The latter included beneficiaries who were either (1) the primary and only earner, (2) the primary earner with the wife a secondary earner, or (3) the wife as a secondary worker. Information was secured on the family expenditures, the relationship between the weekly benefit amount and the weekly wages of the claimant and the expenditures of the household, the availability of other income to the family, and the expedients used to make up the deficiency between income and expenditures.

The results of these studies were consolidated and analyzed by the Department of Labor's Bureau of Employment Security.[10] The outstanding fact, when one looks at the results of these surveys, is that on the average, the claimants reduced their expenditures very little during unemployment. The average reduction in cash outlay during unemployment of single claimants ranged from 7 percent to 20 percent in the different surveys. For the heads of four-person households, the reduction was somewhat similar, ranging from 5 to 22 percent. Reductions in expenditures were limited even though, on the average, income other than unemployment compensation was very small. In order to make up the difference between income and expenditures, 18 to 54 percent of the single claimants drew on savings, as did 14 to 17 percent of the heads of households. About half of the heads of households increased debts to stores, and 11 to 46 percent borrowed money. About the same percentages received help from relatives or friends. Only a small percentage received public relief.

It is obvious that unemployment benefits could not be increased to meet all expenditures of the unemployed without being so high as to reduce the incentive for some to seek work. Unemployment insurance therefore must have a more limited objective. A criterion that is receiving increased acceptance is that unemployment insurance should be sufficient to meet nondeferrable expenses.

A thorough analysis of the data produced by these studies has been made by Father Joseph M. Becker.[11] He used the same list of nondeferrable expenses that was selected by the Bureau of Employment Security, namely, expenditures for food, housing and utilities, clothing, and medical care. On the basis of expenditures for these items, Father Becker concluded that the benefits were adequate for most single persons and secondary workers but inadequate for the heads of four-person families.

[10] *Unemployment Insurance and the Family Finances of the Unemployed,* BES No. U-203, July, 1961.
[11] Joseph M. Becker, *The Adequacy of the Benefit Amount in Unemployment Insurance* (Kalamazoo, Mich.: Upjohn Institute for Employment Research, 1961); and his "The Adequacy of Benefits in Unemployment Insurance," in Joseph M. Becker (ed.), *In Aid of the Unemployed* (Baltimore, Johns Hopkins Press, 1965), chap. 5.

Father Becker would probably be the first to acknowledge that the list of nondeferrable expenditures that he used cannot be described as "scientifically selected." The Bureau of Employment Security had used them earlier as "illustrative" in its analysis of the studies. When the actual expenditures of the beneficiaries in the studies are looked at, it appears that practically no category of expenditures is completely deferrable: the general pattern was some reduction in all expenditures but elimination of none. Indeed, there was less reduction in several of the "deferrable" expenditures than in those considered to be nondeferrable. For example, expenditures were not reduced for personal care. Research appears to be necessary therefore, on nondeferrability and the extent to which such expenditures can actually be reduced without falling below some minimum standard to which beneficiaries adhere.

One approach suggested by the Bureau of Employment Security in its report was to compare the family expenditures of beneficiaries with the City Worker's Family Budget (CWFB) developed by the Bureau of Labor Statistics.[12] It recognized that beneficiary expenditures would normally have to be lower than the CWFB, which provides for a "modest but adequate level of living" for a four-person family of one worker who is *employed,* not unemployed. The Bureau of Labor Statistics is planning to develop a lower-level budget for the needs of families during a temporary period of unemployment of the primary worker in the family. Downward adjustments in the content of expenditures would be made, but the budget would still be adequate to preserve the family's health, efficiency, and social acceptability. While such a budget would be useful as a standard against which the benefits of heads of four-person families could be measured, it could not be used to evaluate the benefits of single persons or of secondary workers in families. A need, accordingly, would still exist to develop such lower-level budget data for claimants representing different family types and for single persons.

Since unemployment compensation varies with earnings, it may well be asked, however, whether any determination of a "minimum adequate budget" is pertinent. One of the important areas for research would be to determine the correlation between size of income and the nature of expenditures. It is known from studies of the Bureau of Labor Statistics, for example, that the proportion of total income spent for food decreases as income rises. If there is a sufficiently well-defined relationship, it might be possible to establish budgets at several wage levels. This, however, would probably be impracticable. About the most that a "mini-

---

[12] U.S., Department of Labor, Bureau of Employment Security, *Unemployment Insurance and the Family Finances,* pp. 46–49.

mum adequate budget" can do is to serve as a guidepost in evaluating the adequacy of benefits.

Maximum Weekly Benefit Amount

The principal factor limiting the adequacy of unemployment benefits has been low maximum weekly benefit amounts. Since the early 1950's, when maximums had not been increased as much as wage increases following World War II, in most of the states too high a proportion of claimants have been receiving less than 50 percent of their wages because of too low maximums. Maximums have been increased since then in every state, and in many states several times. Still, in 1964 more than one-half of the beneficiaries were eligible for the state maximum in twenty-two states. In five states 70 percent or more were at the maximum; in seventeen states from 50 to 69 percent; in only five states less than 30 percent.[13]

There has been increasing acceptance of a device (in fifteen state laws by the end of 1965) by which the maximum benefit amount is increased automatically as the wage level increases. In most of these states this "flexible maximum" is equal to 50 percent of the average weekly wages of covered workers in the state.

The criterion advanced by both Republican and Democratic Administrations since 1954 has been that the maximum should be high enough that the great majority of workers should be eligible for a benefit equal to one-half of their regular weekly wages. Even if this criterion is applied to claimants, whose wages on the average are lower than the average wages of all covered workers, a maximum equal to 50 percent of average wages would not be high enough to meet the criterion. In five of the nine states that had a "flexible maximum" during the twelve months ending June 30, 1965, less than a majority received at least one-half of their average wages; the proportions in the nine states ranged from 32 percent to 77 percent.[14]

The Administration bill of 1965 (H.R. 8282) would have required the states to provide a maximum equal to 50 percent of average covered wages in the state by 1967 and of 66⅔ percent by 1971. The Interstate Conference of Employment Security Agencies, while endorsing the need for a minimum federal standard in this area, recommended that a maximum of not more than 50 percent be required. If this lower standard

[13] U.S., Congress, House, Committee on Ways and Means, *Unemployment Compensation; Hearings on H.R. 8282,* 89th Cong., 1st Sess., 1965, p. 151.
[14] Unemployment Benefit Advisors, *The Advisor* ('66–3; Washington, February 25, 1966).

is adopted, some states will need to have a higher maximum if the great majority of claimants are to be eligible for at least one-half of their individual average weekly wages if the experience of the states now meeting this standard is any guide.

Use of the average weekly wages of covered workers as a basis for setting the maximum benefit is subject to the difficulty that such an average does not necessarily correspond to the average wages of claimants.[15] The average wage of covered workers is used because it is a figure that is readily calculated from regularly reported statistics. It would be an expensive and difficult process to calculate the average wage of the claimants in each state each year. It is possible, however, to determine without undue expense through sample studies what proportion of claimants will be eligible for 50 percent of their average wages. The average weekly wages were reported by the sample of claimants questioned in May and September, 1961, and January, 1962, in the thirteen-state survey of regular claimants previously referred to. On the basis of this data, it was found that a maximum of 50 percent of state average covered wages would have limited the benefit to less than one-half of their individual average weekly wages for 20 to 29 percent of the claimants in four states, for 30 to 39 percent in seven states, and for 50 to 59 percent in two states. If, however, the maximum were 66⅔ percent of state average covered wages, the proportion of the claimants who would have been limited by the maximum would have been less than 20 percent in all the states.[16] If a federal standard is enacted which would require the states to have maximum benefits no higher than 50 percent of each state's average weekly covered wages, the states should make studies similar to the thirteen-state sample study if, after meeting or bettering this standard, more than a small minority of the claimants are affected by the maximum. Through such studies it would be possible to determine in advance what the effect of higher maxima such as 60 percent or 66⅔ percent of the average weekly wage of covered workers would be, which would be of great assistance to the policy makers in the state.

---

[15] At the time of writing (February, 1966), the proposed federal standard in terms of the average wages of covered workers is being attacked because of this, and it is hinted (in *The Advisor, ibid.*) that an alternative in terms of the average wages of claimants will be proposed.

[16] Merrill G. Murray, *Proposed Federal Unemployment Insurance Amendments* (Kalamazoo, Mich.: Upjohn Institute for Employment Research, 1966), p. 20, Table 2; U.S., Congress, House, Committee on Ways and Means, *Unemployment Compensation*, pp. 153–66.

Dependents' Allowances

One other facet of benefit adequacy needs research. Father Becker, finding that benefits were inadequate principally for heads of families, concluded that dependents' allowances would be especially helpful in providing adequate benefits. Dependents' allowances, however, are payable in only eleven states, and many object to the payment of such allowances as injecting an element of need into the program. The efficacy of using dependents' allowances to provide adequate benefits should be explored in all states.

Basic to any research on dependents' allowances would be some study as to the amounts needed by wives and children to supplement adequately the basic weekly benefit. Little or no study preceded the establishment of dependents' allowances in those states that have them, and little or no study has been made as to the value of such allowances in enabling the beneficiary to meet essential expenditures.

DURATION OF BENEFITS

There is a general consensus that, at least for the regular unemployment insurance program,[17] the maximum duration should be at least twenty-six weeks. All but Puerto Rico and two states provide this duration, and nine states go beyond it. But most states vary the duration allowed for each individual, usually from a minimum of ten weeks or more for those who barely qualify for benefits to a maximum of twenty-six weeks for those with a very substantial amount of previous employment or earnings.

Whether the duration of benefits should be varied with the length of time that the claimant has been employed (variable duration) or whether the maximum duration should be available, if needed, to all claimants who meet a basic qualifying requirement ("uniform duration") is the key issue. The view that the duration of benefits should be varied with the amount of previous employment or earnings of the individual has been gaining ground. In 1941, sixteen states provided uniform duration; in 1966, only eight states. New life was injected into the uniform duration cause, however, when the federal Administration in 1965 proposed (H.R. 8282) a federal standard requiring that a state must pay at least twenty-six weeks of benefits if a worker has twenty weeks of employment in the "base year" used for determining the benefits.

[17] An extended benefit program was enacted in the recessions of 1958 and 1961 and a permanent program for longer duration, either during recessions or at all times, for workers with a long record of employment was proposed by the Administration in 1965 in H.R. 8282. (See Mackin, "Extended Unemployment Benefits," this volume.)

One argument made for variable duration of benefits is that the longer a worker is employed, the more he has earned in benefit rights. This argument particularly appeals to employers, who feel that they should be charged with benefits only in proportion to the time that the claimants worked for them.

The principal argument of those favoring uniform duration is that a worker who has had irregular or short-duration employment may need the maximum duration of benefits as much as the worker who has been steadily employed—perhaps more so. It is also argued that variable duration does not effectively meet the needs of the unemployed, as evidenced by the larger proportion of workers who exhaust benefits in variable duration states. In the twelve-month period ending June 30, 1965, for instance, in none of the states[18] that provided uniform duration of benefits was the ratio of claimants who exhausted benefits as high as 20 percent. On the other hand, twenty states with variable duration had exhaustion ratios of 25 percent or more and one variable duration state (Texas) had an exhaustion ratio of 38 percent.

The crux of the question as to whether variable duration is justified relates to the labor market attachment of those who become eligible for less than maximum duration of benefits. Are they workers who are only loosely attached to the labor market and do they leave it as soon as they exhaust benefits?

A number of states have carried out surveys of the post-exhaustion experience of exhaustees in order to determine their characteristics and the extent to which they found employment or withdrew from the labor market two or four months after exhaustion. These studies give much valuable information on the labor force attachment of beneficiaries. Tabulations in twenty-six state post-exhaustion studies during the years 1954–58 showed that only from 5 to 18 percent had withdrawn two months after exhaustion (except for New York which showed 24.5 per cent). The proportions who had withdrawn four months after exhaustion were only slightly higher, ranging from 7 to 20 percent (New York again was exceptional with 25.3 percent).[19]

When these data are distributed by sex, it is seen that a larger proportion of women than men withdraw from the labor market, although the proportion for women is still not very large. Two months after exhaus-

---

[18] Except Puerto Rico, which provides a maximum of 12 weeks.

[19] U.S., Department of Labor, Bureau of Employment Security, *Experience of Claimants Exhausting Benefit Rights Under Unemployment Insurance*, BES No. U-178, 1958, Chart 1; and its *Major Findings of 16 State Studies of Claimants Exhausting Unemployment Benefit Rights, 1956–1959*, mimeo, April, 1961, Table 1.

tion of benefits the proportion of females was below 10 percent in five states, ranged between 10 and 20 percent in eighteen states, and exceeded 20 percent in only three states. The proportions were not much higher after four months. No noticeable difference occurred between states with variable duration and states with uniform duration.

After comparing the percentages of withdrawal from the labor market in the post-exhaustion studies with pertinent census data, Father Joseph M. Becker concluded that the studies understated the number of post-exhaustees, particularly female exhaustees, who had actually withdrawn from the labor market.[20] In support, Father Becker cited a study by Ronald S. Johnson of the University of Michigan who personally interviewed a sample of exhaustees in Detroit in 1948–49. Johnson concluded that only 53 percent of the exhaustees studied were clearly regular members of the labor force with good chances of reemployment.[21]

Post-exhaustion studies should not rely, as they have in the past, on a brief mail questionnaire. Father Becker recommends that more intensive surveys should be made on the basis of personal interviews. Such interviews would make it possible to determine the labor market status of exhaustees more accurately.

The chief shortcoming of earlier post-exhaustion reports is that they give very limited information on exhaustees by duration of benefits. The Bureau of Employment Security's consolidated report of seventeen state studies (BES No. U-178) has only one table in which a percentage distribution of exhaustees is shown by sex and the number of weeks compensated during the benefit year prior to exhaustion.[22] Tabulations are needed concerning the percentage distribution of withdrawees by the duration of their *benefits*. Such figures would show whether a higher withdrawal rate applies to those with short duration of benefits under variable duration formulas. It would also be desirable to analyze the relationship between withdrawal rates and the previous employment records of exhaustees to determine the degree of prior attachment to the labor force. Studies of such exhaustees should also be made in depth through personal interviews, as already suggested above.

The formula used for limiting the duration of benefits in variable duration states also requires additional attention. States that use former

[20] Becker, "The Adequacy of Benefits in Unemployment Insurance," p. 106.

[21] Ronald S. Johnson, *A Study of People Who Have Exhausted Unemployment Benefits in an Active Labor Market* (Ann Arbor, Mich.: Bureau of Business Research, University of Michigan, January, 1951).

[22] Two other tables give the percentage distribution of exhaustees employed, unemployed and withdrawn from the labor force two and four months after exhaustion, but the distribution is given by number of weeks compensated *in the last spell of unemployment prior to exhaustion*.

earnings as a basis for determining potential duration take a fraction (such as ⅓) or a percentage (such as 35 percent) of the claimant's annual earnings and divide this by the weekly benefit amount to determine potential duration of benefits. For example, if the claimant's base period earnings were $1,350 and the fraction ⅓, total potential benefits would be $450; if the weekly benefit were $30, the claimant would then be eligible for fifteen weeks of benefits. If former weeks of employment are used to determine potential duration, then a fraction such as, for example, ⅗ of the weeks of employment in the base period is used. Then, if the worker had twenty weeks of employment he would be entitled to twelve weeks of benefits.

The fraction or percentage of former earnings or employment used in determining potential duration of benefits is therefore very important for the claimant. In Georgia and Indiana, which used a fraction of ¼ in 1963, the proportion of claimants that were eligible for less than fifteen weeks of benefits were 51 and 58 percent, respectively. In California, which used a fraction of ½ in 1963, the proportion eligible for fewer than fifteen weeks was only 10 percent that year.

The fractions or percentages used to limit the duration of benefits are so diverse that they evidently were arrived at by legislative bargaining in each state rather than on the basis of research. If a state is going to have or keep variable duration of benefits, it should analyze the effects of various fractions or percentages of earnings or employment on the potential duration of its claimants. It should also analyze the characteristics of those claimants who become eligible for short durations. Perhaps, some claimants should not receive benefits at all and a higher qualifying requirement should be imposed. Or, perhaps, it will be found instead that the fraction used is unduly restrictive. In either case, a state should know what it is doing and why.

CONCLUSION

The foregoing discussion indicates that there is a great need for much more comprehensive research into the difficult questions involved in establishing the proper qualifying requirements, benefit amounts and benefit duration. Except in some of the larger states, research at the state level is usually handicapped by inadequate allocation of funds by the state agency for this purpose and a shortage of trained personnel. The federal Bureau of Employment Security has been especially handicapped by lack of funds for nationwide studies and by shortage of personnel for leadership and technical assistance in the conduct of state studies. The Administration bill of 1965 (H.R. 8282) contains a provision authorizing $5 million initially and as much as is needed thereafter to contract or carry out directly, or through grants, a comprehensive program of research into all aspects of unemployment insurance. The bill provides, incidentally, for the types of research suggested in this paper.

The Temporary Extended Unemployment Compensation (TEUC) Act of 1961 contained a provision requiring research into the characteristics of workers who drew extended benefits under that Act. About $1 million was appropriated for this research. As a result, a wealth of statistics were produced that are invaluable in planning any future program of extended benefits.[23]

Similarly, funds should be continuously available for comprehensive research into the characteristics of claimants for benefits under the state programs. The thirteen-state sample study (previously mentioned) of the characteristics of regular claimants in comparison with TEUC claimants indicates the kinds of claimant information that would become available for program planning.

This paper, it should be repeated, has been intended less as a guide to researchers than as an aid toward identification of areas of needed research on unemployment insurance issues. Research can, of course, do no more than assist policy-makers. After the research is completed, judgment must be exercised in assaying what the results mean and what specific action would best meet the objective. The same statistics may be interpreted differently according to the viewpoint of the observer: one person views as satisfactory what another views with alarm. In the last analysis, then, value judgments necessarily help determine the kind of an unemployment insurance system we get. More research is badly needed to enable us to make better judgments, although political, actuarial, and other factors enter into decisions regarding the provisions of unemployment insurance. This paper has pleaded for more facts and less guesswork.

---

[23] Mackin, "Extended Unemployment Benefits," this volume.

7

CHARACTERISTICS OF STATES WITH ADEQUATE UNEMPLOYMENT INSURANCE RESERVE FUNDS

EUGENE C. McKEAN

The purpose of this paper is to identify states with "adequate" reserves in their unemployment insurance funds and to consider various contributory factors. The principal question to which attention will be given is the extent to which a relatively low level of unemployment helps to explain a good reserve situation. To the extent that a favorable unemployment record does not seem to be the explanation, attention will be focused on other factors that permitted the attainment of an adequate reserve in these states.

The characteristics that are examined also provide tentative answers to related questions. For example: Are the states with favorable reserve positions primarily nonindustrial in character? To what extent does a relatively strong reserve appear to be associated with a relatively low maximum weekly benefit? Is any one type of financing system especially well represented in the list of strong-reserve states? To what extent do these states reflect a higher-than-$3,000 wage base or a relatively high tax-rate structure?

Detailed analysis would be necessary to provide conclusive answers to these related questions. A number of observations will be made, however, on the situations disclosed by a review of the data in the tabulations. These remarks and the data upon which they are based may be helpful to those who wish to analyze in depth the reserve situation of the states.

RECENT IMPROVEMENT, UNCERTAIN OUTLOOK

The continued expansion of the nation's economy that began in 1961, culminating in virtually "full employment" five years later, has relieved the earlier pressure on many state unemployment insurance reserve funds. Although concern about the level of state funds has largely subsided, the topic should still command our interest in good times, especially for the sake of policy planning.

The reserves of all states taken together reached a peak of $8.9 billion at the close of 1953. Thereafter, attrition was occasioned by heavy benefit outlays during the recession years of 1954, 1958, and 1960–61, so that total state reserves had dwindled to $5.8 billion by the end of 1961. Despite rather substantial benefit payments after that date, state reserves gradually built up to $8.4 billion by the end of 1965. By the close of this year (1966), state reserves will probably have surpassed the 1953 peak by a comfortable margin.

Not all states have shared in the recent steady improvement of reserves. Somewhat surprisingly, eleven states experienced a decline in their state fund balances during prosperous 1964, although in most cases the decreases were small. Even during the boom year of 1965, three states experienced declines, again small ones, in their reserve balances. It must be noted, however, that significance attaches only to those declines which occurred in states with less than adequate reserves, whatever the definition adopted.

The likelihood that reserves will have surpassed their 1953 peak level by the end of 1966 may be interpreted either as a favorable or as a less than favorable development. If one believes that the 1953 reserve was considerably larger than needed, then the current reserve fund may be regarded as large enough to carry the unemployment insurance system comfortably. Such a view may be strengthened by a belief that the recent high level of employment will continue during the next few years.

Other observers will point instead to the considerably higher potential benefit liabilities that the system must carry today because of the substantial increase in employment and payrolls since 1953, a development that presumably calls for greater reserves. They may also point to the possibility of cessation of the conflict in Vietnam, or at least a reduction in the scope of the nation's involvement. Such a development could sharply reduce defense spending and lead to production cutbacks in some industries and to readjustments in others, with at least temporary, and perhaps fairly substantial, unemployment for some states. Moreover, observers of this persuasion will point to a number of states in which the reserve situation is still far from satisfactory, in spite of the nation's vigorous economic advance during recent years. Indeed, foreseeable technological and industrial trends could lead to serious unemployment problems in some states, despite general prosperity. And finally, it is premature to assume that recessions have been mastered.

MEASURING THE ADEQUACY OF RESERVES

These conflicting points of view make it clear that the question of the "adequacy" of reserves is a difficult one. As one observer has said, "The hazard involved is too unpredictable and too little susceptible to actuarial projection." Judgment must remain "the dominant factor in deciding how big a fund should be."[1]

Besides, there are other aspects of the solvency of the state system. Among these are the revenue-producing capacity of the tax structure and the rapidity of response to changes in the balance of the unemployment fund. These too should be taken into account in deciding financing policy.[2]

Despite the questions that might be raised concerning the feasibility or desirability of attempts to measure the adequacy of state reserves by formula, such attempts are inevitable. One of the simplest of the measures employed for this purpose is a comparison of a state's reserve fund as of a given date with total wages paid to covered employees during the preceding twelve-month period. On this basis, the relative position of a state's reserve fund may be measured over time or against the position of other states. The difficulty with this measure, of course, is that it does not directly reflect the state's vulnerability to unemployment.

Vulnerable states presumably should carry a relatively larger reserve than states in which employment levels are less sensitive to swings in the economic cycle. A measure developed by the Bureau of Employment Security of the U.S. Department of Labor attempts to cope with this problem by introducing benefit-payment experience into the formula. It reflects "the adequacy of State reserve funds in relation to potential recession benefit costs." The formula shows the reserve ratio (i.e., the current reserve fund as a percentage of total wages of covered employees during the preceding year) as a multiple of the highest benefit cost rate (i.e., highest twelve-month benefit payments during the preceding ten years as a percentage of total covered wages during the same twelve-month period). This formula, commonly referred to as the reserve multiple, thus relates both the current reserve fund and the record twelve-month volume of benefit outlays to an appropriate payroll base and compares the reserve ratio to the benefit ratio as a multiple. The larger the multiple, the more adequate, presumably, the reserve.

The Bureau itself, however, recognizes the hazard involved in attempting to evaluate the adequacy of state reserve funds by a standard measure.[3] In connection with the reserve multiple concept, it cautions that

[1] Russell L. Hibbard, "As Industry Sees It," *Unemployment Insurance Review,* January–February, 1964, p. 4.

[2] *Ibid.*

[3] U.S., Department of Labor, Bureau of Employment Security, "Financial Developments Under State UI Programs," *Labor Market and Employment Security,* May, 1961, p. 17.

interstate "comparisons of this multiple must take into account whether the circumstances that gave rise to the high-cost period could be expected to recur, at least with substantially the same results."[4]

Despite limitations, the reserve multiple forms the basis for the interstate comparisons of reserve adequacy made in this paper. Use of this formula does not indicate belief that the formula is a true indicator of the adequacy of a state's reserve or of differences among the states in reserve adequacy. However, it does offer a fairly reasonable approach to the problem of making interstate comparisons in this area. From a practical point of view, its use is inescapable in any systematic comparison with respect to reserve adequacy.

The Bureau has suggested a reserve multiple of 1.50 as a minimum adequate reserve. For purposes of this paper, states have been classified as having a satisfactory fund reserve if their reserve multiple equals or surpasses this level. As suggested, it is likely that some states with a multiple somewhat below 1.5 may actually be in a more satisfactory reserve situation than states with a multiple somewhat above it.

As in most tabulations, questions of reliability and of comparability may be raised concerning the data used in the tabulations shown in this paper. Ohio has recently published a detailed list of limitations on the use of data on insured unemployment for interstate comparisons.[5] Some of the characteristics that might contribute to an understanding of a state's reserve situation are not susceptible to systematic cataloging in statistical tables.

OBSERVATIONS ON GENERAL STATE EXPERIENCE

Before the pattern of individual state reserves is examined, a few more remarks may be appropriate concerning recent over-all reserve experience, as disclosed in Table 1. At the close of 1960, the reserve multiple of all the states averaged 1.68, above the minimum level of adequacy. Thirty-six states, accounting for two-thirds of all covered employment, enjoyed a reserve multiple of 1.5 or better. Nineteen of these states, accounting for one-fourth of all covered employment, actually had reserve multiples of 3.0 or more, double the level suggested as the minimum level of adequacy. In this connection, it has been sug-

---

[4] *Ibid.,* p. 25.

[5] Ohio, Bureau of Unemployment Compensation, Division of Research and Statistics, *Limitations of Rate of Insured Unemployment as a Measure of Comparative Economic Conditions,* November 24, 1965.

gested that "a multiple of 3 or more may indicate an excessive reserve fund." [6]

In view of the publicized impact of the 1957–58 recession, the good over-all showing reported for 1960 seems somewhat surprising. The substantial reserves accumulated prior to the 1957–58 downturn evidently carried many states, and especially the nineteen with a multiple of 3.0 or over, quite comfortably through that downturn.

This favorable picture for 1960 deteriorated by the close of 1961. The reserve multiple of the states as a group had fallen to 1.44, a level that also prevailed for the next two years. The number of states with a reserve multiple of 1.5 or more had declined to twenty-eight; the number with a multiple of 3.0 or more had dropped to eleven. During the next two years, only seven states were in this latter, especially favorable, category.

The reserve situation improved again by the end of 1964. The thirty-one states with a reserve at or above the minimum level of adequacy accounted for somewhat over half of all covered workers. The eight states with a reserve multiple of 3.0 or more accounted for 9 percent of those workers.

TABLE 1.
Unemployment Insurance Reserve Multiple, 1960–64

Year	All States		States with Reserve Multiple of:			
			1.50 or above		3.00 or above	
	Reserve Multiple	Rate of Insured Unemployment	Number	Percent of Covered Employment	Number	Percent of Covered Employment
1960	1.68	4.7	36	66	19	25
1961	1.44	5.7	28	42	11	13
1962	1.44	4.3	27	49	7	7
1963	1.45	4.3	27	51	7	7
1964	1.55	3.7	31	53	8	9

High-level unemployment during 1960 and 1961 contributed to the deterioration of the reserve situation of the states as a whole. During 1961, state funds suffered the impact of a sharp rise in the rate of insured unemployment and a 25 percent jump in benefit outlays.[7] How-

[6] Paschal C. Zecca, "UI Financing in Fiscal Year 1964," *Unemployment Insurance Review,* January–February, 1965, p. 29.

[7] Although the rate of insured unemployment reported for the years 1958–64 ran below the unemployment rate as reported by the Department of Labor on the basis of its Current Population Survey, the year-to-year movements were in the same direction and in some cases were roughly of the same magnitude.

ever, as the nation's economic expansion gained momentum during 1962, the insured unemployment rate dropped appreciably. Reflecting also a gradual increase in the average tax rate from 1960 to 1962, tax collections outran benefit payments during 1962 and 1963 by a small margin; the favorable balances were the first recorded since 1956. During 1964, tax collections exceeded benefit outlays by $500 million.

OBSERVATIONS ON STATE CHARACTERISTICS

The Unemployment Record

A favorable unemployment record during recent years was the principal explanation in most states for the adequate reserves reported at the close of 1964 (Table 2).[8] Eighteen of the thirty-one adequate-reserve states experienced a rate of insured unemployment below the all-state average during each of the three years shown. Eight states experienced an above-average rate during one or two of the three years. The remaining five states were on the list of adequate-reserve states despite a rate of insured unemployment that exceeded the national average during all three of the years. The five states were Washington, Idaho, New York, Oklahoma, and Kentucky. The multiple for three of these states fell between 1.5 and 2.0, a level above the minimum level of adequacy but not necessarily one that indicates an especially strong reserve position for these states.

An interesting sidelight of the data shown in Table 2 is that nine of the thirty-one adequate-reserve states could be classified as industrial, in view of the relative importance of factory employment.[9] Since indus-

---

[8] It should be noted that changes over time in a reserve multiple may reflect in part a change in the base period of highest benefit costs. In several states, the reserve multiple for 1962 is based on benefit costs for a period ending during 1961 whereas the multiple for 1960 is based on costs during an earlier period.

[9] As indicated by Table 2, the degree of industrialization of the states is measured by the percentage of factory workers in covered employment during 1963. States with a percentage higher than the average percentage (40.5 percent) for all fifty-one states (including the District of Columbia) are regarded as "industrial."

The use of this measure results in classification of a number of southern states as industrialized, while some northern states commonly regarded as important manufacturing states are not shown as industrial. The vagaries of the classification reflect, of course, the diversified compositions of the covered labor force.

For general purposes, a better indicator of the relative degree of industrialization among states would be a measure that relates a state's factory workers to its population. Such a measure would provide a uniform base for interstate comparisons and would thus afford a more realistic indication of the importance of factory employment in each state in comparison with its importance in the country generally. Under this measure, only two southern states—the two Carolinas—would be classified as industrialized.

trial states are generally regarded as especially susceptible to unemployment, the presence of these nine states on the adequate-reserve list may be unexpected. However, none of the five states with an unfavorable unemployment record during the period 1960–64 was included among the "industrial" states.

Benefit Payments

A relatively low level of benefits appears to be an important factor in maintaining a favorable reserve situation (Table 3). Fourteen states were still paying a weekly maximum benefit amount of less than $40 at the start of 1964. Nine states did not increase the weekly maximum amount during the four-year period beginning with January 1, 1960. During 1964, nineteen of these thirty-one states were paying an average weekly benefit representing a percentage of average weekly total wages that was smaller than the average percentage (33.8) for all fifty-one states.

The generally light benefit load carried by the thirty-one adequate-reserve states as a group is indicated by the last three columns of Table 3, which provide a measure of the composite effect of the volume of unemployment and the size of weekly benefit payments by relating total benefit payments to the total wage bill. During 1962 and 1964, twenty-four of these states experienced a benefit-wage relationship below the all-state ratio. During 1960, twenty-three states were below the all-state ratio.

However, there are many exceptions to the general pattern. Thus, at the start of 1964, twelve of the thirty-one adequate-reserve states were paying a maximum weekly benefit of $45 or more (including dependents' allowances). During 1964, twelve of the fifty-one states provided for a "flexible" maximum weekly benefit, amounting to 50 to 55 percent of the statewide average weekly wage.[10] Eight of these flexible-maximum states were among the thirty-one with adequate reserves. Again, from 1960 to 1964, nineteen of the adequate-reserve states experienced a percentage increase in the weekly benefit paid that was larger than the average percentage increase (9.4) in the country generally.

[10] The maximum weekly benefit in these twelve states was computed according to the formula embodied in H.R. 8282, a bill providing for federal standards, that was being considered in Congress at the time of this writing (March, 1966).

TABLE 2.
Labor Force Characteristics of States with an Unemployment Insurance Reserve Fund at or above the
"Minimum Level of Adequacy" at the Close of 1964[a]

State[b]	Reserve Ratio as Multiple of Highest Benefit Cost Rate[c]			Degree of Industrialization		Unemployment Experience				Average Weekly Total Wages in Covered Employment[f]	
	1964	1962	1960	Factory Employees as Percent of All Employees[d] 1963	Percent of Factory Workers in Durables[e] 1963	Insured Employment as Percent of Covered Employment[f]			Percent of Labor Force Un-employ. April 1960[g]	1964	1960
						1964	1962	1960			
All states[h]	1.55	1.44	1.68	40.5		3.7	4.3	4.7	5.1	$106.47	$ 93.34
District of Columbia	5.61	7.07	8.42	7.4	—	2.0	2.0	2.2	4.1	106.06	90.63
Iowa	5.02	5.15	7.49	38.8	—	1.8	2.5	2.7	3.2	97.35	85.82
Arizona	4.24	4.31	5.36	21.2	—	3.8	3.7	3.5	5.3	104.40	94.12
South Dakota	4.13	4.92	6.19	16.7	—	3.1	2.6	2.7	4.1	85.72	77.63
Virginia	3.96	3.45	3.33	38.0	—	1.5	2.0	2.6	4.2	89.43	76.35
Nebraska	3.76	3.72	4.34	27.2	—	2.2	2.5	2.3	3.1	92.72	83.13
Missouri	3.27	3.25	3.58	39.5	—	3.1	3.9	4.1	4.1	105.64	90.68
South Carolina	3.07	2.94	3.43	57.9	20.0	2.8	3.0	3.3	4.1	78.78	66.84
Georgia	2.99	2.82	3.21	44.3	31.8	2.3	3.2	4.2	4.5	86.89	73.08
Florida	2.92	2.51	3.01	22.5	—	2.4	3.7	3.5	5.0	92.54	80.89
North Carolina	2.91	2.75	3.11	55.1	28.0	3.2	3.7	4.2	4.5	80.27	68.91
Utah	2.76	2.91	3.57	27.1	—	4.0	3.1	3.3	4.1	96.97	85.58
New Mexico	2.65	2.90	4.75	10.3	—	3.6	4.0	4.1	5.9	95.17	87.19
Texas	2.59	2.86	3.30	27.3	—	2.3	2.7	3.0	4.5	96.29	84.55
Kansas	2.55	2.70	3.50	32.3	—	2.6	2.7	3.7	3.7	97.17	85.41

Washington	2.51	2.57	3.15	35.7	—	6.6	5.6	6.8	6.6	112.94	98.09
Idaho	2.36	2.15	2.82	27.3	—	4.7	4.7	5.2	5.7	90.64	81.94
Wisconsin	2.25	2.38	2.80	51.6	64.3	2.8	3.1	3.3	3.9	107.17	94.88
Colorado	2.25	2.56	4.05	24.4	—	2.0	2.9	2.6	4.0	102.42	90.96
Mississippi	2.11	1.56	1.73	45.1	46.3	3.7	4.7	5.7	5.4	76.21	64.77
Louisiana	2.03	2.02	3.17	25.6	—	3.7	4.8	5.2	6.1	96.61	82.74
New Hampshire	1.89	1.78	1.94	56.1	41.4	3.7	3.5	4.4	4.3	89.09	77.22
Maryland	1.84	1.29	1.05	35.1	—	3.0	4.2	4.9	4.8	97.69	85.21
New York	1.82	1.78	1.78	36.4	—	4.7	4.9	5.1	5.2	117.48	102.71
Illinois	1.78	1.51	1.47	44.8	64.6	2.5	3.1	3.4	4.5	116.84	103.29
Oklahoma	1.72	1.49	1.73	23.0	—	3.8	4.4	4.8	4.4	95.98	84.50
Kentucky	1.70	1.68	1.93	38.4	—	4.1	5.4	6.6	6.0	93.06	81.06
Alabama	1.62	1.22	1.36	44.4	48.1	3.1	4.9	5.4	5.7	88.65	75.95
Delaware	1.54	1.09	1.14	46.1	23.8	2.6	3.3	3.1	4.6	117.17	103.15
Hawaii	1.52	1.52	3.37	17.7	—	3.4	4.6	2.4	4.2	91.25	77.75
Nevada	1.50	1.27	1.65	5.9	—	4.4	3.5	4.4	6.2	118.57	99.05

[a] For discussion of the "minimum level of adequacy" concept, see section in text entitled "Measuring the Adequacy of Reserves."

[b] States are listed according to their relative standing at the close of 1964 with respect to the "minimum level of adequacy." Puerto Rico is excluded.

[c] Reserve ratios and cost rates for December 31, 1964, and December 31, 1960, have, as their base, wages for the twelve-month period ending six months prior. Data for 1964 and 1962 from *Unemployment Insurance Review*, July, 1965, p. 6, and April, 1964, p. 33, respectively. Data for 1960 from *Labor Market and Employment Security*, p. 16.

[d] U.S. Department of Labor, Bureau of Employment Security, *Unemployment Insurance Tax Rates by Industry, 1963*, BES No. U-250, May, 1965, pp. 4 and 7.

[e] Covers only states in which covered manufacturing employees as a percent of all covered employees exceed the national average of 40.5 percent. Bureau of Labor Statistics, *Employment and Earnings Statistics for States and Areas, 1939–1964*, Bulletin No. 1370-2, June, 1965.

[f] Bureau of Employment Security, *Handbook of Unemployment Insurance Financial Data, 1946–1963*, BES No. U-73, May, 1964, and September, 1965, supplement, annual tables.

[g] U.S. Census of Population, 1960, *United States Summary, General Social and Economic Characteristics*, PC(1)-1C US, Table 106, p. 1-249.

[h] Data shown on this line for 1964 and 1962 cover fifty states, the District of Columbia, and Puerto Rico. Data for 1960 exclude Puerto Rico.

TABLE 3.
Benefit Payment Characteristics of States with an Unemployment Insurance Reserve Fund at or above the "Minimum Level of Adequacy" at the Close of 1964[a]

| State[b] | Reserve Multiple[c] 1964 | Average Duration of Benefits (weeks) | | Maximum Weekly Benefit as of Jan. 1[d] | | Average Weekly Benefit | | | | Ratio of Total Benefits to Total Wages | | |
| | | | | | | Amount | | As Percent of Average Weekly Total Wages | | | | |
	1964	1964	1960	1964	1960	1964	1960	1964	1960	1964	1962	1960
All states[e]	1.55	13.0	12.7	—	—	$35.96	$32.87	33.8	35.2	1.05	1.26	1.40
District of Columbia	5.61	15.7	12.4	$ 51[f]	$ 30	38.38	26.20	36.2	28.9	.66	.51	.50
Iowa	5.02	11.4	11.4	30-44	30-44	30.30	29.85	31.1	34.8	.43	.68	.72
Arizona	4.24	11.4	10.3	35	35	33.66	30.80	32.2	32.7	.95	.85	.80
South Dakota	4.13	12.9	10.9	34	33	31.10	29.21	36.3	37.6	.94	.75	.81
Virginia	3.96	9.8	9.3	34	28	27.84	23.54	31.1	30.8	.35	.45	.60
Nebraska	3.76	12.1	10.7	38	34	33.61	30.04	36.2	36.1	.76	.83	.75
Missouri	3.27	10.7	10.5	40	33	33.36	28.61	31.6	31.6	.67	.91	.91
South Carolina	3.07	11.6	11.0	37[f]	26	27.29	22.14	34.6	33.1	.76	.81	.83
Georgia	2.99	9.4	10.9	35	30	28.42	24.70	32.7	33.8	.51	.77	1.06
Florida	2.92	11.3	10.8	33	33	27.32	27.37	29.5	33.8	.48	.78	.83
North Carolina	2.91	10.6	10.2	35	32	23.15	20.59	28.8	29.9	.82	.98	1.10
Utah	2.76	12.8	11.1	46[f]	40[f]	37.23	33.18	38.4	38.8	1.26	.91	1.01
New Mexico	2.65	13.7	13.6	36	36	29.72	29.33	31.2	33.6	.98	1.12	1.23
Texas	2.59	12.8	11.5	37	28	29.53	24.27	30.7	28.7	.57	.68	.75
Kansas	2.55	11.6	12.1	46[f]	41[f]	37.59	34.11	38.7	39.9	.88	.89	1.33

State												
Washington	2.51	14.5	12.9	42	42	33.12	32.20	29.3	32.8	1.69	1.42	1.91
Idaho	2.36	11.5	10.5	45[f]	40	37.81	34.95	41.7	42.7	1.44	1.66	1.81
Wisconsin	2.25	12.6	9.9	53[f]	47[f]	42.60	37.58	39.7	39.6	.91	.98	1.06
Colorado	2.25	11.5	13.0	48[f]	43–54[f]	42.76	37.96	41.7	41.7	.60	1.09	.92
Mississippi	2.11	12.0	11.5	30[f]	30[f]	24.54	23.76	32.2	36.7	.93	1.17	1.57
Louisiana	2.03	14.3	17.0	35	35	30.49	30.31	31.6	36.6	.85	1.35	1.60
New Hampshire	1.89	10.4	10.6	40	38	31.50	26.65	35.4	34.5	.95	.91	1.17
Maryland	1.84	12.1	13.8	38–46	35–43	32.93	30.63	33.7	35.9	.91	1.35	1.68
New York	1.82	14.8	14.0	50	45	38.95	35.40	33.2	34.5	1.33	1.43	1.51
Illinois	1.78	12.2	11.8	38–59	32–50	38.04	34.10	32.6	33.0	.69	.97	.96
Oklahoma	1.72	15.0	14.3	32	32	26.47	26.17	27.6	31.0	.77	.93	1.09
Kentucky	1.70	12.2	13.3	40	34	33.01	28.71	35.5	35.4	1.08	1.27	1.68
Alabama	1.62	13.0	12.3	32	28	25.79	23.24	29.1	30.6	.70	1.19	1.30
Delaware	1.54	10.7	11.4	50	40	38.69	33.57	33.0	32.5	.89	1.14	1.01
Hawaii	1.52	13.6	11.7	55	45	39.40	31.74	43.2	40.8	1.07	1.72	.74
Nevada	1.50	11.7	11.0	38–58	38–58	39.22	37.56	33.1	37.9	1.35	1.01	1.49

SOURCE: Bureau of Employment Security, *Handbook of Unemployment Insurance Financial Data, 1946–1963*, and September, 1965, supplement, annual tables; and its *Comparison of State Unemployment Insurance Laws as of January 1, 1964, and as of January 1, 1960*, BES No. U-141, Table 19.

[a] For discussion of the "minimum level of adequacy" concept, see section in text entitled "Measuring the Adequacy of Reserves."

[b] States are listed according to their relative standing at the close of 1964 with respect to the "minimum level of adequacy."

[c] Reserve ratio as multiple of highest benefit cost rate.

[d] Where range is shown, highest figure represents maximum including dependents' allowances.

[e] Data shown on this line for 1964 cover fifty states, the District of Columbia, and Puerto Rico. Data for 1960 exclude Puerto Rico.

[f] Reflects a "flexible" maximum weekly benefit based on a given percent (ranging from 50 to 55) of average weekly wages in covered employment. Absolute maximum of $30 in Mississippi.

The relatively light benefit load experienced by most of the thirty-one adequate-reserve states is reflected in the pattern of financing arrangements that emerges from the data shown in Table 4. Thus, at the start of 1964, twenty-six of these states were still financing their programs on a $3,000 taxable wage base. Only two of the five states with a higher-than-$3,000 base had operated under their higher base ($3,600) during the entire five-year period, 1960–64, inclusive. Thirteen of the adequate-reserve states were still operating with a top tax rate of 2.7 percent. For 1964, only seven of the thirty-one states reported an average tax rate (based on total wages) above the all-state average of 1.26 percent. In nineteen states, the average tax rate levied on employers amounted to less than 1 percent of total wages.

The Five Substantial-Unemployment States

As previously noted, five states with a record of fairly substantial unemployment during the period 1960–64, inclusive, were nevertheless on the adequate-reserve list in 1964. What accounted for the ability of these states to maintain an adequate reserve in the face of a continuing unemployment problem? In order to provide a definitive answer to this question, a detailed review of the various aspects of each state's unemployment insurance program would have to be made. The five states indicate a diversity of practice which precludes generalizations. However, on the basis of Tables 3 and 4 and of some related data, a few explanatory remarks may be offered.

Washington's ability to maintain an adequate reserve position reflected in part its operation under experience-rating suspension since 1960. All employers in the state were paying a flat 2.7 percent tax rate on taxable wages compared with a national rate of 2.21 percent during 1964. Despite the application of that rate, benefits exceeded tax collections each year during the period 1960–64—although by a slight margin in some years. Washington's state fund was also protected by retention of the maximum weekly benefit at its 1960 level ($42) through 1964 while most states raised benefits. The average weekly benefit in Washington increased by less than a dollar compared with more than three times as much nationally. In 1964, the state's average weekly benefit paid amounted to 29.3 percent of average weekly wages, while the national figure was 33.8 percent.

Upward revision of both the tax-rate structure and the tax base after 1960 accounted in large part for Idaho's ability to maintain an adequate reserve. During 1961 and 1962, the state operated under a special maximum tax rate of 3.375 percent, despite a nominal top rate of 2.7

percent. By 1964, Idaho was operating with a maximum tax rate of 5.1 percent. During 1963, Idaho increased the standard tax rate (applicable to new employers) to a level ranging from 2.9 to 3.3 percent. Effective 1963, its taxable wage base was shifted to $3,600. Its average tax rate, based on total wages, ran well above the national rate during the years 1961 through 1964. Tax collections exceeded benefit payments during 1964 for the first time in the whole period 1960–64. In large part, however, this development reflected a drop in benefit disbursements. Idaho maintained its favorable reserve situation in spite of a relatively high maximum benefit amount ($45 in 1964). Its average weekly benefit amounted to 41.7 percent of its average weekly wage in 1964—a percentage exceeded only by Hawaii among the other adequate-reserve states.

A fairly high tax structure contributed to New York's ability to maintain an adequate reserve position. During the period 1960–64, New York's maximum rate was 3.2 percent, to which an additional charge of up to 1.0 percent could be added under certain fund conditions. During this period, its average tax rate, based on total wages, exceeded the national rate—substantially in some years. During 1962, 1963, and 1964, tax collections exceeded benefit disbursements. In terms of the average weekly benefit as a percentage of average weekly wages, New York was close to the national average during the period.

Kentucky's presence on the adequate-reserve list also reflected a fairly high maximum rate (4.2 percent) during the period 1960–64. Earlier, its maximum was 3.7 percent. Its average tax rate, based on total wages, ran above the all-state average from 1958 through 1961; thereafter, it ran slightly below the over-all rate. Starting with 1962, the average weekly benefit as a percentage of the average weekly wage was larger in Kentucky than in the country in general.

A relatively high tax structure did not explain Oklahoma's place on the adequate-reserve roster. In 1964, it was still operating with a 2.7 percent top rate on a $3,000 base. One factor involved here was the state's moderate unemployment level as compared with that of the other four states. Actually, Oklahoma's reported rate of insured unemployment during the period 1960–64 exceeded the national rate by a very slight margin. A primary factor in the state's ability to cope with this average level of unemployment, despite a limited tax structure, was the modest size of benefits. Oklahoma's maximum weekly benefit remained at $32 during the 1960–64 period, the second lowest of the thirty-one adequate-reserve states in 1964. During that year, it paid an average weekly benefit of $26.47, representing only 27.6 percent of its average weekly wage. This was the lowest percentage reported for any of the

TABLE 4.
Financing Characteristics of States with an Unemployment Insurance Reserve Fund at or above the "Minimum Level of Adequacy" at the Close of 1964[a]

State[b]	Reserve Multiple[c] 1964	Type of Financing System[d] Jan. 1, 1964	Taxable Wage Base[e] Jan. 1, 1964	Maximum Possible Tax Rate (percent)		Minimum Possible Tax Rate (percent)		Average Tax Rate (percent of taxable wages)		Average Tax Rate (percent of total wages)	
				Jan. 1, 1964	Jan. 1, 1960	Jan. 1, 1964	Jan. 1, 1960	1964	1960	1964	1960
All states[f]	1.55	—	—	—	—	—	—	2.21	1.88	1.26	1.15
District of Columbia	5.61	RR	—	2.7	2.7	0.10	0.10	.89	.86	.48	.51
Iowa	5.02	RR	—	2.7	2.7	0	0	.77	.61	.44	.38
Arizona	4.24	RR	—	2.7	2.7	.10	.10	1.45	1.33	.83	.83
South Dakota	4.13	RR	—	4.1	2.7	0	0	1.00	.81	.62	.54
Virginia	3.96	BWR	—	2.7	2.7	.10	.10	.91	.87	.56	.59
Nebraska	3.76	RR	—	2.7	2.7	.10	.10	1.26	1.05	.74	.68
Missouri	3.27	RR	—	5.0	3.6	0	0	1.42	1.05	.77	.63
South Carolina	3.07	RR	—	4.1	2.7	.25	.25	1.38	1.13	.94	.84
Georgia	2.99	RR	—	4.2	2.7	.25	.25	1.30	1.36	.82	.94
Florida	2.92	BR	—	3.5[h]	2.9	.10	0	1.33	1.15	.81	.77
North Carolina	2.91	RR	—	3.7	3.7	.10	.10	1.52	1.60	1.02	1.16
Utah	2.76	PD	$4,200	2.7	2.7	.70	[g]	1.38	1.45	.96	.90
New Mexico	2.65	RR	—	3.6	2.7	.10	.10	1.31	1.25	.78	.81
Texas	2.59	BWR	—	7.2	2.7	[g]	0	.93	.90	.54	.56
Kansas	2.55	RR	—	2.7	2.7	0	0	1.43	1.06	.82	.67

State		Financing[d]	Wage base[e]			Min. rate					
Washington	2.51	PD	—	2.7	2.7	[g]	[g]	2.70	2.70	1.44	1.61
Idaho	2.36	RR	3,600	5.1	2.7	.30	.30	2.17	1.66	1.48	1.12
Wisconsin	2.25	RR	—	4.0	4.0	0	0	1.54	1.41	.82	.83
Colorado	2.25	RR	—	2.7	2.7	0	0	1.59	.54	.89	.33
Mississippi	2.11	PD	—	3.2	2.7	.30	.60	2.29	1.96	1.59	1.45
Louisiana	2.03	RR	—	2.7	2.7	.10	.10	1.94	1.56	1.13	.99
New Hampshire	1.89	RR	—	4.0	2.7	.30	.50	1.65	1.65	1.04	1.15
Maryland	1.84	BR	—	4.2[i]	2.7[h]	0	.20	2.85	2.64	1.63	1.67
New York	1.82	RR	—	4.2[i]	3.2[h]	0	0	2.69	2.25	1.39	1.29
Illinois	1.78	BWR	—	4.0	4.0	.10	.10	1.93	2.05	.98	1.15
Oklahoma	1.72	BWR	—	2.7	2.7	.20	.20	1.50	1.20	.87	.76
Kentucky	1.70	RR	—	4.2	4.2	0	0	1.92	2.20	1.14	1.44
Alabama	1.62	BWR	—	3.6	2.7	.50	.50	1.60	1.18	.98	.79
Delaware	1.54	BWR	3,600	4.5[i]	4.5[i]	.10	.10	2.19	2.42	1.22	1.48
Hawaii	1.52	RR	3,600	2.7[j]	2.7	0[j]	0	2.25	1.19	1.51	.81
Nevada	1.50	RR	3,600	2.7	2.7	.10	.10	2.70	2.16	1.71	1.53

SOURCE: Bureau of Employment Security, *Handbook of Unemployment Insurance Financial Data, 1946–1963*, and September, 1965, supplement, annual tables; and its *Comparison of State Unemployment Insurance Laws*, Table 7.

[a] For discussion of the "minimum level of adequacy" concept, see section in text entitled "Measuring the Adequacy of Reserves."

[b] States are listed according to their relative standing at the close of 1964 with respect to the "minimum level of adequacy."

[c] Reserve ratio as multiple of highest benefit cost rate.

[d] Financing systems abbreviated as follows: Reserve Ratio—RR; Benefit Wage Ratio—BWR; Benefit Ratio—BR; and Payroll Declines—PD.

[e] $3,000 except as indicated. Dates of adoption of indicated wage bases as follows: Utah, 1964; Idaho, 1963; Delaware, 1955; Hawaii, 1962; and Nevada, 1954.

[f] Data shown on this line for 1964 cover fifty states, the District of Columbia, and Puerto Rico. Data for 1960 exclude Puerto Rico.

[g] Variable minimum rate.

[h] Excludes supplemental uniform rate.

[i] Includes supplemental uniform rate.

[j] Law provided for rates ranging between 1.0 and 3.0 percent until July 1, 1964.

adequate-reserve states and was well below the all-state average of 33.8 percent.

CONCLUSIONS AND PROSPECTS

The preceding discussion has indicated that four of the five states with relatively substantial unemployment were aided in maintaining their favorable reserve status by a fairly high tax rate structure and, in one case, a taxable wage base above the $3,000 level. Since a number of other states on the adequate-reserve list had a maximum tax rate well above the 2.7 percent level, these states might also maintain a favorable reserve situation if they were to experience a more serious unemployment problem in the short-run future.

Furthermore, states on the adequate-reserve list still operating with a top tax rate of 2.7 percent during 1964 and thereafter might be able to retain a reserve above the minimum level of adequacy, for a while at least, if their unemployment records remain favorable and if they keep a relatively modest scale of benefit payments. Some of these states enjoyed such a strong reserve position in 1964 that they presumably could maintain an adequate reserve for some time, even in the face of a serious unemployment problem. Ultimately, however, such states would be vulnerable to substantial unemployment in case of a general recession, or under special adverse conditions even in the absence of an economic downturn.

Eventually, the states operating with a 2.7 percent maximum rate and a $3,000 wage base could be hard-pressed to maintain their adequate-reserve position even if they endure no substantial unemployment. As wages go up, the states will be under pressure to raise their maximum benefits. With a higher average weekly benefit, the present 2.7 percent maximum applied to a $3,000 base could prove inadequate for meeting the increased benefit costs that develop. This problem would become especially acute if Congress were to enact the benefit-standards provisions of H.R. 8282, establishing additional federal standards for state unemployment insurance systems. Under this proposal, states would be virtually required to adopt by July 1, 1967, a maximum weekly benefit equal to one-half of the statewide average weekly wage. By 1971, the standard would have escalated to a point where the maximum benefit amounts to two-thirds of the average wage. Such an increase in the maximum benefit standard would by itself gradually raise the benefit load for all of these states.

As benefit standards are raised, measures to strengthen the financial capacity of some if not most of the adequate-reserve states would have to be taken. Such action could involve a higher tax rate structure or a higher taxable wage base or a combination of the two.

The issue of whether state financing systems should be strengthened by increasing the tax rate structure or by increasing the wage base has been a controversial one for some time.[11] In general, the states have preferred the higher tax rate approach. By mid-1965, however, 18 states had adopted a higher wage base, but, in most cases, the base to which the states had moved was $3,600. In view of the substantially greater relative increase in wages since the $3,000 wage base was adopted in 1939, a move to the $3,600 base represents only a token increase. Nevertheless, where there has been an increase in the wage base, whether to $3,600 or to a higher level, it has been a positive factor in strengthening the state's financing system.

In any event, the issue will be decided for a number of states if Congress should act favorably upon another of the proposals embodied in H.R. 8282. The bill proposes to raise the wage base for the federal unemployment insurance tax by stages from its current $3,000 level to a $6,600 level for calendar 1971. Twenty-nine states are committed by existing legislation to adopt for state taxing purposes the same wage base that is used for federal taxing purposes. These states, which include a number on the adequate-reserve list, would automatically move to a higher wage base if the federal wage base is increased. Some states not on the adequate-reserve list have already adopted a higher wage base. A number of the remaining states might be expected to increase their wage base also. The widespread adoption of the higher base would strengthen the financing capabilities of the states by enlarging the volume of wages to which tax rates are applied.

In addition, other measures could be taken by the adequate-reserve states to improve their financing systems if increasing benefit disbursements threaten the adequacy of their reserves. Some of these measures have already been adopted by some of the adequate-reserve states. Mention has been made of Idaho's increase to a level higher than 2.7 percent of the standard tax rate chargeable to new employers. A number of states provide for a flat supplemental rate to be charged when the condition of the state fund reaches a danger point. In order to achieve a desired over-all rate, a few states have provisions for adjusting the rates determined for their employers under merit-rating. A perusal of Table 4 indicates that, in 1964, ten of the adequate-reserve states had a minimum

[11] For a discussion of this issue, see Eugene C. McKean, *The Taxable Wage Base in Unemployment Insurance Financing* (Kalamazoo, Mich.: Upjohn Institute for Employment Research, 1965).

rate of zero. Only two states had a minimum rate as high as 0.5 percent. Although questions of equity arise concerning the desirability of charging a minimum rate of 0.5 percent or higher, the application of such a rate would surely help to strengthen a state's fund.

Another feature of H.R. 8282 would aid adequate-reserve states in maintaining their fund adequacy. The bill provides for the federal government to cover two-thirds of a state's benefit costs for years during which such costs exceed 2 percent of total wages. (To qualify, states would have to adopt the bill's benefit standards. No fund solvency criterion would have to be met.) Under such an arrangement, adequate-reserve states would receive financial aid from the federal government in the event of severe unemployment, even though their reserve position had not yet deteriorated appreciably.

8

EXTENDED UNEMPLOYMENT
BENEFITS: FOR WHOM?

PAUL J. MACKIN

A variety of considerations should go into planning extended unemployment compensation programs such as were relied on in 1958 and in 1961–62. Not the least important question is—who should be aided by the program? This paper reviews salient characteristics of claimants aided in the most recent of the two periods in which such benefits were paid; and, on the basis of this experience, it suggests guidelines for future programs. In retrospect, it appears that certain mistakes may have been made, and these might be avoided in the design of a new program. Congressional interest in developing a permanent program of extended benefits is now quite strong despite the nation's recent experience with sustained economic growth.

An analysis of the characteristics of the 1961–62 extended claimants reveals wide variation in their labor force attachment suggesting that more emphasis needs to be given this variable in future programs. The trends in labor force attachment by sex, age, and family status indicate that greater selectivity on the basis of individually demonstrated work experience might have resulted in greater remedial action and a more rational allocation of the funds expended. At the same time, the analysis reveals trends by such factors as occupation, industry, and geographic location that place certain limits on labor market experience as a selection factor. In the discussion that follows, essential notions are introduced, tables summarizing the analysis presented, general policy guidelines indicated, and legislative alternatives considered.

EXTENDED UNEMPLOYMENT BENEFITS

Extended benefits refer to additional unemployment insurance payments that are made under certain specified conditions to persons who have used up their regular benefits without becoming reemployed. Extended benefits took on importance in 1958 when a number of states began paying them during above-normal levels of unemployment within

125

the state. In 1958, Congress enacted the Temporary Unemployment Compensation Act (TUC) which provided interest-free advances of federal funds to states to finance a 50 percent increase in benefits to those exhausting regular benefits during the recession. Seventeen states availed themselves of these loans and five more paid extended benefits under state programs independent of the federal program. In 1961, Congress enacted a somewhat similar program—the Temporary Extended Unemployment Compensation Act (TEUC). All states participated in this second program, which was financed by a mandatory increase in the federal unemployment tax. The principal stimulus during each of these periods was that a large number of persons who had been and would probably continue to be regular members of the labor force had exhausted their regular benefits without becoming reemployed.

LABOR FORCE ATTACHMENT

Labor Force Attachment refers to the degree to which a presently unemployed member of the labor force has been a member of the labor force in the past and in all probability will continue to be in the future. The concept has no part in our general definitions of who is unemployed, but it has a decided part in determining who of the unemployed are to be aided by an unemployment insurance program. All state unemployment insurance programs require at least some minimum amount of past employment and earnings during a specified "base year" in order to be eligible for unemployment benefits.

The concept of labor force attachment takes on additional importance in connection with extended unemployment benefits programs. In the hearings and debates over the passage of the Temporary Extended Unemployment Compensation Act in 1961, a great amount of discussion centered on the extent to which the long-term unemployed who had exhausted their regular benefits were only tenuously attached to the labor force and therefore were not really entitled to consideration, especially under an "insurance" program. What proportion, for example, were youth, married women, pensioners, etc.—these were frequently raised questions, both in and out of congressional chambers. The implication often was that these groups had very dubious attachments to the labor force.

THE DATA

The data used are derived from a nationwide survey of long-term unemployed who were compensated under the Temporary Extended

126

Unemployment Compensation Act of 1961. The survey was conducted by the Bureau of Employment Security, U.S. Department of Labor, in cooperation with the employment security agencies of the various states.[1] The original, untabulated survey data were reprocessed by the Upjohn Institute and analyzed in detail. The empirical findings presented here are based on that analysis. The individuals surveyed had exhausted their regular unemployment benefits after June, 1960, some as late as March, 1961. They drew extended benefits at some time between April 8, 1961, and June 30, 1962. This was during the recovery from the 1960–61 recession, which had reached its trough in February, 1961. As had been true of earlier postwar recessions, the decline in levels of unemployment was not as rapid as gains in productive activity. The seasonally adjusted unemployment rate, slightly under 7 percent throughout most of 1961, finally began to decline during the winter months, reaching a level of 5.5 percent by the spring of 1962. The TEUC program paid out over three-quarters of a billion dollars to 1.7 million men and 1.1 million women.

The TEUC data allows us to look at labor force attachment in at least two ways: (1) the number of months in the labor force during the three years prior to filing their extended claim, and (2) the amount of employment during this three-year reference period. Only the latter factor, or "realized attachment" as we shall call it, is normally used in determining eligibility for unemployment benefits. However, in order to give due attention in our analysis to the supply side, we have chosen to look at "intended attachment" also.

Though in our analysis we consider only the past labor force attachment of the TEUC claimants, common sense as well as the findings of the TEUC research indicate that the past is a good predictor of the future in this case. A subsample of those TEUC claimants who used up all their extended benefits entitlement was polled three months after receiving their final TEUC check. Those claimants continuously in the labor force during the prior three-year reference period were more likely to be in the labor force three months after exhausting TEUC rights than those TEUC claimants who were intermittent members of the labor force. For example, in California 10 percent of those continuing in the labor force all three years were out of the labor force three months later, while 22 percent of those not continuously in the labor force were out three months later.

---

[1] *Characteristics of the Long-Term Unemployed,* BES No. U-207, TEUC Series Nos. 1–7, 1962–63.

SUMMARY TABLES AND ANALYSIS: INFLUENCE OF PERSONAL
CHARACTERISTICS ON LABOR FORCE ATTACHMENT

The personal characteristics of the TEUC claimants exert their influence principally from the supply side. That is, they influence the likelihood that a given individual remained continuously in the labor force throughout the reference period even during prolonged spells of joblessness. In Tables 1–3 we will see rather large variations in propensity to remain continuously in the labor force, indicating that the claimants were somewhat of a "mixed bag" as far as their commitment to the world of work is concerned. There is a strong trend for men to have better employment records on the average than women and for individuals who are the main support of themselves and/or their families to have more employment than those ordinarily classified as secondary earners. However, the wide variations within sex and family status demonstrate that the simple primary-secondary earner dichotomy is a very rough way to categorize individual labor force commitment.

Influence of Sex and Age

Table 1 illustrates the essential relation between sex and age as determinants of labor force attachment. The following points are particularly worth noting:

TABLE 1.
Labor Force Attachment of TEUC Claimants during the Prior
Three Years, by Sex and Age

Age	Percent of Total		Percent Continuously in Labor Force		Percent with 24 Months' Employment	
	Males	Females	Males	Females	Males	Females
All ages	100.0	100.0	83.0	60.3	56.9	46.4
Under 25	11.3	13.3	65.2	30.4	45.8	31.8
25–34	19.6	21.3	86.3	50.0	56.7	39.9
35–44	19.6	25.7	86.5	63.3	58.7	46.4
45–54	18.5	21.1	85.5	72.2	58.3	51.7
55–64	16.0	12.6	84.1	74.4	57.0	56.7
65 and over	15.0	5.9	83.6	78.7	61.5	61.5

1. Eighty-three percent of the men were continuously in the labor force during the three years prior to filing their extended claim compared with 60 percent of the women. However, the difference between the sexes decreases markedly with age. This is because, for women, increasing age is a powerful positive influence over the entire age spectrum, but, for men, age is only a moderate influence after the age of 25. The low *average* attachment of females results because (a) the younger

128

women, those at the family formation stage, have very low attachment, and (b) the average age of female claimants is below that of males.

2. The youngest claimants had extremely low attachment regardless of sex. (More detailed figures suggest that, for young males, being a new entrant to the labor force is an important reason for not being in the entire reference period; but, for young females, intermittent attachment is the predominant cause.)

3. Both men and women over 65 had very high realized labor force attachment. In a very substantial proportion of cases, long-term unemployment for this group may be less the result of business recession and technological displacement and more the result of mandatory retirement policies. For this reason, the bout of unemployment they were experiencing at the time of the surveys was in sharp contrast to their previous labor market experience.

4. There is a basic difference between men and women in the relationship between continuity in the labor force and actual employment experience. This applies to all age groups, but it is easier to see for those 55 and over. Older women had as much actual employment as older men, but their propensity to remain in the labor force was much lower. Either women tend to drop out of the labor force more readily when work is not available, or else relative demand conditions during the reference period were such that for a given degree of intended attachment, women are able to achieve greater realized attachment.

Influence of Family Status

Table 2 considers the relationship between family status and labor force attachment for males and females separately. In addition to the actual attachment ratios we show ratios standardized to the age structures of all males and all females, respectively. The standardized columns suggest what the ratios might be if age were held constant. Note the following variations in intended attachment (percent continuously in the labor force), as well as the variations in realized attachment (percent with twenty-four months of employment), which roughly parallel them:

1. A man living alone and supporting himself is less likely to remain continuously in the labor force than if he is the head of a household, though both are primary earners.

2. Secondary male earners have still lower intended attachment. However, the very low average attachment of the single relatives is due entirely to low attachment among those under 25. More detailed tabulations show that older men classified as single relatives are comparable to other males of the same age.

129

TABLE 2.
Labor Force Attachment of TEUC Claimants during the Prior
Three Years, by Family Status and Sex

Family Status	Percent of Total	Percent Continuously in Labor Force		Percent with 24 Months' Employment	
		Actual	Standard-ized[a]	Actual	Standard-ized[a]
All males	100.0	83.0	83.0	56.9	56.9
Head of household	69.7	85.5	85.1	59.7	59.4
Living alone	16.0	82.2	81.5	54.1	54.1
Single relative of head	8.6	66.6	81.9	41.2	51.0
Married relative of head	2.8	79.6	79.9	54.8	54.8
Wid., div., or sep. relative of head	2.9	79.5	79.0	54.8	54.3
All females	100.0	60.3	60.3	46.4	46.4
Married woman, not main support	64.0	55.4	57.9	42.4	44.0
Head of household	14.1	68.3	66.0	52.3	50.9
Living alone	12.4	73.0	69.2	57.8	54.8
Single relative of head	4.7	60.8	74.0	45.8	54.7
Wid., div., or sep. relative of head	4.8	68.4	63.4	53.4	49.1

[a] Standardized to age structure of all male and all female TEUC claimants, respectively.

3. For women, being married and not the main support of the household greatly lowers the propensity to remain in the labor force. The age factor is very important here. More detailed tabulations show significant numbers of married women (most notably among those 45 and over) with substantial attachment records.

4. For women, being a primary earner increases the probability of remaining continuously in the labor force. This is true if she is the head of a household, but it is even more pronounced if she lives alone. In both cases, above-average attachment is related to above-average age. The fact that female heads of families are more irregularly attached than those living alone is probably attributable to competing demands on their time away from the labor force. In this respect female heads of households are similar to married women who are not the head.

5. While single female relatives have very low attachment, more detailed figures would show that those 25 and over have above-average attachment (for females).

6. The importance of family status as an influence on labor force attachment decreases with age (just as the male-female difference decreases with age). Space limitations prevent showing the detailed tabulations needed to demonstrate this point.

EXTENDED BENEFITS: FOR WHOM?

Table 3 shows several gradations in realized labor force attachment by family status group.

TABLE 3.
Employment Experience of TEUC Claimants during the Prior
Three Years, by Family Status and Sex

Family Status	Percent of Total	Less than 30 Months	Less than 24 Months	Less than 18 Months	Less than 12 Months
All Claimants	—	87.0	47.2	22.1	8.9
All Males	100.0	85.7	43.1	18.2	6.6
Head of household	69.7	84.8	40.3	15.8	5.3
Living alone	16.0	86.6	45.9	20.0	7.1
Single relative of head	8.6	89.9	58.8	32.8	15.8
Married relative of head	2.8	86.7	45.2	21.7	8.6
Wid., div., or sep. relative of head	2.9	87.5	45.2	19.2	5.8
All Females	100.0	89.0	53.6	28.1	12.5
Married woman, not main support	64.0	90.5	57.6	31.2	14.2
Head of household	14.1	85.9	47.7	22.4	9.2
Living alone	12.4	85.2	42.2	19.1	7.5
Single relative of head	4.7	90.5	54.2	31.4	15.7
Wid., div., or sep. relative of head	4.8	87.1	46.6	22.7	9.4

Influence of Occupation

Factors such as occupation, industry, and geographic location influence labor force attachment principally, though not exclusively, from the demand side. The remaining tables will demonstrate that the influence of these factors can be rather important in an extended claimant population, and that they often operate so as to create a rather large gulf between an individual's realized and intended labor force attachment.

Table 4 shows intended and realized attachment by broad occupational categories. The following points should be observed:

1. The relative demand for various classes of labor during the years preceding the TEUC program was such that blue-collar males had considerably less actual employment than those from white-collar occupations. Somewhat more surprising, however, may be the fact that blue-collar workers had a significantly higher propensity to remain in the labor force. As a result, the disparity between intended and realized labor force attachment becomes quite large for blue-collar workers relative to white-collar.

2. Occupation also exerts its influence within blue-collar ranks, where of course most of the male claimants are to be found. The lower skill levels had considerably less past employment than the higher skill levels. (More detailed figures show that the unskilled under 25 have particularly minimal employment records even considering their age.)

131

TABLE 4.
Labor Force Attachment of the TEUC Claimants during the Prior
Three Years, by Occupational Group and Sex

Occupational Group	Percent of Total	Percent Continuously in Labor Force		Percent with 24 Months' Employment	
		Actual	Standard-ized[a]	Actual	Standard-ized[a]
All Males	100.0	83.0	83.0	56.9	56.9
Professional and managerial	4.0	83.9	82.2	68.6	68.1
Clerical and sales	7.4	80.6	80.7	65.7	65.8
Service	8.9	80.7	80.5	60.3	60.0
Skilled	21.4	84.6	83.8	58.9	58.9
Semiskilled	25.8	83.7	83.7	57.8	58.2
Unskilled and other	32.4	82.6	83.7	50.4	51.4
All Females	100.0	60.3	60.3	46.4	46.4
Professional and managerial	2.7	66.2	63.3	62.4	60.8
Clerical and sales	31.8	55.5	57.8	52.2	53.3
Service	12.5	62.2	60.2	50.7	49.3
Skilled	3.0	69.0	63.6	51.7	49.3
Semiskilled	23.6	62.0	61.0	45.5	45.0
Unskilled and other	26.4	62.0	61.9	35.8	35.9

[a] Standardized to age structure of all male and all female TEUC claimants, respectively.

3. Occupation influenced female claimant attachment in much the same way it did male. Women from blue-collar occupations had considerably less actual employment than those from white-collar occupations, and within blue-collar ranks past employment decreased with skill level. And this was despite the fact that the blue-collar women (as well as those from service occupations) appear to have a slightly greater propensity to remain continuously in the labor force.

Influence of Industry

Table 5 indicates the way labor force attachment was affected by the particular industry the TEUC claimant was attached to. The following points are important:

1. Male claimants from durable goods manufacturing and those from construction had much less past employment on the average than men from the trade and services industries; yet men from construction and the durable goods industries had significantly greater propensities to remain in the labor force. Again we note the wide gulf between intended and realized attachment for some groups of claimants.

2. Nondurable manufacturing exerts an influence on female labor force attachment similar to that exerted by durable manufacturing on men. Women from the soft-goods producing industries had considerably

132

TABLE 5.
Labor Force Attachment of TEUC Claimants during the Prior
Three Years, by Industry Division and Sex

Industry Division	Percent of Total	Percent Continuously in Labor Force		Percent with 24 Months' Employment	
		Actual	Standard-ized[a]	Actual	Standard-ized[a]
All Males	100.0	83.0	83.0	56.9	56.9
Construction	18.2	83.4	83.0	48.6	48.0
Durable mfg.	34.3	84.2	84.2	56.8	57.1
Nondurable mfg.	12.7	82.1	82.6	60.6	60.8
Trade	14.8	80.4	80.9	61.8	62.4
Services	7.2	81.1	81.0	58.7	58.9
Other	12.7				
All Females	100.0	60.3	60.3	46.4	46.4
Durable mfg.	22.3	58.5	60.4	43.6	45.5
Nondurable mfg.	31.7	63.1	62.0	41.6	41.0
Trade	25.5	59.8	59.1	50.6	50.1
Services	12.1	60.8	59.5	51.5	50.8
Other	8.4				

[a] Standardized to age structure of all male and all female TEUC claimants, respectively.

less actual employment than those from other kinds of industry but a somewhat greater propensity to remain in the labor force.

State Differences

Table 6 shows the states ranked both in order of the proportion of TEUC claimants continuously in the labor force during the three years prior to filing their extended claims and the proportion with at least twenty-four months' employment in this period. Note the following:

1. There is tremendous variation among states. The percent of claimants continuously in the labor force varied from a high of 86 percent for West Virginia to a low of 52 percent for New Hampshire; while the percent with twenty-four months of employment varied from a high of 67 percent for Georgia to a low of 22 percent for Maine. Differences in sex and age structure among the states is responsible for only a minor part of the variation. A state which measures low in male attachment will generally also measure low in female attachment. Many of the variations in intended attachment are traceable to state differences in statutory eligibility requirements for regular unemployment benefits. This does not make them less significant. In a practical sense these divergences must be accepted as "given" in planning extended benefit programs.

TABLE 6.
Labor Force Attachment of TEUC Claimants during the Three-Year Period, by State.

State	Continu-ously in Labor Force		With 24 Months' Employ-ment		State	Continu-ously in Labor Force		With 24 Months' Employ-ment	
	Per-cent	Rank	Per-cent	Rank		Per-cent	Rank	Per-cent	Rank
United States	74	—	52	—	Missouri	75	22–23	59	7–12
Alabama	78	14–16	56	18–20	Montana	71	35–37	43	45
Alaska	67	46–50	23	50	Nebraska	70	38–40	48	40–42
Arizona	73	27–28	57	15–17	Nevada	70	38–40	45	44
Arkansas	79	11–13	51	31–34	New Hampshire	52	51	35	49
California	68	42–45	49	36–39	New Jersey	67	46–50	55	21–23
Colorado	72	29–34	56	18–20	New Mexico	77	17–19	40	47–48
Connecticut	68	42–45	55	21–23	New York	67	46–50	53	26–30
Delaware	80	8–10	60	6	North Carolina	71	35–37	48	40–42
District of					North Dakota	81	4–7	49	36–39
Columbia	74	24–26	58	13–14	Ohio	77	17–19	53	26–30
Florida	77	17–19	64	2	Oklahoma	70	38–40	51	31–34
Georgia	73	27–28	67	1	Oregon	67	46–50	51	31–34
Hawaii	76	20–21	59	7–12	Pennsylvania	83	2	42	46
Idaho	81	4–7	48	40–42	Rhode Island	68	42–45	61	4–5
Illinois	74	24–26	53	26–30	South Carolina	69	41	57	15–17
Indiana	75	22–23	59	7–12	South Dakota	68	42–45	57	15–17
Iowa	72	29–34	62	3	Tennessee	80	8–10	59	7–12
Kansas	72	29–34	59	7–12	Texas	72	29–34	61	4–5
Kentucky	81	4–7	53	26–30	Utah	67	46–50	51	31–34
Louisiana	81	4–7	54	24–25	Vermont	74	24–26	54	24–25
Maine	78	14–16	22	51	Virginia	80	8–10	55	21–23
Maryland	82	3	50	35	Washington	72	29–34	40	47–48
Massachusetts	72	29–34	56	18–20	West Virginia	86	1	49	36–39
Michigan	79	11–13	49	36–39	Wisconsin	78	14–16	47	43
Minnesota	76	20–21	53	26–30	Wyoming	71	35–37	59	7–12
Mississippi	79	11–13	58	13–14					

2. The states whose claimants have a high intended attachment are generally not the states whose claimants had the greatest realized attachment. Of the ten states whose claimants had the highest propensity to remain in the labor force, only two of these ranked in the upper half in terms of actual employment. The positive correlation between percent continuously in the labor force and percent with at least twenty-four months of employment is very low (R = 0.11).

Local Differences

Although the TEUC claimants sample was not such as to make possible comparisons between localities, it is clear that local differences are as great as state differences and are responsible for them. The prevalence of certain kinds of local areas, such as areas of substantial and persistent unemployment within a state is an important factor in setting one state apart from another with respect to claimant characteristics. Such factors are probably responsible for the low realized attachment ratios in Pennsylvania and West Virginia.

Table 7 illustrates the results of an analysis by local area type. All TEUC claimants who resided in standard metropolitan statistical areas were divided into three groups:

TABLE 7.
Labor Force Attachment of TEUC Claimants during the Prior
Three Years, by Local Unemployment Level and Sex

Local Unemployment Level	Percent of Total	Percent Continuously in Labor Force		Percent with 24 Months' Employment	
		Actual	Standard-ized[a]	Actual	Standard-ized[a]
All Males in Standard Metropolitan Statistical Areas	100.0	83.0	83.0	56.9	56.9
Substantial and persistent unemployment	18.5	86.8	86.5	48.1	48.1
6% or more unemployment during 1961	47.9	81.9	81.9	57.3	57.3
Less than 6% unemployment during 1961	33.5	81.3	81.0	61.4	61.1
All Females in Standard Metropolitan Statistical Areas	100.0	60.3	60.3	46.4	46.4
Substantial and persistent unemployment	11.0	65.2	64.8	42.9	42.0
6% or more unemployment during 1961	49.6	59.9	59.5	47.3	47.1
Less than 6% unemployment during 1961	39.3	60.5	59.3	50.7	49.9

[a] Standardized to age structure of all male and all female TEUC claimants, respectively.

1. Those whose place of residence was classified as one of substantial and persistent unemployment at the beginning of 1961.

2. Those in areas where the average unemployment rate through 1961 was 6 percent or more but excluding the areas of substantial and persistent unemployment.

3. Those claimants in areas where the 1961 average unemployment rate was less than 6 percent.

1. Claimants from chronically depressed areas had an above-average propensity to remain continuously in the labor force. (The relationship

135

applies to each sex separately and to different family status groups.) The finding may indicate a tendency in depressed areas for the more intermittent members of the work force to be weeded out of the unemployment insurance system. Although claimants from chronically depressed areas appear to have a higher intended labor force attachment, their actual employment records are much below average (in both sexes and in most family status groups), due to the lower demand for labor that has existed in these areas sometimes over a number of years.

2. Depressed areas aside, claimants from the areas of low unemployment had considerably more past employment than those from the areas of high unemployment, though their propensities to remain in the labor force are about equal.

GENERAL POLICY GUIDELINES

Under extended unemployment compensation programs of the past, there were no special rules governing the selection of individuals to be aided other than that they had exhausted regular unemployment benefits and were still out of work. Apparently the feeling was that it is a good idea to extend benefits a little bit for everybody when jobs are generally harder to find. In light of the foregoing analysis, this may not have been the best course to follow. There were a significant minority for whom additional payments under a wage- and employment-related program didn't make much sense. This was inevitable since many state laws require only a minimal amount of employment in order to be eligible for regular benefits.

The analysis indicates that if the least firmly attached TEUC claimants had been excluded from the program, a significant shift in total payments from secondary to primary earner groups would have resulted, which would be in keeping with the general aims of the legislation. Hence, Guideline No. 1: *In future extended programs, every consideration should be given to restricting the additional payments to those individuals who can meet an additional qualifying requirement based on their employment records.* This requirement would generally be higher than those imposed by states for the receipt of regular unemployment benefits.

It may not be a simple task to establish a suitable additional qualifying requirement. The analysis presented does not suggest an optimal amount of prior employment that should be required in order to be eligible for extended benefits. The analysis does indicate that economic conditions peculiar to an occupation, industry, or geographic location may render a particular requirement far more burdensome to some classes of workers than to others. For manufacturing workers, lower-skilled blue-collar workers, and those from generally depressed areas, there may be a weak relationship between intended and realized labor force attachment. If the additional qualifying requirement is set too high, a number of workers with a really firm commitment to continuing labor force activity may fail to qualify, and the program will fail to serve those who need it most.

Because of the inherent difficulties in establishing an appropriate additional qualifying requirement, Guideline No. 2 is suggested: *The additional qualifying requirement initially chosen should be considered subject to modification as experience under the program accumulates.*

It cannot be stressed too strongly that proper application of Guideline No. 2 will require that adequate claimant characteristics and other evaluative data be collected on a continuing basis. In some respects the data should be even more comprehensive than data collected under the TEUC program. For example, there is reason to believe that race is an important variable in the labor force attachment equation, particularly from the demand side. The differential between white and nonwhite unemployment rates and the commonly held notion that nonwhite groups are the last to be hired and the first to be fired make this very likely. Omission of data on the race of the TEUC claimants was not an oversight on the part of the planners of the research. Legal requirements intended to protect minority groups prevent unemployment insurance authorities from listing race on administrative records, and this proscription was still being overzealously applied to research in 1961 when the survey was planned. Today, with the more open approach to racial matters, this important factor would not have to be neglected in a major research project.

Both Guideline No. 1 and Guideline No. 2 are meant to apply regardless of whether future extended unemployment benefits programs are federally legislated or state-legislated. However, the question naturally arises whether the wide variations among states, particularly in the discrepancy between intended and realized attachment, is evidence that individual state programs might have certain advantages over a single federal program. The question of whether the states or the federal government is better equipped to legislate such programs is a broad one, and no attempt is made to come to grips with it in this article. The wide variation in individual state experience will certainly be taken as evidence that the states should have full sway to develop their own programs. However, proponents of this argument should keep in mind the following points: (1) The TEUC experience does not suggest that a single federal qualifying requirement is not feasible; it only indicates certain difficulties that may be encountered and should be watched for. (2)

137

There are probably as many variations of this kind within states as between them; therefore, a state could encounter the same difficulties in establishing a suitable qualifying requirement as the federal government.

Guideline No. 3 is an important corollary to the suggested emphasis on labor force attachment as a selection factor contained in Nos. 1 and 2. *In planning future extended benefits programs, it would be unwise to single out certain groups of claimants, such as married women or secondary earners in general, as unfit subjects for extended unemployment benefits.* As our analysis clearly shows, many women, including older married women, had very substantial employment records. Apart from the working of injustices and departing from the wage-loss compensation principle, special disqualifications for these groups would be unnecessary if an adequate qualifying requirement were imposed. Determining the current availability for work of certain classes of workers will no doubt always remain a problem in administering unemployment insurance, but it can be minimized as far as extended benefits are concerned if workers with a previous record of low labor force attachment are eliminated from consideration.

The problem of retirement-age unemployed drawing extended benefits will not yield very much to the technique of applying higher qualifying requirements. Generally, those 65 and over, as our analysis clearly shows, have very high past labor force attachment, and this applies to both men and women and to primary and secondary earners. Most of the groups would qualify for one round of extended benefits under any reasonable requirement that might be imposed. Guideline No. 4: *If it is desired to cut down the number of retirement-age claimants drawing extended benefits, then the exclusion must be based on current availability for work and ability to work.* Another possibility is the reduction or elimination of payments to claimants with retirement income based on past service. Such persons could be barred completely, or retirement income could be offset against benefits otherwise due, thus allowing them to receive some benefits if their benefit entitlement was in excess of their pension income.

Higher qualifying requirements for extended benefits would unquestionably result in a further relative reduction in the proportion of unemployment insurance benefits going to unemployed youth. Our analysis indicated very low attachment in the under-25 age groups. Rather than being an argument against higher qualifying requirements, this finding is further demonstration that the problems of long-term unemployed youth are better served under other types of programs. Guideline No. 5: *The needs of youths who have not yet established themselves in the labor market should be considered beyond the pale of extended unemployment insurance programs.*

ALTERNATIVES IN LEGISLATION

Two distinct approaches to a permanent system of extended unemployment benefits are presently before Congress. It is not the purpose of this article to choose between them. It is felt that the guidelines offered relate to each of the approaches, but in different ways.

The first approach is that of the Johnson Administration-sponsored H.R. 8282 calling for federally financed and determined "unemployment adjustment benefits" to qualified exhaustees of regular benefits who have been unemployed for more than twenty-six weeks. To qualify, the regular benefit exhaustee must have had at least the equivalent of twenty-six weeks of employment in the state "base year" and at least seventy-eight weeks of employment in the three-year "federal qualifying period" (state base year and the two immediately preceding years). A qualified exhaustee would be eligible for a maximum of twenty-six weeks of extended payments during any three-year period after which it would be necessary to requalify. The federal extended benefits would be payable at all times regardless of the general level of unemployment.

Emphasis on a firm labor force attachment is so inherent a part of approach number one that little further needs to be said by way of relating the guidelines to it. But Guideline No. 2 should be emphasized. The additional qualifying requirement in H.R. 8282 should be looked on as tentative and subject to the changes that the accumulation of experience indicates are necessary. In this connection, H.R. 8282 provides for a special advisory council to evaluate the unemployment insurance program in general and the changes resulting from the new act in particular. Evaluation of the federal qualifying requirement after an appropriate period of operation, based on research also provided for in the bill, should be an important function of this advisory council.

The second approach would be to build up the number of states that have their own extended benefits programs. At present, eight states provide additional payments for up to thirteen weeks when unemployment in the state reaches a specified level. The Interstate Conference of Employment Security Agencies (ICESA) has recommended that more states enact such programs. In addition, ICESA has sponsored a federal bill by which the federal government would match state payments of extended benefits when unemployment conditions in the state are 20 percent above normal.

139

The recommended guidelines are perfectly compatible with the second extended benefit approach. However, they would be applied at the state level, where the discretion in determining the program would lie. It might be argued that an additional qualifying requirement is unnecessary under this approach, since the payments are confined to periods of high unemployment within the state, and this in itself would tend to curb the proportion of outlay going to secondary earners. However, why not take advantage of the even greater selectivity which an additional qualifying requirement would afford? If the TEUC program, which of course operated during a period of rather high unemployment, would have been improved by excluding some of the less attached claimants, the same might be true of state-legislated programs. It is interesting to note that the State of California, one of the eight states that already have standby extended programs, has adopted an additional qualifying requirement for the receipt of the additional payments, to go into effect on January 1, 1967.

9

PRIVATE PROGRAMS IN AID
OF THE UNEMPLOYED

JOSEPH M. BECKER, S.J.

Private programs are distinguished from public programs insofar as they are established by the free choice of the persons involved in each particular program and not by the taxing power of government, as is the public program of unemployment insurance (UI). (When the government acts as an employer, that is, when it competes in the labor market for its employees and negotiates with them over the terms of employment, it is equivalent to a private employer, and any program of aid thus negotiated is within the private sphere as here defined.) Of the various forms of aid for the unemployed, the most numerous and important are those which provide some guarantee of income to current jobholders. This essay deals only with programs of this nature and excludes other forms of aid, such as retraining programs or moving allowances.

The task of providing some guarantee of income for current jobholders is divided between private groups and the government. The "proper" division of the task involves basic values and is a highly debatable issue. It is not the purpose of this paper to resolve the issue by determining the proper scope of private programs. Its purpose is a simpler one: to describe and analyze the actual role currently played by private programs.[1] An understanding of the actual is an essential part of any realistic determination of the desirable.

This paper describes the scope of the principal private programs and analyzes the reasons for their existence—an exercise equivalent to looking at the supply of such programs and the demand for them. In the discussion of both supply and demand, emphasis is placed on that type of private program which explicitly supplements the public program and thus raises most explicitly the issue of the proper division of responsibility between the public and private spheres.

[1] The paper draws some of its materials from an ongoing investigation of supplementary unemployment benefit plans that was undertaken with the support of the Office of Manpower Policy, Evaluation and Research, U.S. Department of Labor.

141

SUPPLY OF PRIVATE PROGRAMS

Private programs belong to one of two major families, differentiated by the point of time at which the guarantee of protection begins to operate. In one family of programs, protection for the employee is measured from the time of hire and represents a form of protected employment. In the other family, which has two branches, protection is measured from the time of layoff and takes the form of compensation for lost employment. For easier reference, these divisions may be summarized as follows:

1. Protection measured from time of hire.

2. Protection measured from time of layoff.
   (a) Unemployment not a condition for receipt of benefits.
   (b) Unemployment a condition for receipt of benefits.

Protection of Employment

The first family of plans, where protection is measured from the time of hire, is contained entirely in the private sphere. To this family belongs the seniority system, perhaps the most effective of all protections against unemployment—for those who have seniority. To this family also belong call-in pay and the short-workweek benefit of the supplemental unemployment benefit (SUB) plans. Here also belong schemes for rate retention, whereby a worker moved to a lower-paying job still retains his original rate of pay.

The most widely known member of this family is the guaranteed annual wage (GAW), which attracted much attention during the decade immediately following the war but which underwent a gradual, almost imperceptible transformation into SUB by 1955. Some old GAW plans are still operative in companies like Hormel and Nunn-Bush. In more recent times, a plan was negotiated by the Teamsters Union with some St. Louis employers, and the United Auto Workers has announced that in 1967 something similar to the old GAW will again become a major objective.

Some contracts guarantee employment not merely for a year, but for life. They provide that reduction of force will take place only by attrition—through deaths, retirements, and voluntary quits. Such contracts are usually negotiated in situations where technological changes threaten an entire occupation—as, for example, the firemen and telegraphers on the railroads. Unemployment programs that pay very high benefits for very long periods of time—as in the Alan Wood Steel Company plan mentioned later—are the equivalent of guaranteed employment plans, inasmuch as the high cost of terminating an employee discourages an employer from doing so. In such cases, the GAW proposals that became SUB plans a decade ago have completed a cycle.

Compensation for Lost Employment

In the second family of private programs, protection is measured from the point of layoff; the guarantee becomes operative at the time of fire instead of at the time of hire. This family of plans is much larger than the other and has two main branches, differentiated by whether unemployment is or is not a necessary condition for the receipt of benefits.

Unemployment Not a Necessary Condition. Plans belonging to this branch of the family look only to the past employment relationship. If this connection is broken, and if it is expected to remain broken, the employee receives a benefit whether or not he actually experiences unemployment. All the plans belonging to this branch are within the private sphere.

A leading member of this branch is the severance-pay plan, which may serve two related but distinct functions. First, severance pay may serve as indemnification for what is equivalently a property loss. So much of an employee's time and talent may have been invested in a particular job, with all its rights and perquisites, that termination of employment represents the loss of a valuable capital good. Secondly, separation pay may serve the function of replacing some of the income lost during a period of unemployment. In this latter function, severance pay is particularly appropriate for situations where employment is terminated permanently. Since the benefit is paid independently of actual unemployment, the recipient has no reason to delay his search for another job.

Severance-pay plans, which are to be found in practically every industry and every size of firm, come in many forms.[2] Most severance plans pay the benefit in a lump-sum, but a few plans (for example, some of those in the meat-packing industry) permit payments to be made in

---

[2] The Bureau of Labor Statistics of the U.S. Department of Labor has begun the publication of a series of surveys of collective bargaining agreements. The entire series will comprise between thirty and forty separate bulletins. Among the first to be published were Bulletin No. 1425–2 (March, 1965), which dealt with severance-pay plans, and Bulletin No. 1425–3 (June, 1965), which dealt with supplemental unemployment benefit plans and employment guarantees. These are the most comprehensive surveys available, though limited to the description of major plans at a point of time. Closely related to this series is Bulletin No. 1462 (January, 1966), entitled *The Operation of Severance Pay Plans and Their Implications for Labor Mobility.*

installments. In most plans, the payment is final; but in a few plans (for example, some of those in the drug and communications industries), if the employee is rehired, he repays the benefits, usually at the rate of 10 percent of his wage per week. The most common payment is one week of wages for each year of service, but some plans pay much less while others pay a little more. Many plans pay up to a maximum amount, but about half have no ceiling at all.

Severance-pay provisions appear in about one-third of all major contracts and are most frequent in the contracts of five unions—the Auto Workers, Steelworkers, Communications Workers, Garment Workers, and Electrical Workers (IBEW). The proportion of major contracts containing a severance-pay provision has doubled in the last decade, and these contracts currently cover something more than three million employees. As a guide to the potential role of severance pay, the rising trend line is more revealing than the number of employees currently covered. All severance-pay plans are in the private sphere.

Early pension plans belong to this same branch. Provisions for early retirement are in most instances just a concealed form of unemployment benefit payable until retirement age is reached. Here again there is a marked trend upward in both the number of plans and the liberality of provisions, as exemplified by the Auto Workers' contracts negotiated in the fall of 1964. The provisions for thirteen weeks of sabbatical leave negotiated by the Steelworkers in 1962 may also be included in the category of concealed unemployment benefits.

Unemployment a Necessary Condition. The second branch of the second family represents the purest form of unemployment benefit, inasmuch as the benefit is paid only to those actually unemployed. It has many subspecies, of which the principal ones are SIP and SUB. SIP stands for "supplemental income plan." It is a term appropriated from the cement industry but here given a somewhat wider meaning. SIP plans include those which, instead of pooling risks and resources—as is done in insurance—establish for each employee a fund that becomes his property. In SIP plans, each employee has his own individual account, like a bank balance.

Usually, as in the glass industry, the employer puts into each employee's account a fixed amount, which would have gone into wages if the union had not negotiated the SIP plan. But in some instances, as in the plan negotiated by the Machinists with the Douglas Aircraft Company, the employer adds a percentage (Douglas, for example, adds 50 percent) to whatever amount the employee authorizes to be deducted from his pay, and the total is put into his account. There are also various forms of profit sharing which produce an account on which the employee may draw when unemployed. Available data do not suffice for a firm estimate of the number and coverage of SIP-type plans.

Most of these plans are forms of forced saving, and they usually have no relationship to the public program of unemployment benefits. They operate very simply, as though the employee took a part of his wage and banked it. All SIP-type plans are in the private sphere.

SUB stands for "supplemental unemployment benefit." It includes those plans which use the insurance technique of pooling resources and which are tied more or less closely to the public unemployment insurance system. The latter feature chiefly identifies these plans and may be present in greater or less degree. The SUB plan of the carpenters of Buffalo, for example, is tied so closely to UI that eligibility or disqualification for UI is practically equivalent to eligibility or disqualification for SUB. At the other end of the spectrum is the Dana Corporation, a manufacturer of automotive parts; recently this company cut away nearly every tie to UI while keeping all the other features of what used to be an auto-type SUB plan. Paradoxically, the reason given by the carpenters and by the corporation for their respective choices was the same: administrative simplicity.

In the regular auto-type SUB plan, the dependence of the private plan on the public plan has been steadily loosened by the negotiation of exceptions (called "little romans" because in the contracts they are numbered by small roman numerals) to the general requirement that eligibility for SUB depends on eligibility for UI. By the end of 1965, the number of "little romans" had grown to eleven. Most of them were rarely applied, but all were negotiated and defended with the intensity usually reserved for the defense of "principles."

SUB plans appear in every major industry, although they are most common in the steel, can, aluminum, auto, agricultural implement, rubber, and cement industries. During the past decade the provisions of SUB plans have grown steadily more liberal in the amount and duration of benefits. Traditionally the can, steel, and auto industries have led the SUB parade, but in 1965 the rubber and cement industries moved ahead of auto and basic steel in the liberality of their provisions. As of early 1966 the benefit amount as a percentage of gross wages varied for the major SUB plans as follows: steel, 60 percent; autos, 62 percent; rubber, 65 percent; cement and can, 70 percent. The maximum duration of the benefits in most plans is fifty-two weeks, but long-service employees can draw benefits for three years in the cement industry, four years in the rubber industry, and five years in the can industry.

The Alan Wood Steel Company has the most liberal SUB plan. It pays long-service employees benefits equal to 85 percent of gross wages for as long as unemployment lasts. Although the SUB plan of the Hughes Aircraft Company pays benefits equal to 100 percent of gross wages for as long as six months, only those employees are eligible who are permanently separated from the company.

The cost of SUB is far from uniform. Employer contributions vary from as little as 1 cent per employee hour (plan of the Retail Clerks Local 770, Los Angeles) to 17 cents per hour (plan of the carpenters, Buffalo district).

One of the more interesting developments has been the growth of plans in which a number of employers contribute to a common fund. The SUB plans of the Los Angeles retail clerks (1959) and of the Buffalo district carpenters (1960), both mentioned above, are of this kind. Similar plans have been negotiated by the National Maritime Union (1955) and by the International Ladies' Garment Workers' Union (1960), as well as by the photoengravers of New York City (1957) and by the electricians in Detroit (1963). The multi-employer plan makes SUB possible in situations generally thought to preclude SUB.

Growth in SUB has been slow, and in 1965 existing plans covered only about two million employees. However, during the last several years there has been a perceptible increase of interest in SUB and many new plans have been negotiated.

DEMAND FOR PRIVATE PROGRAMS

Even this brief review of existing private plans suffices to show that there is no lack on the supply side. There are plans to suit every need and every purse, but adoption seems to depend primarily on the strength of demand.

Very many factors enter into the demand for unemployment benefits, and at least seven are worth identifying. This list was compiled in the course of a study of SUB programs but it is generally applicable to most of the other private programs as well.

1. As might be expected, the first factor is experience with unemployment. Only those who have been or who expect to be unemployed are much interested in programs of unemployment benefits. It is understandable that the demand for additional unemployment benefits showed itself most strongly in the auto and steel industries, which have been more than ordinarily exposed to the threat of seasonal, cyclical, and secular unemployment.

A survey conducted by the writer in late 1965 among seventy-five of the larger unions found that the great majority of even these unions rated unemployment benefits low on their scale of values. Many other objectives came before this one. The most usual reason given for the low ranking was the absence of a serious threat of unemployment.

When SUB was first negotiated in the auto industry in 1955, the pattern makers who worked for auto firms were offered the same plan but declined it in favor of a slight increase in wages. They argued that unemployment was a rare experience for them. But in the early 1960's, when they began to experience some unemployment incident to technological changes, they began to negotiate SUB programs. As it has turned out, the current boom has so dried up unemployment in their occupation that some of their members are again questioning the desirability of the program.

A significant determinant in a union's evaluation of unemployment programs can be the age distribution of its membership. The union is less likely to demand unemployment benefits if older workers are in the majority. Older workers are better protected from unemployment by seniority and are likely to be more interested in additional health or pension benefits than in unemployment benefits. Age and seniority also affect the kind of SUB plan chosen. The older workers want the plan to contain provisions which will protect the fund from being drained by those members—presumably the younger and the more recently hired—who are laid off earlier. The Ford Motor Company made a major issue of this danger during the original SUB negotiations in 1955 and devised a benefit formula which canceled credit units faster as the fund shrank, and thus saved more of the fund for later layoffs. The UAW not only agreed but negotiated a further strengthening of the protective mechanism: as the fund shrank, the unemployed with less seniority lost credit units faster than those with more seniority.

The danger of fund depletion presents itself in a special way for those plans which pay both SUB and severance out of the same fund. When a company's operations are cut drastically, heavy severance payments can quickly bankrupt the fund. The danger is the greater of course for smaller companies and funds. Under pressure from the senior union members, some of the established funds—for example, in the can, cement, and rubber industries—have been adding protection against an excessive drain by severance payments.

Unions engaged in essentially the same work may evaluate unemployment benefits very differently. For example, some of the plants of Douglas Aircraft are organized by the UAW and some by the IAM. Yet, although the members of both unions do essentially the same work, in

147

the 1965 negotiations the United Auto Workers chose SUB while the International Association of Machinists chose a form of SIP.

Even more striking is the example provided by the Brewery Workers of New Orleans, who negotiated a multi-employer unemployment benefit fund in 1960. In the negotiations, the union represented four groups of workers—the brewers, the drivers, the engineers, and the bottlers. The first three had experienced relatively little unemployment and were unwilling to sacrifice a wage gain for a SUB fund as desired by the bottlers, who were experiencing considerable unemployment. A compromise was reached whereby two funds were set up, SUB for the bottlers and SIP for the others. Then the economy improved and unemployment dropped even for the bottlers, whose SUB fund grew rapidly in size while it paid out few benefits except to those at the very bottom of the seniority list. Older members of the bottlers grew restive as they saw the brewers, drivers, and engineers build up their individual accounts while the bottlers got nothing from "their" 3 cents per hour contributed by the employer to the SUB fund. In 1965 another compromise was reached: the bottlers' fund was divided into two parts. One cent continued to go into SUB, but the other 2 cents went into a newly constituted SIP-type fund. The total number of members of this union, which needed three funds to satisfy all hands, was less than 1,000.

While unemployment stimulates a demand for unemployment benefits, it can also limit the benefits payable. In 1960, the International Ladies' Garment Workers negotiated a multi-employer SUB fund which pays benefits for only the unemployment that results from the closing of a business. The reason for the limitation is that the ladies' garment industry is subject to heavy seasonal unemployment, so provision for all types of unemployment would take too much out of wages.

2. The second factor in order of importance is wages, or, more specifically, high wages. A high wage encourages a demand for unemployment benefits in several ways. First, the high-wage earner is the one most dissatisfied with the regular UI benefit, because he is the one most affected by the limitation on the maximum benefit. Second, as a man's income rises and he has money left over after satisfying basic needs, he feels he can afford to buy more of other goods—for example, more insurance. Third, the high-wage earner, feeling the impact of the income tax, is the one most inclined to take some of his earnings in the form of fringe benefits rather than wages. The tax advantage of fringe benefits over wages is less for unemployment benefits than for some other fringes, because income taxes must be paid on unemployment benefits when received, but there is still some advantage.

148

Practically all plans of unemployment benefits are found among employees who have higher than average wages. The operation of this factor is seen most clearly in cases where high-wage members of a union have unemployment benefits while lower-wage members of the same union do not. Thus members of the United Steelworkers of America (USWA) who work in basic steel generally have a SUB plan, while many of those who work in foundries or fabricating plants do not. Likewise, members of the United Auto Workers (UAW) who work for the automotive companies generally have a SUB plan, while many of those who work for companies making automotive parts do not. Of the members of the Cement, Lime and Gypsum Workers (CLGW), those who work in cement have a SUB plan, while those who work in lime and gypsum do not. In each of the above examples, the members who have the SUB plan are the higher-wage workers. One division of the Buffalo district carpenters consists of members who work on floor coverings; these members have a lower wage scale and a SUB plan that pays lower benefits than the SUB plan of the other members.

3. A third factor is the degree to which other fringe benefits have already been achieved. If other, more highly rated, benefits like pensions, health insurance, and vacations have already been attained, the union is more likely to be seriously interested in negotiating a plan of unemployment benefits. In some instances an unemployment plan has been negotiated ahead of a pension or health plan, but such instances are rare. Of the 2,500 contracts negotiated by the Steelworkers, approximately 95 percent provided insurance, 54 percent provided pensions, but only 20 percent provided SUB. The respective percentages for the Auto Workers were approximately 90 percent, 54 percent, and 24 percent. In 1963, of the 163,000 welfare and pension benefit plans filed with the U.S. Department of Labor, less than 1 percent provided unemployment benefits, and employers contributed twenty times as much to health funds as they contributed to unemployment funds.

The current tendency of unions to negotiate fringe benefits began to show itself strongly during the Second World War and continued during the postwar period. Especially in the last decade, fringe benefits have grown both absolutely and as a percentage of total labor costs. Since the upward trend shows no signs of slackening, as time goes on and goals are substantially achieved in pensions, health, and vacations, there is likely to occur a significant increase in demand for unemployment benefits. The demand is likely to be greater for the simpler forms of unemployment benefits, such as severance pay or a flat, uniform weekly benefit, than for the more complex SUB plans that characterize the auto, cement, rubber, and steel industries.

4. The size of the firm is an important factor for programs which, like SUB, have the character of insurance. Such programs are better suited to large firms, where the risk can be spread over a wide base. Furthermore, in large plans administrative costs are spread over a larger number of units and hence are lower per unit. In small plans, administrative costs can be very burdensome. For this reason, among others, SUB is not particularly suitable for companies with less than 300 employees.

Unemployment benefit plans are more common among the larger firms. This circumstance is largely explained by the correlation between size and other factors, especially profitability and the extent to which the firm's employees are organized.

5. An employer anxious to introduce technological changes that may involve layoffs finds that an unemployment benefit plan helps overcome employee resistance. This connection explains, for example, the unusually high and long benefits provided in the SUB plan of the Alan Wood Steel Company (1965), which had launched a program of modernization several years earlier. This also explains the liberalization of SUB in the rubber and cement industries in 1965, when these industries were being noticeably affected by technological change.

The desire to avoid the disruptive domino-like bumping inherent in a seniority system is an additional reason why an employer may like the idea of unemployment benefits. If the benefits are liberal enough, the worker may be willing, even prefer, to accept a temporary layoff rather than start the process of bumping. In at least one industry, employers have joined with labor in persuading the UI agency not to disqualify employees who choose to accept a layoff rather than to displace another worker. (The industry is not identified here because the legality of the arrangement has still to be determined.) The combined benefits of UI and SUB are usually necessary to induce an employee to make this choice.

6. The sixth factor may be called, for lack of a better term, institutional uniformity—the tendency of an institution (union or firm) to set up an unemployment benefit plan as part of a general policy. The Auto Workers and the Steelworkers, for example, try to negotiate a SUB plan wherever they have members, no matter how few the members and no matter how slight the danger of unemployment. This tendency explains the existence of plans that have never paid a benefit or that cover only a handful of employees.

Firms, too, manifest institutional uniformity. After negotiating a SUB contract with Union A, perhaps a large industrial union, a firm may extend SUB readily to its other employees, whether or not they have ever demanded it. This is the general policy, for example, of firms in the agricultural implement industry. This institutional policy largely explains the existence of SUB plans for office employees.

Geography makes a difference. In negotiations with the Auto Workers, for example, the nearer a company is to Detroit the more it comes under pressure to have a SUB plan. In the case of the Steelworkers, the vicinity of Pittsburgh is the magic region in which SUB must appear in the contract, no matter what the circumstances of the particular firm.

Management sometimes objects to pattern bargaining because it imposes on all firms provisions like SUB that bear more heavily on "bystander" firms, especially small ones, than on the "target" firms which negotiated the provision in the first place. After the 1965 steel negotiations, R. Conrad Cooper of the United States Steel Corporation voiced this objection publicly.

It is true that strong unions seek to impose the contract with the best terms on the whole industry, but it is also true that the unions are not uniformly successful in this strategy. The statistic quoted above is relevant here: of the 2,500 contracts negotiated by the Steelworkers, only 486 provide for a SUB plan. Most of the metal-fabricating firms have escaped this obligation entirely; and, of those which do have SUB programs, some are liable only for the 5 cents negotiated originally (1956) rather than for the 9½ cents negotiated later (1962) with the basic steel companies. On the other hand, in the cement industry, the very liberal SUB provisions negotiated in 1965 with the target companies of Southern California—which experience relatively low unemployment—have become the obligation of all companies, even those in the East which have been experiencing considerable unemployment.

7. The seventh and last factor is the most elusive. In all affairs involving human groups, the personality and values of the leader can be decisive in the choice of group objectives.

For example, Walter Reuther was personally convinced of the value of unemployment benefits and used all his leadership skills to persuade first his own membership and then the automotive companies to set up the original SUB program. Without Reuther, there would have been no SUB program in 1955.

Burl Phares was president of the Glass Workers in 1955 and had the same ideas as Reuther. Since the Glass Workers negotiated earlier than the Auto Workers that year, Phares thought that he would be the first to negotiate a SUB plan. But he was not able to bring the union members along with him. When they proved unwilling to strike for this demand, he had to settle for something else. The multi-employer SUB plan of the carpenters in Buffalo is attributable almost entirely to the leadership of one man, the district director of the union, whose principal problem originally (1960) was to convince his own membership. The multi-employer plan of the Retail Clerks in Los Angeles is likewise attributable to the personal leadership of one man, the local union's secretary.

SCOPE OF PRIVATE PROGRAMS

Current Scope

In the number and variety of programs, although not in the number of persons covered, the private sphere surpasses the public sphere. Of the programs that provide some guarantee of income to current jobholders, most are in the private sphere. All guarantees of employment (Family 1, above) are in the private sphere, although the public laws that regulate these private arrangements—usually by encouraging them—are an important factor in their spread. Programs of the severance-pay type (Family 2a) are also entirely in the private sphere. Of the programs that provide "pure" unemployment benefits (Family 2b), all the SIP-type programs are likewise private arrangements.

In SUB the private and public spheres overlap, and here the public sphere is easily dominant. Whereas the private programs of SUB cover about two million persons and pay annual benefits in the neighborhood of $200 million, the public program of unemployment insurance covers an average of about fifty million persons a year and pays well over $2 billion in benefits annually. In size, the public program of unemployment insurance dwarfs not only SUB but all the various private arrangements combined.

Potential Scope

The characteristic functions of private programs are innovation and adaptation. When the public program of unemployment insurance was enacted in 1935, private programs had already pioneered in this field and their experience was available for guidance. In the past decade, private groups have experimented in numerous ways with various arrangements, most of which were evoked by the need to adapt the general program to particular situations.

The heterogeneity of all private plans, but especially of SUB plans, is striking. Many differences in provisions that determine costs exist between the SUB plans of the basic steel companies and the fabricators of steel products. Similar differences exist between the basic rubber companies and the fabricators of rubber products, between the Big Three auto companies and the makers of automotive parts. Other differences separate the plans of the basic steel companies from those of the

152

auto companies. Reflecting their unlike unemployment experience, the multi-employer plans of the Garment Workers and of the Retail Clerks differ markedly in most of their provisions. In the Douglas Aircraft Company, the choice of SIP by the Machinists and of SUB by the Auto Workers reflected differences in personal values rather than in economic situations. The Brewery Workers of New Orleans adapted to the variations among their 1,000 members by establishing three separate plans. Presumably, private plans will continue to innovate and adapt.

For the foreseeable future, all programs that provide guaranteed employment, severance payments, and SIP-type unemployment benefits are likely to remain in the private sphere. These programs affect property rights somewhat more directly than they affect income flows, and our society has always been slower to compensate for loss of property than for a loss of income.[3]

Private programs of these three kinds have an almost unlimited potential, a potential likely to be increasingly actualized as other fringe benefits—pensions, health, vacations—are attained and collective bargaining is freed to turn more attention to the threat of unemployment. At this point, a critical choice may have to be made between guarantees of employment and compensation for loss of employment. The choice will depend largely on the kind of labor mobility we wish to foster.

The potential scope of private programs is affected by the public program in several ways. Severance pay has one serious friction point with the public program of unemployment insurance. In twenty-two states, severance benefits are considered "wages" and therefore a bar to the simultaneous receipt of unemployment insurance. Whatever the intrinsic merits of this disqualification, there seems to be an inconsistency in allowing the simultaneous payment of unemployment insurance and SUB—as all states but one now do—and prohibiting the simultaneous payment of unemployment insurance and severance pay. Insofar as it represents indemnification for a property loss, severance pay would seem to be of no concern to unemployment insurance; in its other function as an unemployment benefit it would seem not to be basically different from SUB.

The inconsistency developed gradually. Severance pay antedated SUB by many years and had always been considered disqualifying income in many states. With the advent of large-scale SUB in 1955, the states, seeing the essential similarity between the two programs, declared that

---

[3] The comparison does not rest on an assumption that these programs involve property in a strictly legal sense. The comparison is within the programs themselves and implies only that these three types of programs are more like a form of property protection than unemployment insurance is.

SUB also was disqualifying income. But many more persons were affected by SUB, the political climate changed, and in state after state SUB gradually was accorded the status of nonwage payment. In many states however the original judgment on severance pay remained unchanged. In California, for example, it was only in 1965, after a decade of SUB payments, that the state supreme court declared severance pay to be like SUB and not disqualifying.

The proper scope of SUB is particularly difficult to determine because in SUB the private and public spheres overlap. Unemployment insurance programs exist in both spheres, and expansion of one may occur at the expense of the other.

The most likely way in which the development of SUB could inhibit the development of UI would be by diminishing interest in UI. As more of the powerful unions negotiate SUB plans and thus satisfy their own needs for protection against unemployment, their interest in UI may diminish and their efforts to improve the public program may lose the intensity necessary to secure results. A cursory investigation has turned up little evidence of such a development, but any conclusion had best wait until a more thorough investigation, now in progress, is completed.

The opposite possibility is more likely, that development of UI will inhibit the development of SUB. Obviously, to the extent that UI increases the amount and duration of its benefits, the potential scope of SUB is lessened. In 1966, H.R. 8282 was presented for the consideration of the Congress. If the provisions of this bill regulating the amount and duration of benefits should be enacted into law—now or in the future—they would sharply restrict SUB's ability to extend duration but would have only a limited effect on its ability to supplement the amount.

The proposal of H.R. 8282 is to pay benefits for fifty-two weeks to the core members of the labor force, and this is the present duration limit for much the same workers in nearly all the private plans. The private plans could, of course, go beyond fifty-two weeks, as a few already do; but supplementation beyond a year will probably remain rare. The role of the private plans in supplementing the benefit amount would be lessened by the increase in the UI maximum amount proposed in H.R. 8282, but since UI would still pay only 50 percent of the claimant's wage, there would remain room for supplementation up to the level currently provided by the private plans, which, as indicated, replace from 60 percent to 100 percent of gross wages.[4]

---

[4] The scope of private plans could be affected by the proposed negative income tax, but any effect would probably be slight. As already indicated, private plans appear chiefly among employees who have a higher-than-average wage, and these are the employees who least expect to be helped by the negative income tax.

Of course, the increase in the benefit amount provided by H.R. 8282 is not necessarily the most liberal that will ever be proposed for the public program. More liberal proposals that will further delimit the scope of the private programs are likely to be fostered by the very success of the private programs. Experience under SUB plans has established the feasibility, in at least some circumstances, of paying higher benefits for longer periods than has been attempted by any of the state unemployment insurance programs. Could not the public program pay similar benefits?

> This question cannot be answered on the basis of information currently available. The programs of supplementary unemployment benefits and unemployment insurance are too different for experience in the one to be applied directly and simply to the other. SUB is confined to a more homogeneous work force with higher-than-average wages, has stricter eligibility requirements, has stricter disqualifications in the crucial areas of the voluntary quit and the strike, is under the closer surveillance and control of the employer, and is under the discipline of a stricter kind of experience-rating system. In order to make proper allowance for these differences more detailed knowledge of experience with SUB plans is needed than is now available.[5]

An investigation of SUB currently in progress may throw additional light on the question.

The chief limitation on the potential scope of all private programs is the limitation common to the whole system of private property, the inequality that results. Supplementary benefits generally appear in the industries that can better afford them, not necessarily in those that most need them. The lime and gypsum workers of the CLGW, the workers in the floor-covering division of the Buffalo carpenters, the USWA workers in the fabricating plants, the UAW workers in the plants making automotive parts, and many other similar groups probably have as much need for SUB as their more fortunate union brothers have; but they do not have a full SUB program because, earning lower wages, they cannot afford to give up part of a wage increase in exchange for this fringe benefit.

In a job-oriented society, where unemployment is a major and universal threat, the benefits provided by the public program should be as adequate and as widely available "as possible." In the debate over the dimensions of that possibility, any reasonable doubt among prudent men should generally be settled in favor of the public program. Private pro-

---

[5] Joseph M. Becker (ed.), *In Aid of the Unemployed* (Baltimore: Johns Hopkins Press, 1965), p. 135.

grams should be only supplemental to a truly adequate public program. Nevertheless, since our society has always preferred the system of competitive wages and private property, properly modified by a concern for the public interest, and since this preference inevitably involves the acceptance of some inequality of income, it would be inconsistent to demand equality of private unemployment benefits. In our society, there is and probably will continue to be an established place for private unemployment benefit programs.

III

COMMUNITY IMPROVEMENT

10

SECONDARY AND POSTSECONDARY OCCUPATIONAL EDUCATION IN KALAMAZOO COUNTY, MICHIGAN

HAROLD T. SMITH AND HENRY C. THOLE

Kalamazoo County, Michigan lies at the heart of a well-balanced industrial area with a population of approximately 300,000. The community has always been proud of its educational institutions and cultural level. In addition to the public and private elementary and secondary schools, the usual array of proprietary business, professional, and trade schools, and a number of cultural facilities such as the Kalamazoo Institute of Arts, the Civic Theater, and the Nature Center, it has two excellent liberal arts colleges and the state's fourth largest university. On the other hand, no publicly supported institution, other than the high schools, offers the occupational education programs that an industrial economy normally needs, and the possibility that there is a shortage of occupational training opportunities in the county has become a matter of deep concern. The Upjohn Institute, therefore, has undertaken to examine the existing facilities to determine what gaps do occur and what new educational facilities might best fill them. The findings and recommendations of the study are reported here in the belief that they may be helpful to similar communities throughout the country.

In order to attain an understanding of both future plans and present practices concerning occupational education in Kalamazoo County, conferences were held with school administrators, counselors, and teachers on the one hand and principal employers from industry on the other. This report is based upon these conferences as well as upon available documented data.

OCCUPATIONAL EDUCATION IN THE HIGH SCHOOLS OF KALAMAZOO COUNTY

The conferences held with school personnel involved more than 200 principals, counselors, and teachers of business, industrial arts, and home economics. In each conference, it was made clear at the outset that our concern was the extent to which students of every grade and age level are being prepared for what they will, or must, undertake next. We were not concerned with how well students are being prepared to become nuclear physicists or brain surgeons or any other goals too far in the future to serve as incentives for most high school students. We were concerned with how well students are being prepared for the next course or grade, college or professional school, business, technical training, training or further training for a specific job, or direct entry into a job at the level of schooling achieved. High school graduation was considered of secondary importance, and seldom if ever, an end in itself.

Data indicating what the students believe they need beyond a high school education were made available through a May, 1965, survey of all eleventh grade students in both public and private schools in Kalamazoo County.[1] The survey showed that 46.8 percent of the students were enrolled in the college preparatory course; 14.9 percent in business education; 6.8 percent in industrial education, which is heavily industrial arts-oriented rather than vocation-oriented; 28.4 percent in general education; and the balance, 3.1 percent, in special or unidentified programs.

In answer to a question concerning their future educational aspirations, just under 40 percent of the students said they expected to graduate from college. Just over 40 percent expected to acquire two years of college or some occupational training such as technical training, business education, apprenticeship training, nurses training, or other special training in programs normally offered by public postsecondary institutions, adult education programs, and proprietary schools. The remaining 20 percent did not expect to acquire training beyond high school.

Preparation for the First Undertaking Out of School

How well are high schools preparing students for their postsecondary education aspirations or for direct job entry?

Preparation for Entrance to College. All Kalamazoo County high schools offer college preparatory courses, although not of equal breadth and depth. The larger high schools are able to offer a wider variety of subject matter and frequently courses of greater depth. The private high schools, of course, generally concentrate on the college preparatory program and offer no vocational programs other than secretarial.

[1] Report of Subcommittee on Youth Educational Needs, Mrs. John Shoemaker, chairman, of Citizens Committee to Study Educational and Job Needs in Kalamazoo County, Marvin E. DeBoer, chairman, March 9, 1966 (unpublished).

OCCUPATIONAL EDUCATION

No discussion of the role of the high school in preparing students for college is needed here. The undue prestige of a college preparatory course, parental pressure to take it, the academic background and orientation of many guidance counselors, and the fact that it may be the only well-organized preparatory curriculum in the school program all influence students to take the college preparatory course. The net result is that many students not of college caliber enroll in such courses.

Preparation for Entrance to Postsecondary Vocational-Technical Institutions. No high school offers its students specially designed preparatory courses for entrance into technical institutes or technical programs in postsecondary institutions. Because of the variety of postsecondary technical programs (such as all kinds of mechanical technology, engineering technology, electrical technology, mining technology, and medical and dental technology), the student must know what kind of technician he expects to be in order to know what preparatory course to take. Most technical programs, however, require a broad base of mathematics and science. Postsecondary institutions generally offer the necessary preparatory science courses for students after their arrival. It would save time, however, and be advantageous otherwise, if the student were able to take the preparatory science courses in high school.

Guidance counselors and teachers seem to feel that most high schools could make up acceptable preparatory courses for postsecondary technical programs by selecting appropriate subjects from the college preparatory and general education courses and by including relevant mathematics and science courses. For some programs, it would be well to add such courses as mechanical drawing and drafting, machine shop, and electricity, when available.

On the other hand, guidance counselors seem quite unaware of the need to offer preparatory programs for entry into technical education. They do not counsel students to enter such programs, and they are unable to answer the question: Where do students go for postsecondary technical education? Counselors and teachers in several of the schools seem to feel that the needed preparatory programs could be devised, but the difficulty of counseling students to prepare for postsecondary technical programs that are not readily available would still remain.

The high schools of the county do not offer programs designed particularly to help the student enter postsecondary training for nontechnical but highly skilled jobs. Almost any good high school student is eligible for admission to such courses. Even though shop work offered by the schools is oriented toward industrial education or industrial arts rather than toward job entry, it does acquaint the student with materials and tools, which is good; and if the student takes the full sequence of these courses he may acquire considerable preparation for entering training for most skilled jobs.

Preparation for Direct Entry into Skilled Jobs. All of the high schools offer secretarial and related courses of sufficient depth to enable graduates to enter directly into office employment. Some schools offer a few isolated trade courses such as automobile mechanics and body repair, drafting, printing, and carpentry. Indeed, one group of boys is now having the unique experience of building a house for sale on the market. But this program is exceptional. Furthermore, it is not at all clear that the high schools should provide an array of special preparatory programs for direct entry into skilled jobs. It is probably better for most students to prepare for entry into training for nontechnical skilled jobs upon graduation than to attempt to qualify for direct entrance into such jobs. This assumes again that training for nontechnical skilled jobs is available after high school.

Until 1965–66, all home economics courses offered by county high schools were designed for the homemaker rather than for job entry. Two schools have reported that some courses in occupational home economics have been introduced this year, and two or three others reported that they will introduce such courses next year. This change has been encouraged by federal aid under the Elementary and Secondary Education Act of 1965. It remains to be determined to what extent these new courses will lead to direct job entry.

Preparation for Direct Entry into Unskilled and Semiskilled Jobs. Unskilled jobs are generally considered to be those for which no special training is needed, while semiskilled jobs (such as many assembly line jobs) are those for which training of varying duration must be done by industry on the job itself. The processes involved in both kinds of work are routine, so that any physically and emotionally normal youth should be able to perform them.

The best preparation for both kinds of jobs is a good general education, but this presupposes the existence of other very elementary and fundamental qualifications, many of which should be acquired in home and community. The more fundamental qualifications fall into place in the following order: (1) knowledge of how to work and ability to experience satisfaction in work, (2) ability to cooperate with other people, (3) ability to read functionally, and (4) knowledge of simple

162

arithmetic. The possession of a good general education is more a test of employment competency than a qualification in itself.

Conferences with school personnel in Kalamazoo County confirmed the idea that, for unskilled or semiskilled employment, knowledge of how to work is even more important than reading and arithmetic. In the more rural school districts, high school graduates, except for those with emotional or personality problems, have not gone unemployed. Farm boys learn how to work at home where they experience the satisfaction of achievement and success. They may have done a man's job in many ways from the time they were 14 years of age. Their sense of dignity and self-respect and their status with their peers are bound up with work. The result is that they have experienced no sense of failure from doing poor academic work, even if they have not learned to read adequately. These boys, when they graduate, possessing confidence in their ability to work and, having considerable knowledge of and feeling for machinery, have been able to secure jobs on assembly lines of factories in neighboring towns and to hold those jobs even when others were being discharged.

Knowing how to work and getting satisfaction out of work seem to be important qualifications for unskilled or semiskilled jobs. The individual may find in the long run that he has allowed himself to be short-changed; that he has become chained to the assembly line for life; or that automation may someday eliminate his job at a time when it is difficult to secure another. But, for the present, he is not unemployed.

Our educational programs were formed at a time when every youth learned how to do manual work at home. Today, that is not the case. Almost every teen-age youth needs job experience. He needs it as an exercise in learning how to work at a time when he is physically and emotionally ready for work; he needs it for the development of his own sense of achievement and self-respect; and, in some cases, he needs it to provide the necessities that are incidental to being in school. The opportunity to learn how to work and to experience the satisfaction of work successfully done may provide the key to the education of the youth headed for direct job entry.

The loss of such opportunities is due only in part to urbanization. It is due also to the miscarriage of many of our regulations in regard to child labor and to the reluctance of employers and their employees to teach inexperienced youths how to work. Efforts to protect the child from exploitation have made it difficult for a youth to find a job that will provide him with either proper training or self-respect. If he secures a job, he may be prohibited from climbing a ladder to change a light bulb or from lifting more than thirty-five or fifty pounds, depending on his age. He may not be allowed to ride in his employer's delivery truck, yet he may take the family car out on the highway at any hour of the day or night. A host of restrictions may destroy a youth's respect for his job and damage his own self-image.

Both employer and labor should recognize the necessity for youth to learn to work and should cooperate with the schools in providing real work experience. But to do so is likely to cost the employer something. Many new employees do not pay their way at first. Students as a rule are only part-time, temporary employees. For boys, the problem is aggravated by the military draft. Insurance companies may remind employers that, insofar as the employment of beginners increases industry accident rates, their premiums will also go up. The employer may find the paper work required by the schools and the state troublesome. Experienced laborers may prefer not to work with student beginners, and they may resent the employment of students on jobs that would otherwise be available for men with families. The employment of students may even become a matter for consideration in drawing up union contracts. Without such work experience, however, a youth may find himself entirely unprepared upon leaving school to enter directly into the labor force with any appreciation of the responsibilities of work. This whole matter needs to be taken into account in the formulation and administration of the child labor laws, workmen's compensation insurance, and employer-union regulations.

The Kalamazoo County schools have recognized for a long time that students seeking to acquire a skill profit greatly from work experience. This recognition is exemplified dramatically by the cooperative work-study program in business subjects. Now the schools are appreciating that students expecting to enter directly into unskilled or semiskilled jobs also need work experience as an essential part of their preparation for entry into the labor market. One city district, for example, has introduced an "Employment-Bound Youth" program, designed specifically to provide work experience for the students most likely headed for unskilled or semiskilled employment. Partly because of the restrictions referred to above, and partly because the program is in the experimental stage, the jobs have been provided primarily by the schools themselves: work in school cafeterias and offices, and school janitorial services. Credit is given for some of the work just as it is for a class, and everything possible is done to provide the students with a sense of personal achievement.

Preparation of the Potential Dropout for Direct Entry into Unskilled or Semiskilled Employment. A word must be said about the youth who is so conditioned against school that he becomes a potential or an actual dropout. The term is not intended to apply to the youth who quits school simply because he thinks for the moment that he can get more out of something else and therefore takes a job instead. Such a person is in a position to resume his education at some later time. It is the youth who drops out with nothing, into nothing, who is properly labeled a dropout.

In Kalamazoo County, dropping out of school before high school graduation is no longer general. Michigan law requires that youths stay in school until they are 16 years of age; and child labor laws, employers' liability risks, and employer-union attitudes make attainment of satisfying employment before the age of 18 quite difficult. Home and society exert strong pressure on young people to graduate from high school, and the schools are doing everything they can to encourage them to stay in school until the age of 18 and eventual graduation.

This attitude differs from that of just a few short years ago when a 16-year-old youth could check out of school without challenge or counsel. But even recently, school counsel and other pressures have been aimed primarily at graduation rather than preparation for entry into the world of work.

The causes of emotional block against school and its learning processes are many and varied. Some lie in the physical makeup of the child, others in the social and cultural fabric of home and community. Whatever the causes, they must be detected, diagnosed, and remedied or circumvented—preferably before school age, or certainly early in school. And whatever the causes, the subsequent effects are cumulative, and these in turn become causes in themselves. For example, the failure to learn to read, which is an early result, soon becomes a major cause for further failure; continuous failure results in an emotional block against learning, which then itself becomes a cause. By the time the individual has reached high school, the gap between what he knows and what he needs to know in order to prepare for something he might like to do in the world of work has become wide and deep, and the emotional block against learning very strong.

High schools have come to graduate such an individual because that seems best for him. But, up to the present time, the schools have not made much headway in preparing him for job entry, although, as already noted, they are beginning to try. The hope is to prepare him for entry into unskilled or semiskilled employment by providing work experience and affording him an opportunity to learn how to work, and thereby to gain a feeling of success and self-confidence. If this can be accomplished, the student, like the farm boy who learns to work at home, may become employed; and perhaps out of that employment, he may discover that learning is a lifelong activity that may not be so hateful after all.

Some high schools are introducing remedial reading and arithmetic for these youth with federal aid under the Elementary and Secondary Education Act of 1965. Some success has been reported. But, if these youth can be taught to read in high school, they surely could have been taught to read in the elementary grades. In fact, a large majority of the elementary teachers interviewed seemed quite emphatic in the belief that, if they had the time, the necessary professional help, and the support of the public, they could teach many who are not now learning to read to do so.

Surely this must be done if we are to check the flow of conditioned failures through the elementary grades into high school—a flow that is becoming so great in some areas as to threaten the effectiveness of the school programs in which the youth are enrolled.

In an effort to find a way to reach the embittered dropout and the conditioned potential dropout, an experimental program, known as Youth Opportunities Unlimited, Inc. (YOU), has been set up in the city of Kalamazoo for youths 16 to 21 years of age. The program is a creation of the community, and is financed by private funds.

A number of changes have taken place in the program since its beginning in 1961, but it is now operating generally as follows. YOU has its own shop in which some youth work on products made under contract for industry. The type of work is limited to that which the labor laws and other restrictions permit. The youth are paid by the piece so that they experience the direct relationship between work done and pay received. Except for some of the overhead, each contract is expected to pay its own way. Other youth are found jobs in the community. At first, YOU subsidized employers for using these youth on certain jobs, but such payments are becoming unnecessary. More and more employers have had satisfactory experiences with the program, and they are more inclined to absorb the extra costs of the learning period.

Some of the youth, the potential dropouts, remain half-time in their regular schools. YOU assumes responsibility for teaching these to become employable; and either YOU or the outside employer, as the case may be, provides them with training on the job. Other youth are actual dropouts, and some of these will not participate in any program that requires even entering a regular school building. In lieu of the half-day in school, YOU undertakes to teach these youth to read and to do simple arithmetic.

YOU is operating in an area of great need, apparently with considerable success. The time has come, however, to determine its future role and how it should be managed and financed. We shall refer to YOU later, in our conclusions and recommendations.

Detailed knowledge of a community's industries and their skill requirements is essential to adequate planning for the education and training of workers. Such knowledge should provide a valuable basis for assessing the strengths and weaknesses of industrial training practices. It should also provide guidelines for educators in establishing curricula and for counselors in guiding students. With such information, the community can seek to meet the needs of industry more adequately, and citizens can better prepare to fill available jobs.

The following observations concerning Kalamazoo County industries are based not only on data generally available, but also on information obtained through personal interviews with executives of manufacturing firms employing more than 70 percent of the manufacturing workers in the county. The county's industries are well diversified, requiring a wide variety of unskilled, semiskilled, skilled, and technical manpower, as illustrated by the following discussion.

Types of Manufacturing in Kalamazoo County

Educational and skill requirements of industry are directly related to the types of manufacturing processes used. Most companies in the Kalamazoo area, as elsewhere, may be classified into two major types of manufacturing: intermittent and continuous. Most plants are not wholly in either category, although nearly all may be classified as primarily one type or the other. The major difference between the two types is the length of time that equipment is operable without interruption for change or modification. Intermittent production is characterized by relatively short runs—often lasting only minutes or hours—of many different products that may require frequent changes of tools and fixtures. Continuous production is characterized by long runs of highly standardized products, in plants operating without a shutdown of machinery for extended periods, possibly months.

Intermittent Type. Factories employing intermittent manufacturing processes require many skilled and semiskilled workers but relatively few unskilled workers. Three general categories of firms producing by intermittent manufacturing methods are identifiable in Kalamazoo County. First, there are the jobshops in industries such as printing,

167

machinery, and fabricated metals, which produce in small lots or batches for customer orders. Generally, firms in this category require highly skilled workers who know how to set up and operate several different machines. Such workers often need to know shop mathematics and how to use blueprints and measuring instruments. These companies prefer to hire trade-school graduates whose training and experience enable them to acquire skills within two years by on-the-job training. Some of these companies recruit trade-school graduates from out of the state.

The second category of firms using intermittent-type production includes larger companies, mostly metalworking, which produce precision parts and equipment in large enough quantities so that jobs may be broken down into one or two operations. Inexperienced trainees in these companies can become proficient in their jobs after a year or two of on-the-job training. These firms, of course, also employ some highly skilled generalists and maintenance people.

In the third category, firms utilizing intermittent-type operations are able to standardize production to a considerable extent. Because of longer runs, more uniform products, or less critical tolerances, these companies require fewer skilled workers than the other two groups. They may use intermittent methods because minor variations in product are ordered by customers. Workers in these factories generally become proficient in their jobs in a year or less. However, these firms, like others characterized by intermittent processes, require engineers, technicians, and skilled workers for product design, production control, tool design, toolmaking, diemaking, and other functions. Although capitalization is generally not so high in these companies as in firms using continuous production techniques, it does necessitate either the employment of highly skilled maintenance workers in the plant or the purchase of such services from specialists.

Continuous Type. Most of the larger manufacturing companies in Kalamazoo County are characterized by continuous processes and huge capital investments in machinery and equipment. These firms require many professional, technical, and skilled persons, such as engineers, machine designers, toolmakers, diemakers, plumbers, electricians, and machinery repairmen. Because interruptions in production are extremely costly, preventive maintenance is essential. When repairs are needed, they must be made rapidly to minimize costly shutdown time. Most of the production workers in such industries are unskilled or semiskilled. The learning period on many jobs is very short; often the workers may be trained in a matter of hours, days, or weeks.

Kalamazoo County's paper and chemical companies and certain metal-working companies produce most of their products by continuous production methods. Paper and chemical companies are sometimes called "process industries" because they produce by a set process that often approximates automatic manufacturing. Bulk materials—liquids, powders, or chunks—are processed in mixing tanks and pressure-cooking vessels. They are usually moved by pipe, chute, duct, or stream, as in paper manufacturing; or they are mixed in batches, as in chemical manufacturing.

Of course, not all companies classified as process industries use continuous manufacturing methods for all items they manufacture. The paper companies fabricate paper into many different end products, often using intermittent-type methods. The production of ice-cream cartons or cups and plates for customer orders is an example. The larger companies often have large service departments, such as printing, machinery repair, or machinery building, which produce items by inter-mittent-type methods. One large metalworking company employing continuous manufacturing methods produces many of its own tools and dies for use in special-purpose stamping machines. This one function has the characteristics of labor and machinery common to intermittent-type manufacture; in fact, this company will eventually employ more persons in this activity than all but one or two of the larger metal-working companies specializing in intermittent-type manufacturing.

On-the-Job Training

A survey of training practices in local firms indicates that on-the-job training is offered in most local manufacturing companies. Generally, supervisors or key workers instruct the new employees, remaining with them until they are ready to work alone or with a minimum of guidance. After this initial period, the instructor may leave the new employee on his own, giving help only on machine setups or when otherwise especially needed.

The training time for semiskilled and skilled workmen depends on many different factors, such as the nature of the industry, method of production, the nature of materials being processed, and effectiveness of supervision, and the aptitudes and abilities of the trainees.

Most unskilled jobs require very little on-the-job training beyond orientation, a briefing on safety practices, and such simple instructions and follow-up as are necessary for satisfactory job performance.

The training period for semiskilled jobs varies from a few weeks to a year or more. In companies employing continuous manufacturing techniques particularly, jobs requiring simple assembly or subassembly can be learned very quickly. Rudiments of such jobs can sometimes be mastered by a good employee within a few days, and top proficiency might occur in a few weeks. More intricate assembly jobs—for example, in firms working on aircraft, space vehicles, or transportation equipment—require a longer training period.

Kalamazoo metalworking shops utilizing intermittent techniques in which semiskilled machine operators do repetitive work on one machine find it unnecessary to instruct and to supervise workers closely for more than a few weeks, but up to a year may be needed before an individual is fully proficient on the job. Firms in both metal-cutting and metal-forming industries fall into this category. Some companies have a skilled setup man to install the cutting or forming tool in the machine, so that only the running of the machine is left to the operator. Other companies require workers to learn how to install tools in their own machines. The latter procedure requires more skill on the part of the operator, but many shops with repetitive-type operations indicate that workers still are able to become fairly proficient in a year or so.

Machine-operator training for both semiskilled and skilled jobs generally requires more time in the metal-cutting industry than in the metal-forming industry because it more frequently demands training in blueprint reading, measuring instruments, and shop mathematics. An exception is the tool and die function in the metal-forming industry in plants such as the General Motors Fisher Body plant. This function is, of course, a metal-cutting operation, and employees must be highly skilled journeymen or the equivalent to perform capably.

Most training of skilled workers in the manufacturing industries of Kalamazoo County is conducted on the job in a manner similar to the training of semiskilled workers. Skilled workers, however, may need three or four years, or longer, to become proficient. One company has a ten-year on-the-job training program leading to journeyman status for its employees.

Most companies having collective bargaining agreements develop skilled workers either through a carefully planned apprenticeship program or through such informal systems as job-bidding procedures. There are about a dozen manufacturing companies offering apprenticeship programs for the machine trades. Most of these programs are federally approved, by the Bureau of Apprenticeship and Training. They consist of on-the-job training in all major aspects of the trade, plus related training in one of the local high schools. Some firms located outside of the county send workers to Kalamazoo for this related training. One local company has established an apprenticeship course providing for related training through a contract with the International Correspondence Schools. Employees are given two hours of study time within the working day, during which an engineer is available to help them with their lessons.

Job-Bidding Systems

A discussion of training by Kalamazoo County industries would not be complete without mention of job-bidding systems, which help account for the large amount of on-the-job training. In every contacted local manufacturing company that has a labor union except one, job-bidding systems are written into the contracts. Of the two major manufacturing companies that do not have unions, one employs a job-bidding system to advance workers, and the other advances workers through a merit system. A worker in the latter company has the opportunity to try a new job for two weeks before deciding whether or not he wishes to keep it. If he chooses not to accept a job, he may return to his previous one.

Job-bidding systems in local union contracts require companies to "post" vacant jobs due to expansion, turnover, or other reasons for a period ranging from twenty-four to forty-eight hours. Employees then "bid" for the job, and the person with the greatest seniority is transferred to the new job. Thus, employees proceed from the less difficult to the more difficult jobs.

In a job-bidding system, filling one vacancy may precipitate many additional moves in the factory. For example, a machinist might successfully bid on an opening for a toolmaker's job; in turn, a drill press operator might successfully bid on the machinist's job; and, in turn, someone in a lower classification might bid on the drill press operator's job. One job opening might require up to seven or eight job changes in a company.

A very important side effect of the job-bidding system is that employers find it advantageous to employ only workers with a good basic education even for unskilled jobs. Any employee hired under such a system may apply for a better job as he accumulates seniority. A slow learner, or a worker with low-level skills in reading, communicating, and arithmetic, might easily prove inadequate if he should bid for a better job. Such an employee might need longer training and might be refused advancement. Many companies, therefore, prefer to employ only high school graduates even for unskilled and semiskilled jobs which can be handled easily by persons with less than a high school education.

171

As extensive as on-the-job training is in Kalamazoo County, it does not adequately prepare workers for their jobs in all respects. Although the new workers learn how to do the work on the job, most companies are not set up to teach workers the related subjects necessary for a good academic and theoretical background. The result is that very few all-round craftsmen are being trained by local manufacturing companies, and, except for periods of poor business conditions, critical shortages occur almost continuously.

The medium-sized and smaller companies in Kalamazoo County, many of which engage in intermittent-type production, have special problems in training skilled workers. Many have tried repeatedly to train skilled workers without success. Local company managers report that workers become discouraged because of the long training periods required. In many of the larger production shops, workers can reach pay levels of at least $3.00 per hour in a very few months. Consequently, many workers in smaller companies leave jobs that may have a good long-term future for jobs with larger companies that pay more money immediately.

Smaller companies lack the facilities and resources for the selection, testing, and training necessary for successful apprenticeship courses. A small machine shop cannot afford to pay high wages during the learning period. Neither can it afford to train many workers during periods of good business conditions, since the output of experienced workers is reduced during the time they spend in coaching novices.

Employers point out that facilities and equipment for vocational education in most local high schools are not adequate. Budgets are so small, in some cases, that adequate materials and equipment cannot be purchased. As a result, shop equipment common to Kalamazoo industry is not available in most school districts. For example, although a turret lathe is common to factories using both intermittent and continuous processes, there are very few such lathes in local high schools. Furthermore, there are very few grinders (cylindrical or internal) or radial drill presses. Very little or no equipment is available in most schools to train workers for Kalamazoo County's important fabricated metals industry. There are almost no press brakes or punch presses, very few welding machines, and little welding equipment.

Several employers point out that equipment such as milling machines and lathes presently in school shops often is not heavy enough for realistic training. Equipment in some shops is outmoded and inadequate in amount, variety, and accessories. Emphasis needs to be placed on machines and equipment used both in production and in skilled maintenance

172

and service functions. Additional vocational training facilities and equipment, therefore, are necessary to meet the needs of the county's expanding industry.

Since training facilities are inadequate in educational institutions in the Kalamazoo area, and since very few sequential courses are available in educational institutions, only a few skilled workers are being trained for manufacturing industry. As a result, local companies are often obliged to attract skilled workers from outside the county, or to employ workers with less education and skill than desired.

Additional vocational facilities in the local area, with sequential course offerings, would fill two highly important needs. First, such facilities would enable interested persons to take a complete course in a vocation of their choice. This would go a long way toward satisfying industry's demand for semiskilled and skilled workmen. Graduates would still need on-the-job training, but they would have demonstrated an interest and aptitude for skilled work, and a readiness for additional specialized training. Vocational training, too, combined with education in all-important related subjects, would give trainees background for supervisory and management positions in industry.

Second, vocational training facilities could be used for accelerated short-term training courses in times of booming business conditions, when companies find it necessary to employ workers without sufficient background or training. If adequate facilities were available to train workers on equipment common to Kalamazoo industry, short courses could be offered during hours when facilities were not being used for regular courses. Thus, without detracting from the over-all program, an important contribution could be made to alleviate shortages of semiskilled workers in periods of rapid business expansion.

The bright long-run outlook for Kalamazoo manufacturing underlines the need for additional vocational education facilities frequently mentioned by employers. It is anticipated that Kalamazoo factory employment will increase by 39 percent between 1960 and 1975, compared with a growth of 19 percent for the nation as a whole.[2] The best growth prospects are in many of those industries—both in continuous and intermittent-type manufacturing—that require highly skilled workers. Companies in industries such as chemicals, fabricated metals, transportation equipment, machinery, and printing are expected to grow rapidly. The recent establishment of a Fisher Body Division plant is expected to attract satellite facilities for producing highly specialized tools, dies, and

[2] Samuel V. Bennett, *Manpower Requirements in Kalamazoo, 1975* (Kalamazoo, Mich.: Upjohn Institute for Employment Research; in process).

other equipment, since General Motors plans to produce only 40 percent of its own tool and die requirements.

Management officials are overwhelmingly in favor of additional vocational training in Kalamazoo County. They feel that a good background in vocational education will enable workers to attain skills much more quickly after they are employed. In addition, the vocationally trained workers will be more safety conscious, therefore less apt to injure themselves, or damage expensive machinery. Finally, there is no doubt that additional stress on vocational training in the community would provide greater opportunities, and more higher-paying industrial jobs, for local citizens.

ADDITIONAL NEEDS FOR OCCUPATIONAL EDUCATION PROGRAMS AND FACILITIES

In determining what the additional over-all needs are for occupational education and training programs and facilities in Kalamazoo County, two major considerations emerge. First, what should reasonably be expected of the high schools, assuming that supporting postsecondary facilities become available? Second, what kind of postsecondary facilities would be best for Kalamazoo County? We begin with a consideration of the high schools and proceed to the postsecondary facilities best suited to the county.

Occupational Education by the High Schools

We should expect the high schools to be as comprehensive in their offerings as the community and its economy require. This means that the school should provide each student who has ability with a solid, basic education in communications, the social and political sciences, the physical sciences, and mathematics, and should prepare the student for what he will undertake upon leaving school.

Each school should offer within its own plant all of the needed occupational courses that do not require costly specialized equipment and for which student demand is sufficiently large to permit efficient teaching. These courses should include the usual business subjects, home economics, and industrial arts. Some very essential courses, however— preparatory for postsecondary occupational education, preparatory for skilled jobs essential to the local economy, or needed by students not in a position to take them after high school graduation—are too costly in relation to demand to be offered by any single school in the county. Such programs could be made available only by offering them cooperatively. How this can best be done and how the needed postsecondary occupational education and training programs can best be provided will be considered together, since the two are related.

The high schools must prepare all who, upon leaving school, will enter directly into the unskilled and semiskilled labor market. All members of this group, furthermore, should have such general education as they are willing and able to undertake. Many need work experience under conditions that will help them learn how to work and to attain satisfaction from work. Some of these youths who are ill-equipped and even anti-school will need remedial programs in reading and elementary arithmetic. Some will need help in becoming employable.

Some of the schools have had a brief experience with work-study programs for those preparing to enter the common labor market through the Employment-Bound Youth (EBY) program, and through Youth Opportunities Unlimited, which has already been described. The EBY program is intended for the typical youth, and the YOU program is designed for the potential and actual dropout.

It seems clear that the EBY and YOU programs should be reorganized and enlarged as necessary to accommodate all students who could benefit from work experience. It is not possible to know at this time how much expansion is essential for optimum results; time and experience, of course, will be important factors in determining this.

Each school must conduct its own EBY program insofar as the work done is in school offices and cafeterias and relates to maintenance and other services to the school itself. It is not administratively feasible, however, for each school to seek out part-time jobs in the community for all students who need work experience, or to give close enough attention to students on such jobs. Employers could not deal with so many school representatives, and they would resent being held responsible for the students employed. Individual schools could not have shops, comparable to the YOU shop, where students not employed by industry could be assigned to work on products under contract with industry. Nor could the schools serve the conditioned dropout any more than they can now. An intermediary agency is needed—an agency to which the schools may send their students for work assignments and for supervision, and which will act as liaison with employers concerning jobs and student performance.

Obviously, this agency should be something like an expanded YOU. Its governing board should comprise representatives of employers, schools, and the community at large. It should be industry-oriented and provide an industrial atmosphere. It should endeavor to become self-supporting in its contract work. It should serve the actual dropout by continuing the present remedial reading and arithmetic programs. Some dropouts, moreover, should be introduced to adult occupational courses, particularly those offered by a postsecondary institution, yet to be established. The entire program should be underwritten by the community; private benefactors have carried it long enough.

The full persuasive powers of the entire community should be brought to bear on accrediting agencies to recognize high school credit granted for the work part of the program. The pressure of the entire community should be directed toward improvement of the provisions and the administration of child labor laws and other restrictions to assure the availability of work experience that will help youth to become employable.

In addition to providing the in-school programs necessary to prepare students for their first undertaking upon leaving school, the high schools should continue their community schools and adult education programs to the extent that their regular facilities will permit.

Facilities for Joint Offering of High School Occupational Courses and Postsecondary and Adult Education

Attention is now turned to (1) ways in which the high schools might offer cooperatively the more costly occupational courses that some of their students should have, and (2) the postsecondary educational facilities most suitable for filling the needs of Kalamazoo County.

The first possibility is for each school to specialize in some occupational area in which it may have a special interest and to contract with other schools to take students for training in these classes. This *sharing of facilities* has been tried in some of the larger cities, particularly where the schools are under the jurisdiction of one common board and where financing rests on a common tax base. Such circumstances simplify the contractual problems and make possible a variety of arrangements. For example, the students may either be taken by bus from their home schools to the school offering their specialization, or be required to enroll in the latter for all of their work.

It is difficult to point with certainty to places where this system has worked satisfactorily, and it seems ill-adapted to Kalamazoo County with its nine separate districts and boards of control. Each school would have to contract with every other school for each course. Bussing students to so many places would be quite inefficient. Problems would arise in opening the facilities to adults from all over the county. Furthermore, the total cost to the county of building and operating so many specialized facilities would surely be more than the cost of bringing them all together in one place.

A second way of providing programs cooperatively (common in the Carolinas, Kentucky, West Virginia, Georgia, and neighboring states) is for the community to build a *vocational education center,* for joint use by all of the high schools, where the more advanced and costly courses in vocational education can be conducted. The center is not really a school, but an equipped shop or collection of shops where certain classes can be held. The students remain enrolled in their home schools and receive credit in their home schools for the courses taken at the center. They are transported by bus to the center for the courses offered there.

The facilities of the center, as well as those of the high schools, are made available for adult programs when not in use for regular school programs. Adults may receive high school credit for such programs, if credit is wanted, at their own high schools. No credit for postsecondary technical or other organized programs is available, however, because the center is not a postsecondary institution.

A third kind of facility, one designed to serve the high schools and also to provide a broader program of vocational education and training for adults, is the *area vocational school.* It is owned and governed by a separate board. It operates as a school in every respect: it enrolls its own students, grants credits, and awards diplomas.

The area vocational school may operate on the secondary level, the postsecondary level, or both. Where such schools have been in operation over a period of time, however, as in Minnesota and Wisconsin, they have become more and more postsecondary in character. Their own secondary school graduates and the graduates of regular high schools want the more advanced vocational courses, and adults want to continue pursuit of knowledge and skills beyond the secondary level. Furthermore, where such postsecondary programs are available in a community, there is a tendency for high school students to postpone vocational education and training until after graduation. The reasons are several: the high school curricula are crowded with courses the students want and need; employers favor those who have had vocational training after high school graduation and have thereby acquired broader education and greater maturity; and parents and society generally favor a longer period of education and a later employment age.

The area vocational school provides several community services. One of its very important duties is to serve as the vocational education center for the high schools. It does this by conducting classes for the high schools or by making specialized facilities available for courses offered jointly by the schools themselves. Both are done on a contractual basis. The area school, in a sense, may also serve as an industrial high school so long as it offers a secondary program. In doing so, it establishes its own admission standards and is, therefore, not likely to become a dumping ground for the ill-prepared or the embittered potential dropout. It can provide a whole array of adult occupational training programs and grant secondary or postsecondary credits for them. The postsecondary credits may be accepted for transfer into the appropriate programs of colleges and universities offering such programs at the discretion of the admitting institutions.

Although the area vocational school is certain to offer courses in English, social sciences, physical sciences, mathematics, and other cultural areas, it cannot award the associate degree. Nor can its students transfer into the junior year of colleges and universities on the same basis as can graduates of community colleges.

A fourth way by which Kalamazoo County might make it possible for high schools to offer their students the more costly occupational courses, and at the same time meet the needs of adults, out-of-school youth, and others for postsecondary programs, is through the establishment of a *modern community college*. The modern community college should not be confused with its predecessor, the two-year liberal arts junior college. It is a community service institution offering the programs that the community demands. It cannot operate as a secondary vocational high school, but it can serve as a vocational education center for the high schools and do everything else that the area vocational school does. In addition, it can offer the first two years of college and such advanced vocational-technical programs as are ordinarily offered by a resident technical institute. For these it also awards the associate degree.

It is a basic part of the philosophy of the community college that all high school graduates, adults, and out-of-school youth are eligible for admission and may be enrolled in any program that the counselors believe the individual is prepared to undertake. The college may provide any program that the community wants and is willing and able to support—all the way from the skill programs offered under the provisions of the Manpower Development and Training Act and comparable laws to the more sophisticated technical programs.

The community college as a community service institution has had its longest experience in California, where it has served for more than fifty years. It is now spreading rapidly throughout much of the United States. It is Michigan's only area postsecondary institution, since neither the area vocational school nor the state-supported resident technical institute has taken root in the state.

Both the area vocational school and the community college are eligible for state and federal assistance. At present, the state is providing approximately half of the operating costs of community colleges and half

178

of the costs of new buildings and equipment, subject to a ceiling on each project and an annually budgeted total for the state. The colleges are eligible for federal assistance for construction of buildings under the Higher Education Facilities Act of 1964.

It would seem that the most appropriate institution for Kalamazoo County to use in providing the vocational-technical education and training programs needed by all of its people is the modern community college. It is the one instrument capable of meeting all of the needs, and it is in keeping with the system of postsecondary education developing in Michigan as well as in much of the United States.

CONCLUSIONS

Great need exists in Kalamazoo County for additional occupational education and training programs and facilities. These programs and facilities should be designed for the benefit of youth, adults, and industry, and at both the secondary and postsecondary levels.

First of all, the high schools should reconstruct their curricula around the principle of preparing each student for what he must undertake immediately upon leaving school. For the benefit of students and counselors, the schools should organize preparatory courses for postsecondary occupational education and for direct job entry that are parallel to the college preparatory course.

To accomplish the purpose, a way must be found for the high schools to provide work experience for those who need it as a part of preparation for direct job entry; and a way must also be found for offering cooperatively the needed costly occupational subjects that the individual schools cannot afford. A postsecondary institution is also needed to assure high school graduates, adults, and out-of-school youth access to the occupational subjects that they and industry need and want.

It is recommended that an intermediary organization be established, governed and supported jointly by the schools, industry, and the community, and operated by the schools and industry. It would be most helpful in providing work experience for school youth bound directly for employment.

It is also proposed that Kalamazoo County establish a modern community college that offers the vocational-technical programs needed by the community, as well as the first two years of college. This institution should also serve as a vocational education center where the high schools may offer cooperatively the more costly occupational courses that their students need.

179

11

INDUSTRY PARTICIPATION IN LOCAL PUBLIC SCHOOL VOCATIONAL AND TECHNICAL EDUCATION

SAMUEL M. BURT

THE CHALLENGE

Vocational and technical education, with its emphasis on preparation for jobs and careers in trade, industry, agriculture, business, and subprofessional fields has been likened to a giant astride both the public school system and the industrial economy. Naturally, therefore, vocational and technical educators have, since the earliest days of occupational program offerings in our schools, looked toward industry[1] for counsel concerning the content of these programs.

Recognition of the interdependence of industry and education was reflected in the rules and regulations issued by the U.S. Office of Education as far back as 1922. The description of duties of supervisors of trade and industrial education, then and now, includes cooperation with industry. Some states, notably Michigan, Pennsylvania, New York, and Indiana, have gone so far as to require, by legislation, that advisory committees from industry be appointed to consult with vocational and technical educators. Thus, occupational education, more than any other type, offers unlimited opportunity for involvement of and participation by representatives from industry. The effectiveness of such involvement and participation can well determine the practical effectiveness of the occupational education provided by the public schools for developing manpower resources.

The desirability of involving industry in local vocational and technical education programs is generally accepted. When the former U.S. Commissioner of Education, Francis Keppel, said to industry, "We are counting on you," he was simply reiterating statements made by vocational educators since before passage of the Smith-Hughes Act of 1917, generally recognized as the foundation for our present system of federal

---

[1] "Industry" or "industry people" will hereafter be used to designate representatives of business, the professions, labor, and agriculture.

support of vocational education. When the most recent past-president of the U.S. Chamber of Commerce pointed out that businessmen must keep the educator informed of industry's manpower needs so that better educational programs can be devised, he too was simply reiterating the long-accepted rationale for industry's involvement and participation in vocational and technical education.

Nor has there been much question as to the responsibility of educators to conduct the affairs of the schools and to arrange for effective utilization of industry people in vocational and technical education. Indeed, industry offers its services, its time, its personnel, and its funds in vain unless dynamic and imaginative leadership is exercised by educators in channeling and utilizing industry's interests and efforts. Both educators and industry agree that only through their cooperative effort, in all phases and at all levels of occupational education, can the public school system meet its responsibilities to the students, to the potential employers of these students, and to the public.

THE PROBLEMS

Many case studies have been reported on the successful and effective involvement of industry in vocational education,[2] but, as a general rule, educators have neither had time nor staff to maintain the required cooperative relationships. Efforts of national and state vocational educators to provide guidance in these matters to local school officials have largely been confined to establishment of "advisory committees," and to descriptions of functions and ways to conduct meetings. This emphasis on committee operation has tended to ignore the fact that a great deal of industry-education cooperation takes place through a variety of instrumentalities, and that informal activities arranged by instructors, coordinators, department heads, and other school officials are also pertinent vehicles and techniques. In addition, the literature on advisory committees ignores the realities in that they sometimes are and more frequently should be "operational" as well as "advisory." But, since they require a considerable amount of time and effort to organize on the part of already overburdened and understaffed vocational educators, they often exist only on paper, performing neither operational nor advisory roles effectively. Perhaps there is validity to the unofficial estimate of the American Vocational Association that some 20,000 advisory committees are

[2] The Upjohn Institute for Employment Research, with support by the Fund for the Advancement of Education of the Ford Foundation, has been engaged in a study of industry participation in local vocational and technical education programs.

functioning in schools offering vocational and technical education, and that approximately 100,000 industry people are involved. Nevertheless, the value of many such committees could well be questioned, especially those that meet only once a year for several hours.

The fundamental issue is not whether industry-education cooperating committees should or should not be organized by vocational and technical educators, or whether some other technique is preferable; rather, the basic problem is for educators to arrange for cooperation with industry in helping schools provide the meaningful educational and training experiences needed by young people and adults to become productive and knowledgeable citizens. Various types of committees have proved of value to educators. But other and less formal approaches may also prove effective. Educators need to appreciate the variety of ways whereby industry becomes involved and is persuaded to participate in local vocational and technical education programs. More than this, educators must learn how to develop involvement and participation by industry into something more—into a positive identification by industry with the community's problems and programs of occupational education at all levels of the educational system.

NATURE OF INDUSTRY-EDUCATION COOPERATIVE ACTIVITIES

Industry participation in occupational education is usually concerned with initiation of new programs or expansion or elimination of established programs, interpretation of manpower and skill requirements in terms of curriculum needs, development of curricula, acquisition of shop and laboratory equipment, recruitment of instructors and students, public relations, and evaluation of school programs. Almost every one of these activities includes a range of services which may be classified either as "advisory" or "operational," depending upon the leadership exercised by the school people and the extent to which industry representatives are persuaded to become involved.

An example may be useful. Industry participation in manpower and skill requirements surveys[3] may include:

[3] Many school systems prefer to conduct manpower and skill needs surveys, utilizing U.S. Employment Service reports simply as resource material. There is need for greater cooperation between school officials and the Employment Service to avoid this obvious duplication of effort, and for the Service to obtain in its surveys the kind of information needed by educators in developing curricula. The Vocational Education Act of 1963 calls for such cooperation. Dialogue between vocational educators and the Employment Service, at the national and state levels, should soon result in more effective utilization by schools of the manpower specialists, as well as the testing and counseling staff, and services of the Employment Service.

1. Advising the school staff as to which companies should be included in the survey.

2. Advising the school staff as to specific information to be included in the survey instrument.

3. Providing information requested in the survey instrument.

4. Providing job analysis information.

5. Calling on employers in the community, urging them to fill in and return the survey instrument.

6. Reviewing the survey report prepared by the school people and suggesting revisions where considered necessary.

7. Testifying at meetings of the board of education in support of the findings of the survey.

Thus industry representatives may participate and become involved in vocational and technical education programs operationally as well as in an advisory capacity.

Another example which makes this duality of industry participation clear concerns the problem of equipping a school shop for a particular occupational program. Educators may ask industry for advice on specific equipment to be obtained for a shop. On the other hand, educators may request industry to arrange for donations of the equipment. It is the responsibility and the quality of school leadership which is decisive in determining the nature and extent of industry cooperation.

FACTORS MOTIVATING INDUSTRY TO PARTICIPATE IN OCCUPATIONAL EDUCATION

A variety of factors motivate industry groups and individuals to offer their cooperation, counsel, advice, and participation in school programs designed to prepare students for employability in particular occupations. An understanding of these factors will help educators perform their critical role of leadership.

Generally, industry people would like to have the school assume the burdens of recruiting and training potential new employees; they would like the prestige which accrues to their industry and organization as a result of the offering of their program by the schools; and they welcome the opportunity to engage in an educational activity which satisfies their sense of civic duty and pride in public service.

Unfortunately, industry does not always clearly understand the problems of the educational institution, and vice versa. Here the educators have to take initiative to clarify and resolve difficulties of communication, rapport, and collaboration. For instance, industry may not develop definitive manpower policies, nor feel any commitment to employ graduates of the school occupational programs which they may have even helped establish. Yet industry expects the schools to meet its needs for new employees. At the same time, schools may be providing youth with skills for occupations rapidly becoming outmoded and disappearing. Here again educators have to comprehend and deal effectively with the variety of factors that motivate industry people and trade groups to work with school people. For example, recognition of these factors would lead school officials to include in their catalogs the names of industry representatives who are serving in an advisory capacity to the school in developing its course offerings. Not only would this simple technique afford a great deal of personal satisfaction and pride to the industry people involved, but it would also inform the prospective student, his parents, and guidance counselors that industry is indeed identified with the occupational education program of the school and school system.

INSTRUMENTALITIES FOR
ACHIEVING INDUSTRY-EDUCATION COOPERATION

Three major techniques or instrumentalities have been utilized by educators for involving industry people in vocational and technical education programs:

1. The advisory committee.

2. The school-appointed coordinator or special consultant for industry liaison.

3. The local trade and professional associations in the community.

These instrumentalities are not mutually exclusive. Actually, the extent to which they are interlocked can be indicative of a high degree of industry-education cooperation, with each being utilized where and when best suited to accomplish a particular objective.

These same instrumentalities for achieving industry-education cooperation are also utilized in special types of occupational education. Examples are the advisory committee for occupational rehabilitation programs in hospitals and correctional institutions and the advisory committees appointed under the rules and regulations of the Manpower Development and Training Act. Industry-education cooperation in these programs, as such, are not discussed in this paper for two reasons—

first, our major concern is with the public school system; and second, much of what we have to say concerning industry participation in occupational education applies generally, regardless of the types of program served.

Advisory Committees

The Occupational Committee. Some schools have established an advisory committee for each occupational program offered, e.g., printing, plumbing, data processing, etc. Los Angeles Trade-Technical College has over fifty committees, all of which meet at least once a year; Denver Opportunity School has over eighty committees, which also meet at least once annually. On the other hand, some schools offer a number of programs with only a few of the advisory committees meeting annually.

Practically all of the literature on industry participation and involvement in vocational and technical education has concerned itself primarily with occupational advisory committees formally organized by school officials. The manuals and guidelines published by various national and local industry groups, as well as by educational agencies and organizations, emphasize that these committees exist only "to advise" school officials. The disparity between this "theory" and the practice of educators to involve industry operationally in vocational and technical education has led to considerable confusion among both educators and industry representatives as to the actual role of the advisory committee. Much of this confusion could be eliminated if occupational committees were more realistically termed "industry-education cooperating committees." However, since the "advisory" nomenclature is currently in use, we have no alternative at this time but to continue referring to these committees as "advisory."

Occupational committees have proven to be a cumbersome technique for achieving many of the objectives and benefits which can be derived from industry involvement and participation in vocational and technical education. These committees are not substantially different from the committees to be found in other economic, social, political, religious, and cultural institutions. The committee accomplishes little or nothing without effective leadership and staff work. In vocational and technical education, successful committee leadership may stem from one or two industry members who have some background and experience in teaching, training, or school administration; more frequently it comes from school officials who are assigned the responsibility for developing industry-education cooperative activities—both informally and through formally organized committees. Most schools, particularly comprehensive high schools offering occupational education programs, as well as vocational high schools, are not able, because of lack of funds and/or interest, to assign staff for this purpose. Thus, committees are either not organized or, if organized, soon become inactive. The prodigious amount of time and effort required for educators to develop formal, organized relationships with industry in the form of advisory committees has frequently worked against any continuing effort. No matter how well motivated school officials may be in organizing such committees, often it is only a matter of time, usually a short period of time, until the committee ceases to function except for an occasional *pro forma* meeting. Thereafter, school officials maintain such relationships as they do through personal contact with individuals from industry whose judgment they trust, and with whom they feel comfortable, and who are willing to provide advice when called upon. This is true even in many local schools and school systems where state law requires the organization of local advisory committees. Many of these committees simply exist on paper.

Another problem puzzling educators and industry people is whether or not an occupational committee should be established only when specific problems develop, or as a continuing body. A task-force committee may be appointed by the school or school system to assist in meeting a particular problem, and be dissolved upon completion of the assigned task. Or a committee may be appointed to serve the school on a continuing basis, meeting one or more times annually to discuss and resolve a variety of problems. On occasion such committees may use subcommittees for special purposes. The occasional use of task-force or *ad hoc* committees holds many advantages in that their interest and efforts are confined to resolution of single problems in relatively short periods of time; however, such committees do not provide a foundation, such as offered by continuing committees, to develop long-term participation, involvement, and identification by industry in education. On the other hand, without proper leadership and staff services by the educators, it is better not to use committees at all. Inactive or ineffectual committees of industry people will inevitably develop a group of disgruntled critics of the occupational program and of the leadership of the schools.

While numerous case studies of effective formal industry-education cooperative relationships can be documented, they are still the exception rather than the rule, particularly at the secondary school level. Furthermore, in metropolitan areas, there is woeful lack of an organized cooperative relationship between occupational committees for the various vocational and technical schools within the boundaries of a given school system, as well as between various levels of occupational education, and between schools and industry.

For instance, although most school systems offer more or less extensive programs of exploratory occupational programs, known as industrial arts, such programs rarely have the benefit of the services of any occupational advisory committees which may exist for vocational and technical education programs. The anomaly is that more students are usually involved in the industrial arts programs and more money is spent by many school systems for the equipment and salaries of instructors in industrial arts than is spent on vocational and technical education programs.

Also, in some large school systems with secondary vocational schools, area vocational schools, and technical institutes, each type of school may have different occupational advisory committees for similar programs. Yet no effort is made to coordinate the activities of the advisory committees, nor to articulate the program offerings between the secondary and post-high school levels. Rarely is any effort made to develop relationships between occupational educational programs and their advisory committees in adjacent school systems in a metropolitan area. There are seldom, if ever, any joint meetings arranged by educators to discuss mutual problems of occupational advisory committees from the several school systems involved, unless perhaps a local industry group for that area takes the initiative in calling such a meeting. Usually such meetings or discussions are possible only because some of the members on the various advisory committees are also members of the education committee of the local trade or professional association. Finally, seldom is any effort made to relate the occupational education curricula with on-the-job training programs of industry, despite the fact that advisory committees have participated in developing a specific school curriculum for a particular occupation.

The General Advisory Committee. Effective coordination and articulation of occupational education programs within a school system, and between school systems, is impeded because of strong differences of opinion among occupational educators responsible for various types of programs and the objectives of these programs. What is needed is an over-all *system* of occupational education and training for all the youth and adults in a community who need and desire such education. School administrators acknowledge the need for such systems of occupational education, rather than groups of uncoordinated programs, and it would appear reasonable and logical for an administrator to have the benefit of the advice and counsel of a general advisory committee, composed of industry people from all segments of the community, in developing such a system.

In practice, however, few local school systems utilize such general advisory committees. Most school superintendents are not willing to establish an advisory committee for their over-all vocational and technical education programs because they feel they are already working with so many committees, including their boards, that another committee is simply one too many. To persuade school superintendents of the need for and value of such general committees is a difficult task for vocational and technical educators for a variety of reasons. Not the least of these is the generally unfavorable attitude and lack of interest of a great number of school principals, superintendents, and their boards in occupational education programs. However, now that public attention has been focused on occupational education as evidenced by the variety of federal legislation since 1958 dealing with vocational and technical education and manpower development, school superintendents and boards of education should certainly be more interested in developing ways and means for improving these programs. A general advisory committee can be one of the important techniques.

There is little literature on the subject of general advisory committees; therefore, various school systems will have to experiment with methods for achieving effective utilization of such committees. Nevertheless, some guidelines can be provided—e.g., that special staff be assigned by the superintendent's office to work with the advisory committee; that the committee be organized on a continuing basis and meet several times annually; that it be responsible to the superintendent and his supervisory staff for reviewing reports from occupational committees and recommending priorities for occupational programs; and that it be advisory in name as well as function. This is an important distinction since, as pointed out earlier, occupational advisory committees serve in both an operating and advisory capacity and might better be designated "cooperating committees."

Unless fragmentation of occupational education programs ceases to exist in the schools serving a metropolitan area, both at the school system level and for individual occupational programs, effective involvement, participation, and identification of industry people with occupational education will remain an unattainable goal.

The Local Joint Apprenticeship and Training Committee (JATC). The local JATC exists for many of the skilled apprenticeable craft occupations in a number of communities. The organization of local JATC's is promoted by the Bureau of Apprenticeship and Training of the U.S. Department of Labor (established by the National Apprenticeship Act of 1937) and by state apprenticeship agencies, usually established by appropriate state legislation. The JATC itself is organized through joint voluntary agreement of management and labor unions by means of local collective bargaining agreements. The membership of the committee, for those crafts for which JATC's are formed, usually consists of three representatives from management and three from labor. Educators do not usually serve as members of the committee.

The JATC can be a potent instrument of industry-education cooperation for improving manpower development programs in the skilled trades. It is generally responsible for the selection, training, education, and placement of the apprentices within the craft over which it has jurisdiction. In its relationship with vocational and technical schools, the JATC arranges for the use of school facilities to provide approximately 144 hours or more of instruction during the school year for at least the first several years of apprenticeship. Salaries of instructors, school coordinators and administrators, as well as certain operating expenses involved in apprentice related education, are reimbursable from funds available under federal and state vocational education legislation. In large vocational schools and post-high school institutions and school systems, the school officials provide coordinators to work with the JATC's, which may number up to twenty in a particular school according to the variety of apprentice programs offered. The Los Angeles school system provides nine coordinators for some sixty JATC's in the area.

In addition to its responsibilities to the apprentice programs, the JATC is utilized by many schools as the occupational advisory committee for their regular day-school programs. When so used, there is created the novel problem of adapting an administrative body to serve in an advisory capacity. Most school officials prefer to keep the JATC as a separate group, even though some of its members may serve on the occupational committee. Since the JATC is established by management and labor to work with the schools under legislative sanctions, and is not a "creature" of the schools per se, it is obvious that relationship problems can develop between the school and the JATC's, particularly since these committees can bring the weight of union leadership and pressure to bear on school officials. Such pressures are not usually welcomed by educators. However, some educators have learned to utilize this "political pressure" of the JATC to the benefit of their particular school program in obtaining funds from the local board of education and state agencies.

In recent years there has been a growing trend for local JATC's to employ full- and part-time coordinators or training directors. Salaries and expenses of this staff are paid from educational trust funds established by management-union collective bargaining agreements and maintained by contributions from employers on a per employee basis.[4] These funds are also used to purchase equipment and supplies, and to subsidize instructors for the apprentice-related education programs in the schools. Rarely is this equipment permitted to be used by regular day-school students.

Some interesting questions are posed by providing local JATC's their own operating funds, particularly since many economists and educators believe that apprenticeship is declining as a technique for developing skilled manpower. The first set of questions is concerned with public policy: Should schools continue to provide space as requested by the JATC for equipment belonging to the committee and used only by apprentice and journeymen members of the particular union with which the JATC is connected? Classroom and shop space is in critical shortage in vocational and technical schools. Can school administrators afford to give up this space for use by special groups for only part of the school day?

A second set of questions is concerned with the role of the JATC coordinator as the staff member of the committee. Among his responsibilities is the maintenance of records of employment and age groupings of journeymen and apprentices, and projections as to manpower needs in their crafts. Coordinators are also beginning to involve their JATC's more and more in the regular day- and evening-school programs affecting their craft. Will they exercise leadership to continue or change union practices in restricting entrance into the trades, including discrimination against Negroes? Furthermore, will they be able to persuade their local unions and JATC's to expand the infrequent practice of shortening the apprenticeship period by providing credit towards journeyman status for those who have completed school pre-apprentice programs? Such recognition, recommended by most international and national unions, would in effect be an endorsement of vocational education in the schools. This action, more than anything else, can help attract young people into the skilled trades and boost the prestige of vocational education generally. If the JATC coordinators can help JATC's to accept these challenges and perform their responsibilities so that the best interests of young

---

[4] Some unions are using these funds to establish local union-management–operated training centers for apprentice and skill upgrading programs. Unions are also beginning to conduct training programs as prime contractors under the Manpower Development and Training Act.

people, the schools, and the nation's economy are properly served, their influence and leadership in occupational education and training in schools and industry will be beyond measure.

While the JATC currently plays a minor role as an instrumentality of industry-education cooperative effort in developing occupational education programs in the schools, it must be noted that the meetings of the JATC's are generally well attended and that, for the most part, the members are deeply involved in the business of the committees. Apparently having "something to do," plus the constant promotional effort from federal and state apprenticeship agencies and from education directors of the national unions, helps to develop in committee members a sense of identification with the manpower education and training program of their industry. Vocational and technical educators might find many useful parallels and guidelines from the JATC movement in developing more effective occupational and general advisory committees for their schools.

The Industry Coordinator or Special Industry Consultant

The term "coordinator" is usually applied to teachers associated with distributive, diversified, and cooperative education. Coordinators are responsible for developing relationships with employers for part-time job placement of their students, supervision of the students while on the job, and for some classroom instruction. However, in this paper the term coordinator is applied to staff assigned to supervise several related departments comprising an entire industry or group of related industry or technical education programs. For example, there could be one coordinator for all health service educational programs, one coordinator for all construction industry educational programs, and one coordinator for all graphic arts programs such as printing, commercial art, and advertising production. If the number of students and instructors in a related group of programs is not sufficient to warrant a coordinator, then the coordinator is assigned additional programs. Formulas for assigning responsibilities to such coordinators vary among the schools and school systems. It is the coordinator, generally, who is directly responsible for developing relationships with industry people and advisory committees for school programs under his jurisdiction. While instructors and department heads also develop and maintain their own industry relationships, they usually keep the coordinator informed of any direct contact made for a specific purpose, such as placing a student in a job, obtaining a donation of some expendable supply item, etc.

The coordinator's interests and abilities are those of an administrator. He enjoys organizing, attending, and speaking at meetings of industry groups, interpreting industry manpower needs to school people, and helping translate these needs into school programs. He is comfortable in dealing with industry executives as well as with teachers and is skilled in the leadership techniques of group dynamics.

The coordinator is particularly helpful, through his daily contacts with industry people, in determining which individuals are in a position to assist the school concerning a particular problem, and who should be asked to serve on advisory committees and subcommittees. For example, if the problem is one of developing or revising a curriculum or course of study, the coordinator would want to utilize plant superintendents, foremen, and supervisors. On the other hand, if the problem is concerned with obtaining costly equipment which the school cannot afford to buy, the coordinator would want to go to employers and top executives of cooperating industry organizations.

School people assigned the full-time responsibility for industry liaison are unquestionably extremely important in gaining industry-education cooperation for vocational and technical education programs. Most post-high school institutions offering vocational programs, particularly the comparatively new institutions such as junior and community colleges, assign coordinators and/or departmental heads or industry consultants to staff their occupational advisory committees and to develop both formal and informal cooperative industry-education relationships. Part of the salary of this staff, better designated as industry consultants than coordinators, is reimbursable under provisions of the Vocational Education Act of 1963. This is also true for the secondary-level school vocational and technical education program staff assigned to industry liaison. Hopefully more school systems will take advantage of this provision of the Act.

Local Trade and Professional Associations

Frequently, the initiative for developing industry-education relationships emanates from local trade and professional associations. These associations exist for almost every occupational and professional activity of our industrial economy. Many of the organizations concerned with the improvement of their industry or profession establish educational committees. One of the major committee activities is sooner or later connected with vocational and/or technical education.[5] Many industry

[5] The U.S. Department of Labor is encouraging national and local trade associations to become prime contractors to conduct training programs under the Manpower Development and Training Act.

members of school and MDTA (Manpower Development and Training Act) advisory committees are selected from the educational committees of these associations.

If the association is large enough to have a paid executive secretary, he usually provides for a continuing relationship with school instructors, department heads, and coordinators for his association and the industry it represents. He is intimately acquainted with most of the individuals and companies comprising the membership of his association, and thus the school people find him a ready source of information and assistance concerning any industry-education cooperative relationships. The executive secretary provides staff services to the association's education committee, and the membership expects him to represent them in all their official relationships with the schools and the general public. Depending on his initiative and interest, the association executive may become very active in occupational education programs. At the very least, he can be helpful to school people when called upon.

Frequently, the education committee of a local association is chaired by a member who is vitally interested in educational matters and is willing and anxious to devote considerable time to school affairs. The other members of the committee will usually follow his recommendations and support his efforts. When an association's education committee chairman and the executive secretary are both interested in developing working relationships with the schools, there is almost no limit to the extent of the cooperation the schools will receive from that particular industry or professional group.

Local associations of professional people, such as chemists and engineers, usually do not have an executive secretary. However, it is not unusual to find their educational committee members extremely active. Membership on the educational committee is frequently sought as a "prize" assignment. These groups usually prefer to work with post-high school educators in order to establish and conduct technician level programs for their professional field of interest.

Local associations obtain from their members, and from the national associations with which they are affiliated, a variety of instructional and career opportunity literature and material which they distribute, usually free, to instructors and guidance counselors. Filmstrips, slides, transparencies, motion pictures, recordings, displays, texts, suggested curricula, career literature, maps, charts, research reports, model construction kits, and bulletin board material are provided. Local associations are also very helpful in any school and local employment service effort to conduct industry manpower and skill needs surveys, recruit students, obtain donations of supplies and equipment, and evaluate effectiveness of the school program for the specific industry or profession represented by the association.

Area and state regional industry-development commissions and local chambers of commerce, in recent years, have become deeply interested and involved in the general problems of vocational and technical education. These organizations, particularly the local chambers, have established special committees of industry and community leaders to cooperate in conducting areawide surveys of industries' manpower needs and relating these needs to curricula offered by the vocational and technical education programs of the public schools; they have supported bond issues for building new vocational schools and community colleges and have been involved in a host of other activities designed to improve the supply of skilled manpower in their communities and areas.

It should be noted that a great deal of local employer, labor organization, and professional association activity connected with school programs is promoted by the national associations with which they are affiliated. A number of national associations and labor unions maintain close working relationships with the U.S. Office of Education and the American Vocational Association as well as the American Association of Junior Colleges, the American Industrial Arts Association, and the American Personnel and Guidance Association. In cooperation with these educational organizations, the industry and professional groups develop curricula, instructional, and career literature and materials for distribution to school people, as well as guidelines for affiliated local associations in developing local industry-education cooperative relationships.

In an effort to coordinate the numerous local industry-education cooperative activities at the regional level, California educators, businessmen, and labor leaders have formed two regional groups—the Southern California Industry-Education Council and the Northern California Industry-Education Council. They are currently serving primarily as clearinghouses for dissemination of information about specific local industry-education cooperative activities. They also held annual conferences of industry leaders and educators to explore development of more effective means for industry-education cooperation, and to encourage the formation of local school system advisory committees. Both Councils have full-time, paid executive secretaries. Membership dues provide operating funds for the Councils, with the major share coming from companies in the area.

SOME DIRECTIONAL GUIDELINES FOR THE FUTURE

The school officials responsible for occupational education who find the task of developing industry-education cooperation too burdensome, should not complain when such cooperation is lacking. Neither should they be surprised by criticism that the occupational education programs of the schools are failing to meet the needs of the community and its industry, nor in seeing the vocational school, at the secondary level in particular, decline as an important facet of the manpower development, utilization, and training program of the community. Those educators interested in involving industry in occupational education have a variety of techniques and instrumentalities available for achieving effective industry-education cooperation.

A first step to be considered is the appointment of a general advisory committee by the superintendent of schools and the board of education. This committee should meet periodically, on a continuing basis, to review the over-all occupational education program of the community and its schools and to advise on new requirements and priorities. The general advisory committee should be composed of leading members of the industrial, business, professional, labor, and educational organizations in the community. To assist them in their deliberations and recommendations, resource staff from the public school system, industry, and the behavioral sciences should be provided as needed.

Specific occupational "cooperating" committees would be the second major step, if the schools and school system can arrange to provide staff services to such committees. Such staff may be designated as coordinators or industry-liaison consultants where the school system is large enough. In smaller school systems, time should be provided for this activity on the part of supervisors, department heads, and/or instructors.

Industry liaison, both formal and informal, is a vital responsibility of vocational and technical education, and cannot be left to haphazard and accidental arrangements. This has been recognized by the U.S. Office of Education in providing that part of the salary of personnel involved in coordinating industry-education acitivities is reimbursable under the provisions of the Vocational Education Act of 1963. Those schools and school systems which seriously desire to enlist industry participation in their vocational and technical education programs have found such co-ordinating staff a *sine qua non* in developing effective industry-education cooperative efforts.

Particularly important to the development of effective industry involvement in vocational and technical education is the need for educators to provide cooperating industry people with detailed checklists as to how

196

they may best serve the various needs of schools. Providing a checklist to industry groups has proven extremely helpful in terms of initiating and establishing new programs in the schools. Criteria checklists such as those developed by the American Council on Education can be just as helpful to industry groups in evaluating the effectiveness of individual occupational programs, as well as the over-all vocational and technical education program, of a particular school and school system. In other areas of industry-education cooperation, such as recruiting students, curriculum development, and participation in manpower needs and skill surveys, checklists should be developed which would indicate desirable goals to be achieved. A few examples of such goals are: the articulation of school curricula to correspond to industry in-plant training programs; closer relationship among, and rationalization of, employer hiring practices, manpower and skill requirement studies, and job placement efforts of the schools; more industrial experience as a phase of the out-service training of instructors; simplification and standardization of industry job titles and school curricula offerings; and conduct of community or area industry-wide recruitment and public relations efforts in cooperation with schools.

Crucial to the development of effective industry-education cooperation is the need for correcting the woeful lack of organized cooperative relationships among the advisory committees of the various types of vocational and technical schools within the boundaries of a given school system or metropolitan labor market area. It appears to be the rule rather than the exception for school systems to develop and offer occupational education programs without regard to what is offered in the neighboring school systems. Yet each of the programs is attempting to meet industry's needs for a particular metropolitan area. There is also the need for articulating the occupational programs of the secondary schools with post-high school as well as industrial arts programs within the community. Perhaps even more importantly, there is the need for developing some formalized relationships between local school system advisory committees—whether established voluntarily or by state mandate—and the state advisory councils established in accordance with provisions of the Vocational Education Act of 1963. Where effective local industry-education cooperation is found, much of its great potential is negated by many state advisory councils which are either inactive or unaware of such local programs. The need for state level guidance, leadership, and coordination of industry-education activities is very great. This need can be met only if the state boards of vocational education, the state directors, and the state advisory councils accept in full measure the responsibilities assigned to them by the Vocational Education Act of 1963. These responsibilities include developing all-inclusive statewide programs of vocational and technical education, as well as developing cooperative working relations with other manpower utilization and education- and training-centered agencies such as the state employment services and their local and state advisory committees.

The U.S. Office of Education, through its rules, regulations, and reporting requirements for state boards and directors of vocational and technical education, as required by the Vocational Education Act, is playing an important role in stimulating the development of more effective state planning, supervision, and coordination of local programs. National, state, and local educational organizations can be of material assistance in this movement by urging their members to be constantly on the alert to participate in and provide necessary leadership to develop effective, coordinated industry-education cooperative relationships, both formally and informally. An entirely new body of literature is called for. What is particularly needed is a continuing series of case study reports in the journals and at the annual meetings of these organizations.

National employer, professional, and labor organization which have been or will become involved in vocational and technical education programs must also provide their state and local affiliates and memberships with guidelines and case study reports rooted in good practice rather than in the rhetoric of much of their present literature. There is certainly the need for urging local industry and professional people to participate in community and statewide programs of vocational and technical education; but without "how-to-do-it" guidelines and case-study reports, local industry groups and individuals, as well as educators, are left to develop their own trial-and-error techniques. There is no need for such haphazard methods because numerous examples of good local industry-education cooperative programs can be documented, as illustrated in the Upjohn Institute for Employment Research study of local industry-education cooperation. Thus, we see a need for closer cooperation at the national level between educational agencies and organizations and industry associations in developing, publishing, and disseminating on a continuing basis the "how-to" literature of industry-education cooperation so sorely needed at the local and state levels.

In calling upon industry for advice and assistance, vocational and technical educators have recognized that their responsibilities can be better discharged with the help of those segments of our economy which have a vital stake in the education and training of youth and adults. As this country enters the last third of the twentieth century, educators are beginning to recognize that developing rational manpower utilization policies and programs are woven into the whole fabric of our extremely complex economy and society, and that they need the advice, counsel, and guidance of individuals and groups other than those connected with industry. The time has come to broaden the "industry-education team" to include economists and other behavioral scientists such as psychologists and sociologists. The disciplines represented by these professions will assist educators in resolving many of the problems plaguing them—how to involve industry more effectively in their programs, how to meet the manpower and skill needs of industry, and how to motivate youth and adults to prepare themselves for the world of work and its changing needs in order to become productive and knowledgeable participants in our nation's economy and culture. In addition, these "new" team members may help educators and industry to add a new dimension to vocational education—that of job creation. If there is any validity to the thesis that occupational education is an integral part of the total educational program of our schools, as well as the manpower development program of our nation, then local vocational and technical educators, as well as industry people, will find the insights and expertise of the behavioral scientists advantageous in broadening their vision and scope.

This, perhaps, is the greatest need of educators today. They must broaden their vision to recognize that industry participation and involvement in the occupational program of our public school system is not a goal in itself. Rather it is the means for developing a sense of identification on the part of representatives from all segments of our economy in the programs and problems of the schools. To achieve this identification, more than occasional meetings and sporadic cooperative activities of educators and industry people is required. Educators must provide ways, means, and strategies so that industry people may identify themselves with, and feel themselves full-fledged partners in solving, the problems of the schools and school systems of our nation. Only through such a partnership will our schools and our communities be in a position to offer purposeful, meaningful, and effective education for the world of work.

12

ECONOMIC VIABILITY OF COMMUNITIES IN A CONTEXT OF NATIONAL CHANGE [1]

A. HARVEY BELITSKY

This paper uses a case study of community adaptation to alterations in market demand and industrial location as a basis for generalizations on the problem of local adjustment. The community is Erie County, Pennsylvania. Its experience in a national environment of continuing economic change provides some insight into present and future situations, challenges, and opportunities common to other areas as well. Since the discussion is concerned with community welfare, it necessarily takes account of many factors in addition to manpower resources and manpower policy.

ABILITY TO COMPETE CRUCIAL TO ECONOMIC GROWTH

The geographic diffusion of industry has made many communities more vulnerable to nationwide economic fluctuations and more dependent for survival on the ability of local industries to compete.[2] Several recent government programs reinforce this interarea competitive trend. The diffusion of industry has, of course, helped to diversify the economic base of many localities; and, while such diversification is

[1] Several of the generalizations in this paper are based upon selected findings in *The Job Hunt: Job-Seeking Behavior of Unemployed Workers in a Local Economy* (Baltimore: The Johns Hopkins Press, 1966) by Harold L. Sheppard and A. Harvey Belitsky.

[2] New and growing industries are still arising and they will surely continue to develop. At the same time, however, research findings of the Department of Commerce, Resources for the Future, Inc., and the National Planning Association have disclosed a diffusion of industry mixes over broad regions of the United States during recent decades. The existence of national markets for numerous products denotes substantially improved efficiency in transportation and communication media. In addition, national corporations have recognized that economies result from the establishment of branch organizations. Hence, there has been a tendency for growing, constant, and declining industries to be more equally distributed over all economic regions. Under such conditions, growth of an industry in any region or local economy depends upon that industry's ability to *compete* effectively against rivals located elsewhere.

actually desirable, it also enlarges the domain in which a community must compete and therefore does not assure local prosperity. In this new setting, the well-being of most workers depends not only upon the competitive success of local industries but also upon the individual's capacity for making necessary adjustments in the local labor market. Recent government measures for providing greater equality of opportunity may help individuals to make more satisfactory present and future economic choices.

Obviously these trends toward heightened and more subtle competition in local industries and local labor markets will not be expressed in a completely automatic or uniform manner throughout the economy.[3] The passage of legislation aimed at equalizing opportunities will not readily or significantly diminish the relative advantages held by established firms and individuals. And some communities, firms, and individuals will for various reasons (including the imperfect transmission of information) simply fail to apply for available government assistance. Nevertheless, the labor force and the business management of a community may be extensively upgraded in response to environmental changes and opportunities. This improvement could signify both a better utilization of persons already employed as well as the acquisition of jobs by unemployed persons, who, even during relatively prosperous times, qualify only for the least demanding jobs.

GENERAL CONDITIONS FOR MAINTAINING SOUND LOCAL ECONOMIES

Our study of the Erie experience indicates the wide range of factors that bear on a community's economic well-being, especially its ability to meet the challenges of intensifying intercommunity competition. These factors are important for other communities as well as Erie. They are stated as five generalizations below.

1. Local entrepreneurship, including interfirm or community innovations, can support and even diversify a local economic base; and indigenous manpower programs aimed at the more effective and full development of individuals can be as crucial as the introduction of new

---

[3] It might appear that the increasing importance of the service industries as sources of employment could act as a counterforce to the more extensive competition obtaining in several industries, since many services are highly personal, which naturally signifies that the location of such industries must be diffused to practically the same extent as population. However, the relative growth of service industries within a locality will be strongly related to the success of other industries which do face competition in regional and national markets.

products and processes. Mutual benefits are achievable for businessmen and employees through, say, the improvement of labor skill projections and the greater participation of youths in secondary school education and on-the-job training. Moreover, a local economy can still attain a "comparative advantage" in one or another industrial field through the more imaginative and more comprehensive development and use of its human resources.[4]

2. A local community must be alert to new opportunities for bolstering its economic base through benefits from federal and state programs (e.g., with respect to highway transportation, training, all levels of education, area redevelopment, and technical assistance). In addition, the aid provided by any one program should not be considered merely an isolated gift but, instead, a potential link to, and reinforcement of, other public and private programs.

3. Some federal and state programs will strengthen the economic base of particular localities, and not necessarily the "disadvantaged" ones. Whereas, for instance, certain of the unaided communities may be relatively indifferent to the allocation of defense contracts to electronics firms, other localities will be affected, and only special alertness or "defensive" responses may insure that a previously established economic position does not deteriorate.

4. Significant changes in technology and the shift of population can require substantial adjustments for the continuing viability of local economies. For example, since some new technologies will be less capital-intensive or less dependent on indigenous resources, proximity to growing markets can assume paramount significance as new or expanded facilities are constructed.

5. The federal government's contributions to high levels of total economic activity will ensure that competition among communities does not take the dominant form of mere "piracy." Structurally oriented programs, such as those initiated under the Economic Opportunity Act, can also enlarge local competitiveness and lead to a higher level of national output than would have occurred in the absence of the public expenditures. In a real sense, then, the government can be an entrepreneur or innovator; it may directly enhance employment to meet social needs, and it may, through contracts and through impacts upon private costs and profits, induce firms to establish new industries, diversify product lines, and supply new services.

---

[4] This statement is consistent with Dr. Harvey Perloff's finding that the availability of an adequate work force has become less important as a force attracting new firms and industries.

THE ERIE ECONOMY, 1954–64

The economy of Erie County has, like most others, been based on a diversity of industries in the past. Previously important industries—shipbuilding, fishing, and railroad and port activities—have waned. Each of these industries and numerous others could, at different times, have been classified in the growth category, i.e., their employment or value of output increased at faster rates than the average for all industries.

But for several decades the metals and machinery industries have remained major sources of employment. Paper manufacturing has also been important, while firms in the rubber and plastics group have been developing rapidly. Furthermore, in Erie, as elsewhere, nonmanufacturing employment surpassed the total number of jobholders in manufacturing in recent years.

Despite substantial declines, durable goods manufacturing continues to occupy a key position in Erie's economy. This relatively volatile and cyclical sector was responsible for most of the heavy unemployment during 1954–64; the unemployment rate ranged from a high of 13.2 percent in the 1958 recession to a low of 5.4 percent in both 1956 and 1964.

In 1954 and the following years, employment declined (although not consistently) at a much sharper rate than the local labor force. A lagging, but ultimately forceful response to declining employment opportunities is illustrated in the volume of outmigration, which during the years 1960–62 exceeded the total for the entire 1950–60 decade.

The period of substantial unemployment in Erie was one of generally slow growth in the national economy. Weakness in aggregate demand was reflected especially in the employment record of industries that manufactured durable goods. In fact, nationally, between 1955 and 1963, the output of such industries increased to only a minor extent; and employment was practically constant.

Erie's important manufacturing sector has been especially sensitive to the transport element of costs. An estimated 50 percent of Erie's manufacturing employment has been regarded as heavily dependent on transport costs in national markets. This figure contrasts with 35 percent for manufacturing employment in the entire United States.[5]

---

[5] Based on special tabulations for 1958 by the U.S. Bureau of the Census for the National Industrial Conference Board. For the actual development of various "dominant locational factors," see Robert M. Lichtenberg, *One-Tenth of a Nation* (Cambridge: Harvard University Press, 1960).

Plant Shutdowns

Besides the impediment of slow national growth, the local economy lost about 8,500 jobs between 1955 and 1963 when several manufacturing firms moved their facilities from Erie or simply terminated operations. The loss in this period was about 19 percent of average employment in Erie manufacturing for the years 1950–54. On the other hand, approximately one-third of this loss was offset by new manufacturing operations introduced during the same period.

The most significant industrial loss occurred in June, 1955, when General Electric, the county's major employer, completed the move of its refrigerator production facilities to Louisville, Kentucky. The company cited numerous reasons for its move, but the most important attraction was apparently the opportunity of relocating close to expanding markets.

Several studies have observed that the more rapidly expanding durable goods manufacturing industries were locating in the South and West during the decade 1950–60. This phenomenon has operated to Erie's disadvantage. Erie's experience has been somewhat similar to that of the Pittsburgh region, which has also specialized in electrical equipment but has not realized much gain in such fast-growing branches of the industry as household appliances and electronics.

In time, General Electric did find it technically and economically desirable to centralize most of its motor and generator division in Erie. This decision accounted for much of the offset to the 1955–63 job loss cited above. Nevertheless, intraplant adjustments resulted in a large net reduction in the number of female blue-collar workers.

Job-Order Firms

In addition to plant movements to more favorable markets, the job-order or contract basis of the operations of many local manufacturers helps to explain the employment contraction. Since firms that normally placed contracts with the Erie job-order manufacturers were experiencing their own declines, the Erie firms were necessarily affected adversely. Moreover, certain non-Erie firms that usually contracted some of their work preferred to use their own underutilized facilities.

Innovation

Limited innovativeness was still another detrimental factor. According to a widely-held belief, Erie firms employing about 10 percent of the work force in 1960 were at a special disadvantage because their products or production facilities were obsolete.[6] The volume of profit reinvestment was considered inadequate. Some owners were apparently unaware of the deteriorating demand for their products. One firm had operated with equipment twenty to thirty years old, and maintenance costs were perhaps greater than the required outlay for installing new machines.

Other firms, which remained sole proprietorships or partnerships, had been founded by inventors or men who combined creativity in engineering with aggressive salesmanship. The increasing fragility of many such enterprises with the passage of time is, of course, generally appreciated. Also (according to one industrial developer) a few sizable Erie firms have operated as family institutions and do not exhibit normal economic behavior. Some might continue in business merely to maintain a family tradition, even though for years they had been unable to find "a winning new line." It was also reported that some absentee owners "simply patched," and the managers, who were primarily from the local area, were unable to update the plants.

Irrespective of the form of company ownership, failure to innovate undoubtedly has an adverse impact upon employees. If new products or processes are not introduced, employment ultimately declines. Moreover, the updating of worker skills would probably lag in such firms, and this lag would be an additional disadvantage when these workers were laid off.

Community Participation in Industrial and Manpower Development

Although productivity advances and technical innovations are typically generated by the firms themselves, various types of private and public programs of encouragement have also been tried. The Erie Manufacturers Association has engaged an active, elderly engineer to promote a bonus plan that shares cost-savings so that workers would not object to innovations. Four plants had adopted such a plan by the summer of 1964.

On occasion, a useful "innovation" consists simply of information concerning the possibilities of expansion of existing local firms. For example, the Erie Manufacturers Association has compiled a detailed index of the products of local firms so that more of the local establishments could make purchases in Erie.

There have, of course, been still broader programs in support of local economic development. Public or community provisions for adequate

---

[6] Based on individual conversations with some forty industrialists or their representatives and community leaders and the findings of S. Howard Evans, *The Erie Workbook for Community Development Action* (Washington: Chamber of Commerce of the United States, September, 1960), pp. 126, 129.

housing and transportation, effective manpower development programs, and cultural amenities are important for attracting new firms and industries and for assisting firms to compete.

Erie might have utilized funds available through both the Area Redevelopment Administration and the Pennsylvania Industrial Development Corporation to strengthen its industrial base. In fact, however, Erie lagged in its use of matching public funds; and an industrial development park was established tardily because of inadequate private contributions and loans. Part of the failure is ascribable to the opposition of local manufacturers and labor unions,[7] and part to the relative lack of interest on the part of important merchants and bankers who would normally be the dynamic leaders in such programs.

Differences over the strategy of industrial development have been sharp. The Erie Manufacturers Association evidently believed that each firm serves the community best in dedicating its efforts to profit maximization. The Chamber of Commerce, on the other hand, favored participation by its members in a broad community program. In a sense, then, the absence of an aggressive leadership meant that Erie did not keep pace in interarea competition for industrial development. By the fall of 1964, only one major employer (a manufacturer of knitwear) had moved to the industrial park, and only a few of the smaller firms had relocated there in expanding their operations.

Just as industrial development was lagging, a comprehensive approach to manpower and training programs was absent in Erie County during 1954–63. It was not until 1964, when unexpected shortages arose in certain blue-collar occupations, that a community manpower committee was established to conduct a survey of training facilities and to recommend ways of adjusting to changed market conditions. The unanticipated shortage reflected an uneven local interest in manpower projections. In a survey conducted by the Upjohn Institute during the summer of 1964, 60 percent of the responding firms reported activity in projecting manpower requirements. However, nearly half of the projections being made did not provide occupational breakdowns and were therefore of limited value as guides to training.

Some employers reported that, even during the period 1954–63, it was necessary to purchase certain material inputs in Buffalo, Cleveland, or Pittsburgh because engineering and skilled trades and machine shops were comparatively scarce in Erie. The failure of many firms to project

---

[7] Several manufacturers were convinced that existing wages would be raised by the entrance of other firms into Erie. The president of one of the largest local unions, however, was certain that any new firms would be of the "minimum-wage" variety.

their manpower needs probably curtailed their ability to exploit profitable opportunities. These labor shortages reflect an attitude toward manpower development that contrasts with the meticulous planning that is invariably involved in the installation of new equipment or the introduction of a new product.

The supply of trained workers was, naturally, also conditioned by workers' attitudes toward training. Some personnel officers complained that many workers, including younger men, were not interested in enrolling in company (on-the-job) training programs. These workers did not recognize the long-term benefits of skill enlargement as adequate compensation for a temporary cut in earnings during the training period. Furthermore, the "educational" efforts expended on the young men by industry and labor leaders were minor and ineffective.

The volume of on-the-job training would have been somewhat greater if more firms had been aware that such training was partly compensable under the Area Redevelopment Act and the Manpower Development and Training Act. Only one-third of the firms in the Upjohn Institute's survey of 1964 were even familiar with these Acts' provisions; the relatively smaller firms were the least informed.

Enrollments in education and training courses in evening school varied according to economic conditions. They were actually higher in the years of greater unemployment. Evidently many recent high school graduates who had no specialized skills found it necessary to enroll in such courses. Also, employees were more anxious to broaden their skills in the face of layoffs. Finally, employers encouraged their workers to train as the decline or disappearance of overtime made it easier for workers to attend night classes.

Recovery for Erie?

Despite the economic difficulties that beset Erie in 1954–63, the prospects are not altogether gloomy. One hopeful sign is the upturn of employment in manufacturing that began in the summer of 1964. In August of that year, the Erie unemployment rate declined to 4.3 percent in contrast with 7.1 percent in 1963 and 11.2 percent in 1959. These changes suggest that the long-term decline of Erie need not be irreversible.

A second favorable indicator is the comparative performance of sixty-two Erie manufacturing industries and their national counterparts in the period 1959–63. An analysis made by the Upjohn Institute of the sources of employment change (according to the so-called "employment shift" technique[8]) indicates for Erie a decidedly favorable "competitive effect" (one of the three components of the "employment shift").

Important qualifications remain, however; and these should not be neglected in appraising the outlook for Erie. The earlier discussion has already noted weaknesses in the industrial base, manpower development, and community programs. Furthermore, since Erie's employment was more depressed in 1959 than that of the national economy, the 1964 advance largely represented a mere "catching up." In addition, since many Erie firms are job-order producers, their recent gains in output are partially attributable to the approach to full-capacity utilization elsewhere.[9] Consequently, later expansions of capacity elsewhere or a substantial cutback of national output rates could, unfortunately, have a sharp impact upon Erie's revival.

IMPLICATIONS OF ERIE'S EXPERIENCE FOR LOCAL ECONOMIES

Erie's experience indicates that communities have to take positive action on many fronts to remain competitive. The fact that communities increasingly recognize this need for positive action in itself intensifies the competition among them and places laggards in most precarious positions. The action has to include steps by industrial and union leaders, by the workers themselves, and by community leaders and the local citizenry. Communities cannot rely simply on expanding government programs and increasing federal expenditures for local improvement. They have to take constructive advantage of government provisions through complementary and supplementary actions of their own. Indeed, unless communities are motivated to improve their economic resources and prospects, government measures are likely to prove ineffectual and even to accentuate disparities.

It is worth repeating that community efforts may prove unavailing in the absence of a generally favorable national economic climate. Governmental programs that aim at community improvement are more likely to contribute to local advancement when business conditions are buoyant in the nation as a whole. Indeed, the government's fiscal and monetary

---

[8] Daniel Creamer of the National Industrial Conference Board made some early applications of the employment-shift technique. Edgar S. Dunn, Jr., of Resources for the Future, Inc., presented the first formal statement of the method and its refinements in "A Statistical and Analytical Technique for Regional Analysis," *The Regional Science Association Papers and Proceedings,* Vol. 6 (1960), pp. 97–113. Victor Fuchs independently arrived at an approximation of Dunn's method at the same time. Lowell D. Ashby, of the U.S. Department of Commerce, Office of Business Economics, applied the model to statewide and national data.

[9] Newspaper accounts did indeed relate the quickening of Erie's industrial activity to the pickup of orders from firms located elsewhere.

policies can facilitate local improvement by fostering high level employment in accordance with the objectives of such noncommunity legislation as the Employment Act of 1946.

On Exploiting "Obvious" Opportunities

Certain measures for strengthening a local economy's position may appear obvious, but the fact that they did not occur sooner in Erie suggests that other communities might also be failing to act in good time. Some of these measures might, of course, not have been economically feasible for Erie until a recent period, and some need not yet be practical for other communities. Furthermore, measures that promise only modest advantages for individual firms but considerable advantages for the local economy as a whole require interfirm or community cooperation for implementation.

One "obvious" line of action is to support and expand existing firms and industries. For instance, in the case of Erie, there has been belated recognition of the possibility of rejuvenating its port activities. Also, construction of a superhighway from Pittsburgh to Erie got underway only after years of state inaction; the development of important regional markets for several industries and the possible attraction of new firms have been hampered by the absence of a good highway between these important industrial centers.

The desirability of avoiding excessive local dependence upon one major employer should also be "obvious." Private, state, and federal funds (e.g., the currently minor appropriation under the State Technical Services Act) can be used to advantage to determine what additional industries could naturally complement or supplement existing ones. For instance, sizable salt deposits are supposed to underlie Erie. Their exploitation could support a basic chemical industry and thus lead to the formation of other industries and also to the expansion of the local plastics industry.

Some communities may want to improve the balance of their economies by establishing new industries that are relatively insulated from national markets. An Erie County economic development plan, prepared as a requirement for aid under the Area Redevelopment Act, has advocated establishment of "light and assembly-type industries, and small industries based on local markets," plus greater development of recreation facilities.[10] Finally, a committee of business and community

[10] *Overall Economic Development Program,* a preliminary statement prepared by Northwestern Pennsylvania Conference for Economic Development, September, 1961, p. 16.

leaders has suggested that the increasing attraction of industries to communities having cultural and other amenities requires "balanced community development," that is, an "organized effort to make Erie a better place in which to live and work."[11]

Public Programs

As stated earlier, private initiative could be bolstered by public support. Some recent government programs—including the Area Redevelopment Act, Accelerated Public Works Act (both replaced by the Public Works and Economic Development Act), the Appalachian Regional Development Act, the Manpower Development and Training Act, and the Economic Opportunity Act—provide special opportunities for motivated communities and individuals that have been disadvantaged in the past. These opportunities cannot be realized without local or individual efforts. Furthermore, failure to take advantage of these opportunities can impair the competitiveness of indifferent communities and persons.

Human Resources Development

Erie's experience indicates the desirability of an explicit and comprehensive approach to manpower development. Industry can do its part through sustained innovativeness (which would allow workers to have more meaningful careers), on-the-job training, and participation with vocational schools in the design of utilitarian curricula. Workers should take advantage of opportunities to improve their skills and other qualifications for more satisfying work. Parents should encourage children to acquire more than basic literacy and to realize their educational and training potentials more fully. Community governments should provide an appropriate spectrum of educational and training institutions, be alert to programs sponsored by state and federal governments (including the Employment Service), and facilitate and foster interfirm cooperation and other actions benefiting the economic prospects of the locality as a whole. Other influential local entities, such as unions, also have unique contributions to make and should cooperate in joint constructive endeavors.

Because the preceding remarks are in the nature of an exhortation, they should not be discounted as platitudinous or "obvious." Perhaps the greatest gaps in behavioral research still exist in the realization of the "obvious." To achieve joint participation of all concerned is an outstanding challenge at any time, whatever may be the currently fashionable name for the challenge.

[11] Evans, *The Erie Workbook,* p. 123.

Manpower Projections

Only a minority of the firms in the Upjohn Institute's sample favored establishment of a government manpower projection service. Yet adequate manpower projections, under either public or private auspices, could provide a useful basis for training programs. By looking only two years ahead, firms would not have to resort to self-defeating piracy efforts and makeshift or crash training campaigns. They could also avoid in some measure the splintering or simplification of jobs because of unavailability of skilled persons, and could establish more realistic programs of apprenticeship.

Data on Training

As in most other communities, the training of skilled workers in Erie has largely been accomplished under formal and informal employer programs. Unfortunately, meaningful figures on the number of trainees and on the quality of training are lacking. The deficiency of such data on investment in human resources is uneconomical and inconsistent with the new concern for the fuller development of the individual. The proposed "Human Investment Act," incidentally, would grant tax credits for training outlays of business firms and require the maintenance of detailed records on training.[12]

Industry and Union Stakes in Training

As noted, only a minority of the Erie manufacturing firms in the Upjohn Institute's sample were aware of on-the-job training provisions under the Manpower Development and Training Act (MDTA). Therefore, at the least, local offices of the Employment Service should be more active in disseminating information about existing government training programs. But even when there is greater knowledge of existing programs, the volume of training may still be very deficient. Thirty-six percent of the firms in our sample expressed an interest in on-the-job training with government financing of the costs of instruction, supervision, and materials. The interested number of firms rose only to 50 percent when it was suggested that the government might in addition pay part of the trainee's wages.

In short, many firms, in Erie as elsewhere, attempt to secure trained personnel without assuming a proportionate share in the training load.

---

[12] The tax credit would be for costs associated with the training and upgrading of employees in new job skills. The proposed Act "is patterned closely after the investment credit provisions of the Revenue Act of 1962, which permitted a 7 percent tax credit toward investment in certain depreciable plant, equipment and real property." See U.S., *Congressional Record,* September 9, 1965, pp. 22401–402.

Furthermore, they are understandably motivated to train their personnel for specialized occupations. What accords with an individual firm's apparent self-interest, however, may limit the future occupational mobility of the workers involved. In view of the continuing changes and uncertainties that condition the operations of industrial enterprises, a firm may not, moreover, appreciate its true long-range interests in manpower development and training in a community.

The fuller realization of employee potentials is, of course, as much a matter of concern to unions as to industry. As special representatives of workers, unions may contribute signally to achievement of at least one of the three principal objectives announced in 1966 for the government's "active manpower policies" by the Council of Economic Advisers: "to augment the supply of scarce skills." Accordingly, they should promote collaborative opportunities with management for training and retraining, perhaps under the aegis of the MDTA when such support is available. Furthermore, it would seem desirable from the individual's standpoint for unions in the manufacturing industries to encourage a trend away from specialized training.

In cooperation with the offices of the Employment Service, unions and management might strive to give reality to some of the possibilities for individual improvement suggested by the 1965 edition of *The Dictionary of Occupational Titles*. Specifically, they might make it easier for individual workers to move vertically within occupational groups. While both unions and management will usually not find it to their interests to foster mobility across occupational and industrial boundaries, they might occasionally be able to facilitate the geographical mobility of workers. Enhanced occupational mobility (or an improvement in "the efficiency of labor markets") is another of the government's announced objectives for "active manpower policies."

These observations point up the roles of labor and management, but all of the economic groups in a community have a common interest in upgrading individual abilities. The common goal is to minimize chance factors restricting vocational development and occupational choice. To minimize these factors in career determination, communities must first of all offer and seek to ensure basic literacy for all. Beyond this aim, they should participate energetically in the fulfillment of the third principal objective of the government's "active manpower policies": "to fit the unskilled for better jobs," including unskilled persons who are unemployed or lack basic literacy. Since communities, in the last analysis, are the places where the majority of individuals are to be found, the self-interest of communities in manpower development and training is "obvious."

13

CITIZEN ACTION AND COMMUNITY PROBLEMS

HENRY E. HOLMQUIST

LEARNING BY TEACHING

This paper describes an approach being taken to help a community to help itself, especially with reference to manpower improvement. The program is experimental; and, while not entirely research-oriented, it does have important ingredients of learning. Ideally, experience gained under the program ought to upgrade the quality of the service that can later be provided. Indeed, the program is in harmony with the original concept of the Upjohn Institute's activity: research for the benefit of community improvement.

More specifically, the enterprise here described has two basic aims that are not truly distinct. The first is to define and test a constructive intermediary role for people (say, Upjohn staff members) who are more likely to be classified as research-oriented than as "political" activists. These people, however, do have a distinct bias toward utilization; they wish, if possible, to bring their specialized knowledge and other capabilities to bear on community decision-making processes affecting, say, employment and training. They try, through intellectual intercession as benign "outsiders," to assist communities in organizing for timely action directed at local problems. They apply, demonstrate, and try new ideas, including pertinent results of earlier experience or research.

The second aim is to find out, through direct participation in the community setting, just what needs to be learned for more effective attacks on the real local problems of employment and training. The information so obtained provides a basis for establishing valid new research objectives and the design of new research projects.

In short, the exercise may be regarded as a style of research that is goal-oriented insofar as practicable. It could be respectably described, if a grant were at stake, as a form of field work, or case study, involving the dynamics of small groups composed of representatives of the various community subcultures. Furthermore, the lessons learned in one geographic area are expected to be useful to some degree in many others.

Among the things learned early in this kind of endeavor is that local inertia has to be overcome, that key persons have to be activated, that face has to be saved all around, and that an external trusted agent may be very helpful in such matters. Actually, a community has to be "taught" what it might and can do for itself, and it has to be helped in this direction. Goals have to be stated and have to be made credible. The comment made by a colleague with respect to the poverty program is very fitting:

> The war on poverty is basically a process of education, education of both the individual and society. It is intended to educate the individual to the point of lifting him out of his poverty, hopelessness and defeat and of helping him become an employable, self-supporting member of society, and it is intended to educate society to the point of believing that this can be done.[1]

THE CHARLESTON CASE

The program first discussed refers to Charleston, West Virginia. The focus is, as already indicated, employment and training. The main object is not to prepare an "expert" report but to aid local businessmen and the leaders of educational institutions and of the employment service to improve their joint contributions to the community. These persons have to identify roles, establish relationships, and engage in constructive common endeavors. They must survey available local, state, and federal resources. They must analyze the local needs and determine which alternatives are preferable for remedial action. They must establish appropriate channels of communication. The inputs for decision have to be collected and put into place.

The Group Conference

In any community, most persons in key positions already are busily occupied, and they may not be on familiar terms with each other. For this reason, the Upjohn staff member on the scene has a vital role to play as a catalyst, a middleman, a legman, a broker of names and ideas. He sets himself the task of determining the potential leaders of relevant local interests and lists a relatively small number that might cooperatively address the selected problems.

Thus, a group of from fifteen to twenty persons is assembled informally for studying the manpower conditions of the Charleston community. It is committed to meet one full day each month for a period of nine to

---

[1] Harold T. Smith, "Putting the War on Poverty in Economic Perspective," Annual Conference of Michigan Welfare League, November 16, 1965.

twelve months. Initially, members learn from each other's experience. Out of the exchange emerges a redefinition of problems, roles, and resources. Eventually, a felt need crystallizes for specific data, new programs, and changes in existing programs. Then the group begins to act.

What kind of action is taken? Subcommittees are formed, for example, to organize surveys of job vacancies, skill requirements, and training needs in particular employment fields. These surveys are to be conducted under the auspices of the employment service or the local business association. Furthermore, consideration is given, through enlistment of the cooperation of institutional representatives, to the coordination of welfare agency requirements and programs for the supply of better total service.

The Upjohn contribution to the work of the conference will continue to be the provision of liaison for advancement of the work of the group. The motivating theory, which still seems justified, is that concentration on the longer-run self-interest goals of the community (and of its leaders) will inspire needed support as well as encourage new relationships, needed changes, and fresh approaches with respect to training, education, and other manpower problems.

The group thus becomes a focus for the organization of community information and energy. It is concerned with a set of complex problems of recognized importance and it is, therefore, likely to command wide attention and interest. The idea is hardly new, but wide-spectrum organization on a local basis for the achievement of manpower objectives is not necessarily obvious or compelling in the context of other pressing daily issues.

The Charleston experience may also be viewed as an effort to bring the supply and demand sides of the local manpower situation into a more constructive relationship. Before this effort, it had been assumed that the market mechanism worked effectively, smoothly, and rapidly enough. Indeed, the demand for labor was considered to be an active force assuring achievement of a satisfactory equilibrium. Unhappily, "structural unemployment" remains a reality for communities even if unemployment can be exorcised at the national level by the stimulation of "aggregate demand." The Upjohn approach, it is hoped, will provide insights for helping communities to "institutionalize"—to reduce to routine—the flow of information and energy needed to balance supply and demand at higher employment levels.

The group conferences accordingly become part of the supply-demand mechanism and also give a projective dimension to the labor market. Information is obtained from employers not only on current openings and skill needs but also on future openings and needs—for the short run and the long run (three or more years). Projected skill needs are translated into vocational training proposals (including curriculum changes, if necessary), requirements for combination of institutional and on-the-job training, and requirements for retraining. They may suggest not only that a different number of persons should enter the training stream but also that need exists for more effective outreach, increased resort to work-related testing, and greater involvement of industry representatives in trainee selection and actual training.

The Charleston effort is taking special account of the problems of drawing the unskilled and disadvantaged into industry. Adequate preparation with respect to education and training would, of course, expand the potential number of workers for local and nearby firms. A long period of generally favorable business conditions provides a good setting for the stimulation and maintenance of community interest in manpower development.

Broad involvement is sought to foster a community-wide belief that Charleston's future depends largely on the decisions of its own representative citizens. The group conferences include not only members of the more prosperous elements of Kanawha County society but also spokesmen of the less articulate and disadvantaged components of the population. This does not imply a token "representation of the poor." These spokesmen, in addition to having direct experience with and knowledge of the problems of poverty, were actually selected for ability to communicate.

How does the approach described here differ from that of Alinsky's Industrial Area Foundation? This program, like Alinsky's, seeks change, but it assumes a certain degree of readiness for change on the part of the existing "power structure." Instead of organizing the poor for pressure on the "establishment," it takes advantage of a latent desire for reform from within, based on local experience. The concept may lack dramatic appeal, but it retains demonstrable functional value.

Local "Data," Hard and Soft

Why does any community postpone remedial action, or tend to ignore socioeconomic problems until a crisis is reached, or wait for an external force to intercede? This is a complex question that is answered in part in this section. The answer points up the value of the middleman's participation. It also points up the fact that, in Charleston as everywhere else, attitudes and opinions are as important as facts; indeed, they too *are* facts that help to explain the inertia to be overcome.

The local businessman or agency head is no exception. He operates on the basis of information filtered or colored by cultural bias and supplemented by guesswork, hunches, and appeals to experience. His ordinary concerns keep him well occupied, and he is not eager to assume large new responsibilities for solving difficult, long-standing problems posed by the environment. Even if he were eager, he is unsure of his own capabilities and the community resources that could be marshaled for the job. He is normally aware that, in the sphere he knows best, manpower is at a premium and the day is not long enough. He has his personal and family cares too. He rationalizes: "I'm only one man. What more can I do?"

Little wonder that it is firmly held in some quarters that Kanawha County, all of West Virginia in fact, "has no Negro problem" and "the Negro population is small and happy." Percentages may indeed be small, but the degree of contentment is easy to exaggerate or misinterpret. Housing and jobs are limited. Aggravating the normally difficult job situation for the Negro is the flight of bright young persons to larger cities of the North, where opportunities may be better. Therefore, as local business does open an inviting door, qualified Negro candidates may be lacking. Such circumstances tend to prolong the uneasy status quo and support the separateness that excludes Negroes from fuller participation as citizens.

Acceptance of such conditions on the part of the poor, Negro or white, is of course no longer assured. Perhaps most difficult for the more affluent or more successful members of a community to comprehend is the fact that, as education increases and as economic conditions improve for the poor, a point is *not* reached at which these persons are content. Instead, such improvements only stimulate their awakening to the vast areas of opportunity that in theory belong to all but in practice are denied to some.

The businessman who believes or hopes that "good times" will take care of the poor must realize that education and training and opportunity for satisfying work in our complex economic system do not "just happen." A man cannot pick himself up by his bootstraps if he lacks boots. Where there are surplus workers—uneducated, untrained, and displaced by technological change (as in the case of the coal miners)—time will not bring a remedy.

Those who do not migrate tend to maintain a cycle that resembles the urban ghetto cycle of poverty. Relatively isolated families, conditioned to hard times for generations and living on relief rolls, still beget children. Ignorance, filth, and lack of motivation do not necessarily spell contentment; they may instead reflect an inability to cope with the environment. Without special measures to bridge the gap, the margin between the "haves" and the "have-nots" increases.

The need for special measures may be illustrated by the case of the mother who is benefiting under the Aid to Dependent Children program. After training, she refuses job placement, deciding that she is "not available at this time." This attitude, which may seem "irresponsible," could actually reflect foresightedness based on grapevine or other information. She may be protecting herself against the loss of assistance. She may have heard of disturbing precedents—about difficulties in reinstating persons who, after training and placement, had lost their jobs. A wait of ninety days for reinstatement of payments for her children may be too long for the mother to endure.

When a community like Charleston tries to take stock of itself, the leaders are frustrated to find at first that needed information is not at hand. The problems to be overcome loom large, although they cannot accurately be assessed. The number and variety of jobs are not known with any certainty; and, as a result, existing training programs may not be realistic. If a surplus labor pool does exist, its size and composition may be a question mark. Information developed in Charleston shows that greater demands for skilled workers lead to out-of-state recruiting while outside firms seek workers among the Charleston unemployed— the "surplus." Furthermore, for lower-paying jobs, local recruitment proves difficult despite the number of unemployed persons. What may seem like lack of motivation acquires a different aspect on closer inspection: A man with a family to support may find $40 a week very inadequate, certainly not enough to encourage him to forgo welfare alternatives.

Other gaps in knowledge handicap business planning; and some gaps (with conspicuous exceptions, however) are reducible with the middleman's aid. Auto dealers in need of mechanics may be unaware at first of the existence of pertinent programs under the Manpower Development and Training Act. Retail merchants may need advice on arrangements for replacing tailors and seamstresses approaching retirement age. While new job opportunities are seen for the Charleston area in recreation, reforestation, health, and education under federal programs, the state civil service system languishes. A complementary development of state government would seem essential for fuller realization of the potentials suggested by the magnitude and diversity of federal assistance.

The interstate highway system illustrates a tendency to rely on a nucleus as though it were the economic whole. This system will reduce the isolation of West Virginia from the rest of the nation, but the great benefits anticipated from an improvement in transportation do not come automatically. The handicaps of an area long impoverished are not suddenly overcome by a single undertaking, however significant this might be. Progress will depend on what else is being done, especially by the resident leadership. A new highway network, unless it is complemented by changes in attitudes, by worker training and retraining, by state planning, and so forth, will not necessarily, say, increase tourist business as much as provide a higher-speed route through Appalachia. Indeed, for those who lack the training and skills to take advantage of a new Appalachia, the new highways may not even provide a better escape route.

BROOKINGS COMMUNITY PROGRAM

Experience by the author in 1960–62 with the Committee on Problems of the American Community (CPAC) at Brookings Institution contributed to confidence that the current Upjohn effort at Charleston would advance constructive changes. The Brookings project demonstrated that, together with the local leadership based on perceived self-interest, outside social scientists could contribute to the improvement of a metropolitan environment. With proper support established, a basis is laid for beneficial cooperation.

Conferences similar to those described for Charleston were held in Cincinnati, Baltimore, Newark, and Lansing. A series of meetings was held, each lasting a day and a half, every four to six weeks over a period of seven months.

To promote maximum participation and understanding, the meetings were kept informal and confidential. The local press was included, but it did not report the proceedings. The agenda for each meeting was prepared jointly by the participants and the CPAC staff. This arrangement assured discussion of specific local problems and also illustrated the possibilities of the collaboration of the social science representatives with metropolitan planners and policy-makers.

When the program was completed in an area, additional meetings were planned by the participants under local sponsorship. A forum was thus established for exchange of ideas and for communication of these ideas to action organizations in the community.

Something more should be said about the importance of rapport. A primary lesson learned in the CPAC program was that social scientists, practitioners, and policy-makers can have a mutual impact only if there is sustained exposure over a fairly long period of time. The development of effective exchange among these "types" is difficult and uphill all the way. Biases and prejudices have to be overcome. For example, most key persons involved in these programs initially expressed doubt as to the value of the conference series. As busy men already aware of each other's existence, they saw little need to spend one and a half working days together every few weeks. Changes in opinion did come about, however, when it was illustrated how community problems did affect the participants' industries or agencies.

COMMUNITY ASPECTS OF FEDERAL PROGRAMS

The existence of federal, as well as other governmental, programs having large impact on community manpower problems hardly diminishes the importance of local organization for self-help and of the contributing role of the middleman. On the contrary, the existence of these programs enhances the importance of, and may even facilitate, local self-help efforts. They need not be administered independently. They could strongly complement local efforts and do not rule out nonlocal and nongovernment mediators. As in the programs of the Office of Juvenile Delinquency and the Office of Economic Opportunity, the authorized new instruments for community participation may not successfully involve the various relevant strata of the citizenry. Organizations that are representative on paper only can lack authenticity, serve as rubber stamps, and be mere aliases for an officialdom that has already failed in its own right. On the other hand, the encouragement of local rivalries through establishment of parallel local institutions with federal support could also have harmful effects.

Illustrative Situations

Community improvement involves a painful learning process through constant interaction. In this process, respected neutrals or professionals can help reduce the barriers to effective cooperation. The barriers may include differences in auspices as well as differences in cultural background, social functions, immediate interests, and field of education. Some instances of interaction difficulties will now be described, to serve as a reminder that "creative Federalism" need not be a euphemism for dictation from above. The term should designate a constructive partnership for solving problems where most people are—in communities.

In his dealings with the school superintendent, a local poverty program director failed to remember that change does not come about as a result of suggestion or threat. The superintendent could not be expected easily to disavow the policies and philosophies he basically favored merely to please others. Rather than effectively encouraging citizen groups to pressure the schools, the director misjudged his power and threatened to have the superintendent fired if he continued to impede change. The superintendent, with faith in his tenure, decided to "sit the program out." The director left town months later, while the superintendent remained more firmly entrenched and better prepared to fight off other forays into his domain. The subsequent director of the poverty program and his board chose not to further antagonize the schools. Instead, they called upon the schools to analyze, evaluate, and design their own program of change!

A director of urban renewal, troubled with general citizen rejection of his program, inquired into factors operating to his disadvantage. Lack of understanding and poor communication were found important impediments to cooperation. Dealings with representatives of the Negro community had been conducted in such a manner as to maintain public images rather than realistically face issues. On the question of integration, the director discovered as much interest in and support of a "quota" system by Negro representatives as by his own office. The director accordingly ceased to play the role of the idealist planner, and the Negro representatives no longer needed to maintain a position of "better housing for Negroes first, then solve community housing problems." All realized a need to deal with the community as a whole in an effort to correct problems of specific parts, even the problem of eliminating racial ghettos.

Closely related to this case was the involvement of a leading real estate broker who began to see his interests in the light of renewal efforts taking place in the city. Early in the program, he viewed his business as isolated from these slum areas. However, he began to understand how clearance and renewal and the relocation of slum dwellers could have a direct and favorable influence on his business practices. Renewal areas might offer sound investment opportunities; changes in land use did not depend solely on the decision of the renewal agency; and areas of the city which would be receiving the majority of relocatees need not be written off as blighted areas if proper service were made available. He concluded that he, as a broker, and others of the industry stood to gain a great deal by working with the renewal agency rather than around or against the program.

In the administration of the Area Redevelopment Act (ARA), it was found that qualifying communities were best able to take advantage of the federal program when local leadership was developed to the degree that local initiative could be exercised. Comparisons made of some neighboring communities, equally eligible to establish ARA programs, found projects in one but not the other. Investigations showed that citizen involvement (by representatives of industry, labor, and social agencies) accounted for the difference in participation.

After the Studebaker shutdown in December, 1963, at South Bend, industrial, labor, and civic leaders, together with state and federal officials, analyzed conditions and took cooperative steps to meet the crisis. Welfare programs were realigned. The Department of Labor sent a task force to work with local industry and labor on retraining programs. The Federal Housing Authority and Veterans Administration dealt with problems of mortgage forebearance in community-wide meetings. Precooked programs were not handed to the city. Each step was carried out by local residents utilizing the available resources deemed most appropriate.

CONCLUDING OBSERVATIONS

It is clear from the Charleston and Brookings experience that outside agents can play a useful role in encouraging and facilitating community self-improvement with respect to manpower. Information is a valuable tool at the disposal of the intermediary. If he is accepted, he may be an effective go-between in establishing and maintaining needed local communications.

Impressive action taken after a shutdown shows that much latent ability exists for community development that ought to be stimulated and organized sooner. To supplement the South Bend example, we may cite a project, Project Able, developed under the United Community Services of St. Joseph County to deal with the problems of older workers left jobless by shutdown. The goal was to provide total services to these workers. The tasks of direct job placement, financial aid, referral for training and vocational rehabilitation, and contact with welfare and social service agencies, all required extensive community cooperation and coordination.

The growing interest in the "systems" approach to the solution of complex problems suggests that large firms having staff capabilities in this line might wish to reappraise more imaginatively the challenges and opportunities of modern business citizenship. Specifically, major firms that have to decide whether to move to the suburbs or to rebuild downtown ought to consider staying; and, if they have so decided, they might wish to go beyond consideration of the immediate burdens of crime, taxes, and blight to a consideration of the longer-range potentials implicit in better housing, education, training, and jobs for the numerous poorer urban residents. Firms have to be responsive to economic factors above all; but, within a certain range, reweighting may be optional, and it could, perhaps, lead on occasion to alternative decisions that are socially more satisfactory.

In addition to the spectacular operations of shock troops, and even after such operations, the action of plodding infantry is required. Granted, many heads of "bureaucratic" institutions appear immovable and may have no intention of changing what they believe is the "best" or most practical of all possible programs. One response to this situation includes both a demonstration of new ideas *and* attempts at direct involvement of key persons related to the problem in question. Key citizens are effectors of change—as well as keepers of the *status quo,* which may not be maintained through direct effort so much as through inaction and noninvolvement.

"Good" manpower programs—those that stand the best chance of success—require participation by members of the community in design, initiation, and conduct. Packaged programs, presented to community leaders from above for endorsement, are not likely to command the necessary understanding and support.

IV

INFORMATION NEEDS AND TOOLS

14

RESEARCH STRATEGY FOR
MANPOWER POLICY

HERBERT E. STRINER

The increase in the scope of government action in behalf of more effective development and use of manpower requires complementary forward strides in public and private research strategy. This paper explores some of the broader research implications of the order-of-magnitude changes already registered or expected in the federal manpower commitment.

CHALLENGE AND RESPONSE

It is easy to document, of course, the government's expanding effort to raise the quality of this nation's manpower resources and to improve prospects for productive employment. The unprecedented and successful resort to strong fiscal action in 1964 to implement the objectives of the Employment Act of 1946 is sure to encourage other bold steps in the future. Another landmark that promises to become the point of departure for additional ambitious or experimental undertakings is the Economic Opportunity Act, which reflects a new concern over the persistence of widespread poverty in our land of plenty. Earlier striking evidences of growing government involvement might also be cited, such as the National Defense Education Act (1958), the G.I. Bill of Rights (1944), and the Morrill Act (1862). The important thing is that historical perspective reveals a trend, a progressively more comprehensive commitment; the new legislation, moreover, is no longer based on the rationale of improving the manpower basis for national defense.

It is not easy to meet the challenge to research posed by the increase in scale and diversity of the total federal manpower program, although some of the directions to be taken in a strategy of response may readily be defined. The base of statistical and other pertinent information will have to be expanded, some additional types of data will have to be developed, and new ways to use existing data will have to be devised. The electronic computer will become an indispensable tool for the manpower analyst, assisting in his multivariate studies and his design and test of economic models. New institutions, such as the federal data center discussed in Morton's paper, will have to be given serious consideration. The supply of manpower specialists is already strained; and new legislation, affecting such related fields as poverty, health, and education, expands the needs for the kinds of people that might otherwise seek careers as interdisciplinary manpower analysts. Most important, perhaps, is a required shift in attitudes toward statistical and other data, which will have to be seen more as tools for the planning and control of future events than for the autopsy of past events. Administrative uses of data for public programs and for public-private cooperation will feature priority selection, comparison of alternative approaches, and evaluation of costs and probable social returns.

The brunt of manpower policy demands will obviously be felt before the appropriate responses of research strategy can be fully developed and implemented. But this kind of gap, of course, always exists, and it may, as usual, require some compromises between aspirations and capacity, some adjustment in chronological horizons. It is with both reassurance and uneasiness that the dictum on the title page of Alfred Marshall's *Principles of Economics* should be recalled: *Natura non facit saltum.*

The rest of this paper is devoted to a look ahead that takes due account of policy needs and research realities. It discusses five objectives of research strategy that will prove important in the next half-decade. These five, which are hardly exhaustive and not necessarily independent of each other, will surely command much attention:

1. Redefinition of manpower problems in a "systems" context.

2. Clarification of new requirements for local socioeconomic data.

3. Increasing collaboration among the disciplines—social, behavioral, and physical.

4. Increasing service of private, independent research organizations in a catalytic role.

5. Development of new techniques to facilitate implementation of research results.

MANPOWER PROBLEMS IN A "SYSTEMS" FRAMEWORK

During recent years there has been an increasing use of such terms as "systems analysis" and "operations research," which may suggest to some a laboratory science, perhaps devoid of humanity or humanism.

230

Frequently, the social scientist who looks a bit beyond the first page of a relevant article in a professional journal is confronted by phalanxes of difficult equations. The appearance of articles has certainly changed since World War II, when the systems approach began to prove itself valuable for the analysis of large, complicated problems, especially in the realms of defense and military operations. The concept has spread to other fields. The number of systems organizations has increased, and one of these, the RAND Corporation, has in a relatively short period established a worldwide reputation in both methodology and practice.

Any close evaluation of the work of "systems" organizations reveals that less quantitative or hardware-oriented techniques are also used as required. Institutional and subjective inputs must be, and are, utilized where relevant. In particular, the extension of the systems approach to the manpower field will, of course, require many "soft" inputs to complement quantitative "facts" for the attainment of results that seem sensible to the ultimate decision-maker.

The systems approach, then, involves the use of quantitative techniques, but not exclusively; and, more importantly, it draws on all relevant disciplines to help solve a problem in its most logical operational context. Interestingly enough, this novel approach was used in the social sciences even *before* World War II (when the concept was used effectively in solving convoy problems and in assigning priorities for bombing missions). Many years earlier, economic theory had been concerned, for example, with *general* equilibrium analysis, which is actually a close relative of the systems approach. The economics profession has probably developed *partial* equilibrium analysis to a higher degree only because of the lack of data, the limited human ability to handle large numbers of equations mentally, and the limited methodology available until recently even for nonmental operations. The technical handicaps are in the process of reduction, and great advances are achievable in the foreseeable future, even with equipment in which the sums invested are not unreasonably large.

In the manpower field, the increasing feasibility of the systems approach makes it easier, for example, to view a federal agency's program in the light of a major purpose rather than in terms of established patterns of accepted ways of "doing things." The approach also facilitates conception of an agency program in terms of other concurrent government objectives. Suppose that an agency's charter calls for the conduct of "optimal" employment programs, for the development and utilization of the individual's abilities to the fullest extent. Its responsibilities could be interpreted as: (1) conceiving of all meaningful program alternatives, (2) estimating differential costs and benefits of these alternatives, (3) translating this "costing operation into budget and organizational implications," (4) making a policy decision which translates the accepted alternative into a total, multiyear budget, and (5) phasing the program into an annual budget activity category, with continuing review and evaluation of costs and benefits.

This approach has in a brief period of five years converted the Defense agencies (the Army, Navy, and Air Force) into a far more efficient and "unified" organization for accomplishment of their joint objectives. For those who see the Defense establishment as primarily a hardware-type organization, it is well to recall that among its most important activities are the training, retraining, assignment, and effective use of manpower resources. As in the deployment and control of the Polaris submarine network, the systems approach to defense as a whole brings within the reach of rational decision-making the psychological "nightmare" problems involved in operating man-machine combinations of great size, complexity, and power.

By virtue of Bulletin No. 66–3, issued October 12, 1965, by the Director of the Bureau of the Budget to the heads of all federal departments and agencies, the Defense example will be generally adopted. This bulletin directs that the "program package" or systems approach become the point of departure for program planning.[1] Of course, this approach is essentially an improved tool, but still only a tool. It provides the decision-maker with a better basis for considering the plausible alternatives which are available and their relative costs and benefits. But no research technique should ever be viewed as a substitute for, or as an automatic guide to, courageous policy, correct evaluation, or sound programs.

The research implications of the systems approach in the manpower field are formidable. In the Department of Labor, Office of Education, Social Security Administration, and Department of Commerce, there is no tradition of cost-benefit analysis. Accordingly, no easy movement of Defense establishment experience to these civilian agencies can be taken for granted. Staffing and state-of-the-art problems abound. Though some techniques and personnel are transferable, value criteria and data are not, and special methods also have to be developed. First efforts have already been made along these lines by the new Economic Development Administration of the U.S. Department of Commerce, and the Office of Economic Opportunity. But most agencies in the manpower field still have much to do, and they will have to build on the experiences of private industry as well as the government's Defense organizations. Since

---

[1] See also RAND Corporation, *Program Budgeting, Program Analysis and the Federal Budget,* 1965 (for sale by the U.S. Superintendent of Documents).

the early 1950's, the program-package approach has had broad application in the electronics, machine-tool, petroleum, and chemical industries, and it would be well for manpower researchers to adapt and adopt what is usable in this experience.

The systems approach will tend to be more expensive than correctional, unidisciplinary, or fragmented research approaches to the problems of unemployment, training, or education. But relatively low-budget research is in reality quite costly if it does not result in a product which can help to deal effectively with a given problem in its pertinent aspects. A higher-budget research project which provides the means of developing effective manpower programs is actually a less costly way to use brainpower to social advantage. Of course, the systems approach still has to prove its efficacy in the manpower field; the payoffs, which are potentially high, will always have to justify the outlays.

NEW REQUIREMENTS FOR LOCAL SOCIOECONOMIC DATA

Major advances in equipment and techniques are sterile in the absence of data permitting significant application. The research needed for dealing with the complex problems of urban change, transportation, manpower mobility, or the economic development of disadvantaged regions is handicapped by information lacks. The limitations in the supply of local data often are critical.

During the next several years, much more attention will have to be given to major gaps in manpower data at the state, city, county, and neighborhood levels. The new federal manpower programs are being addressed to the sorts of problems requiring true local data rather than merely adjusted or manipulated national data. Manpower projections for the nation will offer little help to vocational schools in the determination of course variety and content to satisfy the needs of local industry. The "area skill survey" has accordingly been developed for the purpose. A national unemployment figure is meaningless for projecting the needs of a metropolitan area for training, public-works, or unemployment compensation benefits. Even an unemployment average for a large urban area may be of limited value for a local program—say, one focusing on the job needs of a city section heavily populated with Negroes. Detailed information—e.g., on age-race distribution of inhabitants of census tracts—would increase sensitivity to dangers latent in socioeconomic problems and could also facilitate timely preventive action.

Recently enacted training, education, regional development, and poverty programs will exert pressure for the multiplication of local "tape" centers to help meet demands for disaggregated manpower data and correlative information. Data storage centers, located mostly at local universities, will have a significant role in regional and subregional exploitation of interindustry matrix design and analysis. The "community action" approach, which seeks to involve individuals throughout the socioeconomic spectrum for the common advancement of all, should receive stronger research support as the supply of local data becomes better organized and more accessible.

Improvement of the supply, quality, usability, and coordination of local manpower information will itself provide a test of statistical leadership. It is always contended that detailed area data are expensive to gather and tabulate; but, in view of the outlays required for the management of the programs, such costs are relatively slight. Indeed, a comparison of expenditures on data with the budgets for operating the manpower and related programs, which must now rely on an inadequate data base, makes it seem that the nation is intent on buying a current-model Cadillac with a Model-T engine.

Statistical programs will be forced to complement the changing manpower programs, which are now aimed at local problems. Better articulation of national and local information, as well as improvements in supply, will be needed if policy requirements are to be jointly satisfied at all levels.

INCREASING COLLABORATION AMONG DISCIPLINES

Unfortunately, manpower problems do not fit into unique disciplines, especially the ones that happen to be represented by interested professionals. An adult who is functionally illiterate is not simply a candidate for help by an expert in remedial reading or education. Experience discloses a role for psychological counseling, too, if this adult is to be readied for further skill training to facilitate his adjustment in a complex urban society.

For years interdisciplinary research was the hallmark of an "in group." It covered a multitude of sinners—sociologists who practiced abominable psychology, economists who preached ridiculous sociology, and public administrators who felt equipped by six credit hours in four different social science survey courses to speak authoritatively on all of the subjects. In more recent years, a reaction against "scientism" and "dilettantism" has prepared the way for development of a more serious multidisciplinary research capability, certainly in the field of manpower. This change, to which Sheppard's paper in this volume is addressed, reflects not only the better education and increasing sophistication of social scientists but also the upgrading of managers. Decision-makers

234

who seek help have already become more demanding, more discriminating, and their standards are likely to advance significantly in the next few years.

The Upjohn Institute's experience with interdisciplinary efforts have proved encouraging. A study was conducted, for example, in Erie County, Pennsylvania, by a team comprising a sociologist, a psychologist, and an economist, which gave a more penetrating insight into the factors influencing the work-search patterns of the unemployed than could have been obtained if the representative of only one discipline had undertaken the inquiry.

In research on employment, training, and manpower mobility, the limited involvement of social psychologists, sociologists, demographers, geographers, and political scientists is noticeable—and regrettable. Psychiatric counselors and cultural anthropologists should be encouraged to broaden their horizons to become better equipped to understand and deal effectively with the manpower and training problems of minority groups. The economist who plans large-scale educational and training programs to raise the economic status of residents in Negro, Puerto Rican, or Mexican ghettos should know about subculture mores and about the techniques of community organization. The social worker or sociologist who knows little about the local labor market and projected job opportunities is hardly equipped to help plan for employment security in a community's trades and skills.

Nowhere in the manpower field, perhaps, is there greater need for multidisciplinary research than in the area described as "structural" unemployment. Roughly, the so-called structural factors are (1) technological, (2) demographic, and (3) cultural. Brief comments on these factors show why a many-sided competence, in an individual researcher or a team, is desirable or even essential.

The technological factors may be hardware-oriented or procedure-oriented (or contain elements of both). Fork-lift trucks, computer-controlled production lines, and coal-cutting machines are illustrations of the hardware factors. Accounting, management, and quality-control systems illustrate the procedural factors. Both varieties are subject to evolution and innovation that may result in higher labor productivity and also call for new work skills and for a change in familiar occupational proportions. How can displacees, especially those actually separated from payrolls, be motivated to retrain for radically different skills? How can redundant personnel who are foreign-speaking and accustomed to life in three-generation households be induced to move to other cities and mingle with different subculture groups? What are the determinants of management decisions in the innovative process? Questions such as these are worthy of address by many disciplines working together.

The relevance of demographic and cultural factors is also hinted at in the questions already asked. Shifts in population and in the cultural mix characterizing urban areas nowadays prevent manpower programs from becoming the exclusive research preserves of the labor economist or the urban sociologist. Psychological and anthropological techniques are pertinent for involvement of indigenous leaders. Vocational schools must relate more directly to the business community to assure that company representatives become and remain a constant source of help in designing curricula, anticipating changes in skill needs, and developing effective placement channels. But there are few successful models, and examples of research cutting across traditional professional boundaries are badly needed. Indeed, the future may require an entirely new strategy of skill training, one that combines the institutional and on-the-job approaches. Training and placement may be rendered more effective through design and use of new nonverbal testing techniques and post-placement evaluative techniques that permit determination of just how much and in what ways different test scores really matter. Here, too, the challenge to several disciplines is evident.

A relatively ignored research area, that of measuring and affecting motivation, ought to prove attractive to the social scientist, life scientist, and physical scientist. The motivation of a hard-core unemployed person with a poor educational background and low communication ability is neither easy to assay nor easy to stimulate by techniques currently available. Teams of social and physical scientists have sought to establish correlations between physical properties (e.g., biochemical characteristics of blood) and observed levels of work motivation. Another opportunity for interdisciplinary inquiry is suggested by the finding that physical illness is related under certain conditions to employment changes or work-study patterns having elements of stress.

CATALYTIC ROLE OF PRIVATE ORGANIZATIONS

"Balkanization" of responsibility is a familiar phenomenon in legislative and philanthropic arrangements for aiding the jobless, the poor, the sick. Many manpower problems, at first glance or upon analysis, are seen to involve other problems that are covered by different government programs—e.g., unemployment compensation, education, training and retraining, mobility, motivation, health, or adequate housing. Furthermore, the conventional division of interests and responsibilities means that manpower problems do not lie wholly within the province of one

236

governmental (or private) organization as a rule. Even when government has clear responsibility, the level may be unclear; federal, state, and local jurisdictions may have to be taken into account, and there may be interstices as well as overlaps. Besides, disputes and rivalries between private and government organizations—and even between government agencies—are not unknown.

Too frequently in the past, research programs have actually been stultified or limited because of overlapping jurisdictions, gaps, and disputes as to control. In numerous instances, the timing of certain types of research would seem inopportune; or the objective evaluation of the validity or adequacy of a manpower or unemployment assistance program would seem incompatible with the interests of the organization actually doing the research or responsible for operations. Consequently, the research may not be done at all, or only superficially enough to justify previous organizational commitments.

As manpower programs require that increasing attention be given to sensitive minority problems, the difficulties of securing a proper research base or a proper research review become more painfully obvious. A bad situation is being aggravated as government fund allocations rise. The absence of adequate research efforts prevents the establishment of sound operating programs and policies and hampers the evaluation of what is being accomplished.

How can matters be improved? Large organizations (both within and outside the government) that deal with thorny manpower problems will have to look increasingly for research assistance to private institutions which are relatively independent. The research should be innovative, bold, and objective, even if it "hurts" the sponsor's self-image and preconceptions. In recent years, universities and nonprofit research institutes have begun to fill this gap. Nowhere is the existing research gap more critical than in the development of methodology, models, and evaluative techniques for judging the effectiveness of manpower programs.

A common complaint of government as well as business organizations concerned with employment, training, and education problems is that their own research staffs have too little time for deliberation on basic issues or for the conduct of long-term reviews. Research organizations, including some connected with universities, are available for this sort of help and are already being used to some degree. Greater use of this kind of contract service is in prospect, in view of the difficulty that large governmental or business organizations have in undertaking intensive research whose results are not influenced by the values implicit or explicit in the very designs of such institutions.

Defense needs have occasioned the acquisition of some useful experience involving close, though still independent, relationships between private research institutes and government organizations. Though such relationships can be compromised, many independent research organizations (e.g., the RAND Corporation, the Institute for Defense Analyses, and the Research Analysis Corporation) have doubtless been able to perform valuable, objective research oriented to the problems of their prime clients. Professional standards have been kept generally high in these organizations.

The Defense precedent will probably be imitated by civilian manpower agencies in the next few years. These agencies already have needs that will encourage moves to provide support for independent research institutions. It would indeed be desirable to meet the basic manpower research needs of government and, at the same time to be sure that independent, high-quality, professional services are being devoted to the task. Contract arrangements with independent research groups, including those in universities, would help keep research efforts in step with the demands of the programs and policies of the agencies.

In addition to the growing use of private research resources, the expansion of "in-house" government research capability will have to be encouraged. An adequate internal staff must remain available regardless of the prospect of contracting more of certain work to outside groups. As the demand increases for manpower research, government cannot allow itself to become excessively dependent upon outside resources. Higher salaries and more senior grades in federal, state, and local agencies have already improved government competitiveness with other claimants for the relatively scarce manpower available for manpower research.

A significant development of the past decade has been the growing cooperation between large foundations and government organizations. Manpower research of interest to both has been advanced thereby. For various reasons and at various times, government agencies cannot either undertake or provide needed research support for certain types of manpower problems. On such occasions, foundations may be able to step in and provide the financial support to guarantee that the necessary research will be done, at least for a while. In the years ahead, manpower research may receive increasing support from the joint efforts of foundations and government agencies.

Private research organizations and academic bodies can obviously serve as intermediaries between government and the foundations. Indeed, they are also well situated to develop programs that logically draw private business and union support too. They can thus help to arrange for a broader, more comprehensive national base for ambitious research programs commanding the interest of all parties concerned.

RESEARCH IMPLEMENTATION

Good research often fails to register an impact because it is completely distinct from operations. This divorce is regrettable. "Applied" manpower research will not affect operations unless it is undertaken with specific applications in view. The research itself can be most meaningfully designed and performed only if it is to be tested on the anvil of reality. The sponsor must "care."

While most social scientists are probably interested in the application of what they have learned and the utilization of research results, they are not necessarily in positions to encourage acceptance and affect practice. Typically, the end product of research is, and remains, only a final report—a volume handed to "someone," placed on a shelf, or deposited in a library. This sort of experience may result in making action-eager social scientists content with sublimation, with the applause of other professionals in the field, or with a favorable review in a learned journal. The highest prize that many seek may thus become blurred: the use of the research results for dealing with the problem that motivated a sponsor to request or support research in the first place.

At the present time, effective means for translating manpower research into action are not too much in evidence. One Federal agency that has definitely striven to build a bridge between inquiry and practice is the Department of Defense. In almost every instance, research supported by the military is viewed as only half complete when the research team has finished its work and presented its report. The next step, or the beginning of the second half of the task, is to ensure communication of the research results to those individuals who must evaluate and eventually translate the research into action. A whole series of briefings is started. The most senior individuals responsible for the programs that logically relate to the research results take part in the early briefings. Additional briefings are conducted for individuals at the lower echelons.

This concept is worthy of adaptation in manpower research funded by federal, state, and local governments. After the research itself has been completed, the research team should develop a suitable strategy of communication with the executives and others responsibile for evaluating and eventually carrying out the manpower programs that the research seeks to aid. Thus, at the very outset, every research project that has a potential application in the view of the funding organization must be designed so as to include not only the research phase itself but also the communication phase. Without adequate advance provision for communication, the research will probably not be addressed to the individuals most concerned with the development of more effective manpower programs.

Communications must be oriented toward obtaining results rather than the mere distribution of written reports or summaries. This emphasis undoubtedly will mean face-to-face briefing sessions with individuals at the highest manpower policy levels as well as with functionaries at the field and operating levels. For example, in the case of research concerned with education and retraining of older workers, the research results must be communicated by the briefing of senior officials in the Departments of Labor and Health, Education, and Welfare, as well as by the briefing of officials in state and local organizations entrusted with development of retraining and educational programs for older persons. The briefing sessions should also include state and federal legislators concerned with problems for the solution of which the research was supported.

Effective communication of manpower research results to those for whom the results are of value calls for the development of skills that combine research with communication. This combination may be regarded as "interdisciplinary" too, although the usual assumption made nowadays is that communication art is natural and requires no cultivation. The schools have to give more attention to this matter, whatever the diploma or degree one seeks.

Above all, the numerous organizations now funding manpower research at unprecedented levels, in addition to financing research, must insist on the eventual utilization and appropriate distribution of results. This has not, as a rule, been one of the objectives of research in the manpower field. Independent research organizations, including academic ones, may well have a role to play here: to undertake limited or pilot demonstrations which provide the basis for more comprehensive or full-scale approaches by public agencies and private firms to their composite research-application-communication tasks.

15

THE EMERGING INFORMATION SYSTEM
AND MANPOWER RESEARCH

J. E. MORTON

Our topic recalls a famous essay by Savigny, the great jurist,[1] in which he addressed himself to a universal question: What are the appropriate circumstances and the right time for codifying the rules of law emerging in a society that itself is in flux and changing? Although he was concerned primarily with the formulation of a civil code, the problem is so general that it also applies to manpower research. Indeed, it applies to the principles and procedures involved in the production and distribution of federal statistical information as a whole, which we shall first have to consider here. The timely promulgation of a body of pertinent rules is important not only because a field of research benefits from the guidance that is offered but also because norms once established prove difficult to abolish as they become irrelevant and dysfunctional.

THE CHANGING CONTEXT

A consideration of future directions of manpower research has to begin with an understanding of trends affecting the federal statistical system in general. The first trend that we note and discuss is *the growing recognition that federal statistical data constitute a national resource*.

This recognition manifests itself in a much greater concern than heretofore in *the selective preservation and the multiple use of historical statistics*. The interest in such statistics is twofold. First is the analysis of economic time series to ascertain trends and structural changes in the economy at large and in its components. Second, the increasing cost of the information encourages the belief that data for the past as well as the present may have an unutilized analytical potential. Accordingly, although new tailor-made information and *ad hoc* surveys may be preferable in the search for answers to a current problem, it is also

---

[1] Friedrich Karl von Savigny, "Vom Beruf unserer Zeit für Gesetzgebung und Rechtswissenschaft" (1814).

recognized that a great deal may be learned from new analyses of existing data. This "secondary recovery" activity usually can be performed at considerably less cost than the development of new special-purpose information for each case. Furthermore, it is now generally conceded that, apart from the direct dollar expenditure, an additional (although usually not directly measurable) cost element is to be taken into account: the psychological and financial burden on the respondent. This cost affects not only the quality of the response but the very willingness to supply the answers in the first place.

Another important fact is *the introduction of automatic data processing equipment.* The facilities now generally available for computing are gradually being considered for other uses too, such as information storage and retrieval. Thus, we may look forward to fuller exploitation of the capabilities of electronic data processing machines in the field of statistical information. Among the first experiments in fuller utilization is the endeavor of the Bureau of Labor Statistics in the area of manpower statistics.[2]

We should also acknowledge *the stimulation of the demand for quantitative information exerted by the new management sciences.* The quest for quantitative information has been rapidly expanding through the data specifications and requirements of operations researchers, systems analysts, users of linear-programming techniques and decision-theoretic models, and econometricians. Until recently such investigators would have been left in their proverbial ivory towers, but suddenly they are becoming welcome and even essential occupants of the office buildings of large government and private organizations. This change is not only leading to a much more ambitious and energetic exploitation of existing data but is also encouraging demands for large amounts of new quantitative information.

Another pertinent feature of our time is *a gradual lowering of the walls separating the traditional problem areas,* with a corresponding weakening of the autonomy of any single discipline. This tendency toward interdisciplinary approaches has resulted in a rising demand by the analyst for data derived from various, often independent and uncoordinated, statistical sources. These data have to be put together, rearranged, matched, and reconciled. Manpower analysis offers but one example of the importance and complexity of the interdisciplinary ap-

[2] See, for instance, J. E. Morton, *Analytical Potential of the Current Population Survey for Manpower and Research* (Kalamazoo, Mich.: Upjohn Institute for Employment Research, 1965).

proach. It must rely on bits of information originating in different statistical operations, agencies, and programs. Major analytical efforts to date still tend toward unidisciplinary approaches, but this source of limitation on the availability and use of information is bound to give way as researchers become more sophisticated and more insistent.

In the manpower field as elsewhere, we may expect more often in the future the development and adoption of systems-oriented concepts emphasizing "the need for organizing a method of data collection to define the system."[3] The relegation of other than conventional economic variables to the class of exogenous ones, their typical omission in the design of a particular model, is now more frequently deemed objectionable. It is recognized as a serious, though often unavoidable, inadequacy of partial models, an inadequacy that may hamper analysis and policy formulation. Other papers in this volume, by Harold C. Taylor, Herbert E. Striner, and Harold L. Sheppard, touch on the need for comprehensive approaches to manpower issues.

Public recognition of many long-festering problems of industrialization and urbanization has led to *new concern for the scope and quality of state and local area data*. Such interest sometimes requires, on the information side, the disaggregation of statistics already published. In such cases, attention is directed not to production of new data (which may also be needed) but to the appropriate processing and presentation of information being collected. Thus, the new quest for local area data stimulates a reexamination of the very nature of statistical operations and of the organizational structure within which such operations are taking place.

The more intensive exploitation of available data is being complemented by efforts to utilize quantitative information in *the development of new and more imaginative analytical problems*. Some of the present shortcomings may well exist on the side of the demand for data, i.e., in the analyst's shop, rather than in that of the data-producer. To generate imaginative hypotheses and to develop significant analytical problems and theoretical models—these are tasks that can be pursued even with the statistical information collected for more immediate purposes and uses. In the long run, speculative uses of quantitative data in the behavioral sciences may well become an integral part of forward-looking basic research. Such possibilities are being spurred by the development of computer science and applications.

[3] J. Van Court Hare, "Systems Analysis," in David B. Hertz and Roger T. Eddison (eds.), *Progress in Operations Research* (New York: John Wiley & Sons, 1964), II, 127.

PROGRAM BUDGETING

The foregoing and similar factors have surely helped to shape present expectations concerning the functions to be fulfilled by the government's statistical information system. They have found expression, for example, in the President's announcement (August, 1965) to the Cabinet of a new planning-programming-budgeting system and in the completion (April, 1965) of a report by the Committee on the Presentation and Use of Economic Data to the Social Science Research Council.[4]

The two events reflect concern about quite different objectives, the first about fiscal administration by the government and the second about data requirements of research institutions and universities. Both events are symptoms of the growing interest in issues regarding information, including the nature of data pertinent to the problems of the interdisciplinary manpower analyst.

The President's announcement and the elaboration of its ideas and concepts in Bureau of the Budget Bulletin 66–3 (October, 1965), which stresses "program budgeting," have important implications for the use and analytical exploitation of quantitative information. Thus, the introduction of the concept of "basic program categories" may open the way to interdepartmental approaches, including the definition of interdepartmental information requirements. Since present statistical data obviously are not adequate to meet all the needs of the government's new management philosophy and procedures, the development of an appropriate information system to satisfy the recommended techniques of decision-making becomes a respectable objective, even if only partly achievable.

In the jargon of the academic community, program budgeting portends a turn toward interdisciplinary, systems-oriented, and strongly quantitative decision-making efforts by the federal government. The manpower analyst may, therefore, expect changes in the design, production, and processing of federal statistical information which will modify not only content but also concepts and classifications. He may find more sympathy than heretofore with his quest for statistical data referring to comparable units of inquiry (say, the individual or the family), even though the data originate in different agencies and bureaus and overlap traditionally separate subject matters.

---

[4] The Committee was appointed early in 1962, at the recommendation of the Executive Committee of the American Economic Association following the annual meeting in December 1959. The members of the Committee were Richard Ruggles, chairman; Richard Miller, secretary; Edwin Kuh, Massachusetts Institute of Technology; Stanley Lebergott, Wesleyan University; Guy Orcutt, University of Wisconsin; and Joseph Pechman, Brookings Institution. The report is also referred to as the "Ruggles Report," after the Committee's chairman.

INFORMATION FOR MANPOWER RESEARCH

TOWARD A RESEARCH DATA CENTER

While the presidential directive set the scene for the treatment of statistical information on highest policy levels, the report to the Social Science Research Council raised related questions on needs and opportunities in the light of evolving information storage and retrieval technology. This report, together with a review by Edgar S. Dunn as a consultant to the Bureau of the Budget,[5] is concerned primarily with the data-using researcher and addresses itself to his problems in technical detail. Both the report and the review reflect awareness of the statistical implications of efforts to increase the analytical exploitation of quantitative information generated by the federal government. They indicate directions of present thinking in the behavioral sciences in general, and are, therefore, also directly pertinent to the field of manpower research.

To concentrate on a manageable portion of the very broad problem, the report was deliberately restricted to bodies of information currently available in machine-readable form. In other words, the report deals with data collected by agencies of the federal government and available on magnetic tape or on punched cards.

It would be futile to try to do justice to the report short of complete reproduction, including the two useful appendices, one on evaluation of the machine-readable materials held by federal agencies and the other on the initial inventory of materials held at the end of 1964 by a number of agencies. Incidentally, over 25 percent of the nonagricultural items listed in that inventory contain materials of concern to the manpower analyst.

The report noted the absence (in the United States in contrast with many other countries) of a single statistical agency which, among other things, should also be responsible for the record-keeping of the nation. Added to this decentralization is the existence of a mass of so-called operating statistics, i.e., statistical information accumulated as a by-product of the administrative and regulatory activities of various agencies. The manpower analyst is too familiar with the resulting problems; he is accustomed to searching for valuable statistical data, not only in the output of, say, the Bureau of the Census or the Bureau of Labor Statistics, but also in the operating, or by-product, data of the Social Security Administration, the Internal Revenue Service, the Veterans Administration, the Public Health Service, and so forth.

The report also points out, as most users of employment data have experienced at one time or other, that it is now extremely difficult to

[5] U.S., Bureau of the Budget, Office of Statistical Standards, *Statistical Evaluation Report,* No. 6, December, 1965.

find out what data exist and where. Failure to provide access impedes effective utilization of the large amount of information obtained at public expense. To remedy the situation, the report proposes immediate establishment of a *Federal Data Center,* a step which may well require additional legislative authority.

The review by Dunn seems to agree with the major diagnosis of the Social Science Research Council study. However, it goes beyond the therapeutics there recommended and suggests the establishment of a *National Data Service Center.* In addition to being a comprehensive data storage facility, such a center would have as its primary mission the provision of certain services. Among other advantages, it would provide computer services of particular interest to the manpower analyst, such as the matching of records from different sources, and the bypassing of the confidentiality (or disclosure) problem. Many of the present information problems in manpower research could be solved or greatly simplified if micro-data from individual records could be reaggregated in forms different from those now available in publications and elsewhere, or if information pertaining to given persons could be matched across schedules from different surveys and other individual records.

The confidentiality (or disclosure) problem mentioned above is a special nuisance to manpower analysts. One of the traditional obstacles in attempts to gain access to micro-data is the privileged status of much of the information. Agencies are of course careful to avoid violation of disclosure laws and rules, but the manpower analyst is rarely, if ever, interested in information pertaining to an individual identifiable as such and often is not interested in the identity of a firm. A device which bypasses the disclosure problem is, therefore, of immense help to him. An organizational intermediary such as the proposed National Data Service Center also might assure that an agency is not unduly burdened with requests encouraged by any liberalization of disclosure practices.

Existence of a center would also help dispel misgivings of some bureaus about the use of released data. In defense of restrictive policies, agencies sometimes claim a responsibility for preventing misuse of data by an analyst who obtains micro-information from them directly or exclusively. The center would be a useful intermediary between such agencies and, say, clients whose research objectives may lie outside the analytical interests of the agency controlling access to the data.

On the other hand, many limitations will become more explicit and acute if the available data become inputs into a comprehensive information storage and retrieval system. Among these inadequacies of foremost concern to the manpower analyst are those affecting the uniformity of concepts, the consistency of definitions, and the taxonomic comparability of data originating in statistical programs now administratively independent. Although much progress has been made in this respect within the Bureau of the Census, for instance, the same cannot be said for the comparability of data across bureau and departmental lines.

In manpower research, the removal of deficiencies is important not only for facilitating analysis but also for matching records in the first place. The creation of a simple data bank, of a physical storage facility, or a repository of statistical records (even if in machine-readable form) is far from a solution of the manpower analyst's information problem. He will, therefore, welcome Dunn's proposal for the development of standards for the classification and coding of statistical data, with special attention to respondent units and other statistical building blocks.

To achieve Dunn's objectives is no minor task. The proposed National Data Service Center accordingly envisages a resident research function for evaluation of user requirements. A clear grasp of anticipated data uses is an indispensable element in the design of an information system, in the construction of taxonomy and reference codes, and in the definition and the revision of standards. Here the manpower analyst's readiness and skill in presenting his requirements in precise and specific language becomes crucial. To hold his own in the competition with other data users, he will have to "do his homework" before going to class.

STATE AND LOCAL INFORMATION

So far we have discussed only the problem, which is difficult enough, of providing statistical information within the direct purview of federal agencies. To complicate matters, our period is also one that demands considerable statistical information on state and local levels. The integration of state and local statistics—with each other and with national data in turn—presents a most complex challenge for the information systems engineer. Such data would constitute a rich resource. Their analytical potentials, however, are hardly indicated by the present supply of information, which lacks coordination and standardization.

To form even a superficial idea about the magnitude and diversity of nonfederal information resources, we should note that there are at present over 90,000 state and local governments in the United States, each with its own file cabinets and collections of records. In principle, these records contain some information, in many instances a good deal, on everyone, but they are now widely dispersed and unusable for analytical purposes, with rare exceptions and for strictly limited purposes.[6] They span a wide range—from information on voter registration, law enforcement, parole, and probation to data on income tax, health, welfare, education, and employment. The information may originate in observations recorded by government personnel, in reports made by an individual to a government agency, in application forms, in inspection and investigation reports, or in registration forms. Taken as a whole, the mass of resulting records doubtless is the single most nearly complete information source on individuals. The telling limitations are not so much the gaps in content as the statistical deficiencies, such as doubtful quality and lack of comparability.

Some of the reasons for inadequacy of the data are obvious. One is the mobility of the individual across the boundaries of local government jurisdictions. Another is the traditional autonomy of local governments. Then there is the departmental autonomy of offices headed by different elected officials. Still another factor is poor communication, both horizontal and vertical, between the agencies of local governments.

The improvement of subfederal data systems has recently attracted much attention with the expansion of Great Society programs. These programs entail a substantial increase in federally funded expenditures for information-gathering. The activities are usually uncoordinated, however, and the circumstances in which they have been initiated have precluded a proper account of concepts and policies.

To the extent that the call is heeded for more and better manpower specialists in local labor market analysis,[7] a lax approach toward fundamentals of the information problem is particularly disturbing. Aside from the neglected opportunity of gearing expensive information collection to the standards required by serious analytical uses, the data gathered may often give to the analyst only the materials for a limited case study. It would be better for him to have the opportunity to place such findings into a more general reference frame. On the other hand, the growing emphasis on regional and urban problems points in the direction of more disaggregation and more micro-analysis. More stress on persons and on specific areas and localities is inevitable. It is hard indeed to visualize how the educational, training, and manpower programs recently authorized by Congress can be carried out effectively without reference to local job needs and opportunities as reflected in technically adequate and

[6] See E. F. R. Hearle and R. J. Mason, *A Data Processing System for State and Local Government* (Englewood Cliffs, N.J.: Prentice-Hall, 1963).

[7] See Herbert E. Striner, in National Planning Association, *The National Program for Domestic Progress; Its Character, Cost and Economic Consequences, Proceedings of Seventh Annual Conference of the Center for Economic Projections* (Washington, 1966).

economically comparable "local socioeconomic data." It is essential "to obtain information on the characteristics of the unemployed that is adequate for coordinated national and local remedial programs."[8]

To complement our present information with data pertaining to lower levels of geographic aggregation, to states, and to even smaller areas will prove an enormous task. The need is now widely acknowledged, and so is the requirement of small-area data for successful analysis.

Among recent manifestations of recognition that interest the manpower analyst is the Atlantic City meeting in summer, 1964, of the National Association of State Budget Officers. This conference endorsed ongoing efforts toward interstate standardization of statistics. The Association also participated early the following year in a joint endorsement with representatives of the Council of State Governments and of federal agencies. Subsequently, the Council created an *ad hoc* committee on automation, technology, and data processing to explore the utilization of electronic equipment and the interstate exchange of quantitative information. Finally, attention should be drawn to the Minneapolis meeting of the National Governors Conference in July, 1965, which agreed to sponsor a national conference (held early in 1966) on comparative statistics to be attended by federal, state, and local officials. Quite apart from motivation by research interests at large, these organizational efforts are responses to the rapidly increasing data requirements of new and expanding federal programs in such areas as education, health, welfare, housing, and transportation.

Present needs and deficiencies below the federal level were succinctly summarized in an address to the above-mentioned National Governors Conference by James E. Webb, Administrator of the National Aeronautics and Space Administration.[9] At the end of his address, he suggested that state units be established to supervise statistical standardization within states and comparability of data between states, and to examine the applicability of modern information technology at state and local levels. He also advocated the national conference on the comparability of statistics among states, mentioned in the preceding paragraph.

NEXT STEPS BELOW THE FEDERAL LEVEL

What strategy should now be proposed to facilitate development of a modern integrated system of state and local statistics? Three different

---

[8] *Ibid.,* p. 60.
[9] "Decision Making and Statistical Standards," *The American Statistician,* December, 1965, pp. 16ff.

approaches suggest themselves. Again, we should recognize that these approaches are pertinent to manpower as well as other statistics.

First, *data relating to state and local areas may be collected by federal agencies.* The Bureau of the Census has had considerable experience in this activity. Indeed, a population census seems an ideal vehicle for accumulating certain manpower information for small, analytically relevant units or classes. Analogous enumerations are occasionally undertaken by other agencies, too, in their respective areas of responsibility. Furthermore, by-product data may accrue to an agency for the special population covered by its operations.

The situation is more complex when acquisition and tabulation of the data are not the only or primary tasks; when, as in sample surveys, additional steps, computations, and estimation procedures are involved. Sample size, allocation of different-order sampling units in multistage designs, and the like must be considered, and only rarely will a self-representing sampling unit coincide with the particular locality for which the analysis is undertaken. However, resourceful manipulation of the data can sometimes go beyond these limits. For instance, strata of sampling units may be formed such that each stratum includes localities which are uniform with respect to the desired characteristics. Although the resulting estimates would not describe specific single areas, they make it possible to draw useful inferences with respect to areas of the same kind. Some interesting work along such lines has been going on in the Bureau of the Census for several years.

Second, *data relating to geographic subareas may be collected directly by the agency exercising jurisdiction over these areas.* Thus, data for a given city could be collected by the local government units having immediate jurisdiction. This approach would seem especially feasible where the area of statistical interest and the administrative area coincide.

Unfortunately, this is only the beginning of the process by which data might be assembled through local or state government offices. A major task that remains is to provide guidance for such efforts, in the interest of comparability of the data across local and state areas, and to meet statistical standards. At present, no existing organization fills this void on the local level. Even on the state level, provision is rarely made for the maintenance of statistical standards, although the importance of this function is often recognized. Pressure for comparability and for data satisfying statistical standards is likely to increase with the increasing cost of such programs. The fact that cost is frequently shared by the federal government is also favorable to eventual improvement of data quality and coordination.

According to a third approach, a variant of the preceding one, *state and local governments would collect certain kinds of information, but only after a carefully developed, comprehensive information system has been designed and put into operation.* Most state and local governments are not equipped to participate effectively in the development task, and the preparatory phase is bound to be protracted. Limited systems of this kind are now in operation (e.g., state-federal programs in the field of unemployment insurance), but the order of difficulty involved in the realization of a comprehensive system cutting across several independent jurisdictions and traditional subject matters is formidable. The problem is not unlike the one facing the builder of a federal information system, and considerably more challenging.

STAKE OF MANPOWER ANALYSIS

More than ever before, the manpower analyst of today and tomorrow has to depend on an information base that is interdisciplinary, intertemporal, and interterritorial. As other papers in this volume emphasize, the present scope of manpower research is far broader than economics. Its topics have to include population and psychology, and its tools are not altogether distinguishable from those of the demographer and the student of attitudes and motivation.

Unless the format of the manpower analyst's data is flexible, his efforts to come to grips with the complex problems of manpower research will be frustrated. He will be limited to conjecture or to an empirical analysis that is too often confined to surface issues. The building blocks that compose the information system must be made more usable for his purposes in addition to serving traditional needs.

Indeed, the manpower analyst should have data in a form enabling him to take full advantage of the new information technology. The need, for example, for disaggregating and reaggregating information as now published, for matching and linking schedules, and for developing tailor-made measures and new series has transformed the traditional problems of concept, comparability, and taxonomy from predominantly academic problems to eminently practical ones. Since it is acknowledged that the situation is acute with respect to the government's statistical information system in general, major remedial moves are likely, and these should benefit manpower analysts.

On the other hand, the manpower analyst must consider that planned alterations of the information system also have long-range implications for his research that could be adverse. Alertness to proposed legislation and major administrative steps is accordingly required. Not being one of the traditional and established subject-matter representatives, the manpower analyst must watch for signals of impending change in the information structure on which he depends so much. He may not be consulted; he must make his voice heard beforehand, lest he be advised only after the accomplished fact. The reality of the problem posed by Savigny cannot be ignored by people interested in research on vital issues of society.

For effectiveness in attempts to make his voice heard, the manpower analyst must be prepared to specify his data requirements and he must communicate these in a form intelligible to the data producers. His efforts must be timely, selective, and well directed. He cannot simply hope that all necessary data will routinely become available, for example, on the county level of detail. He cannot expect that a complete census, taken frequently enough, will provide needed current data. But, where statistics are being compiled, where new series are being proposed, he should try to have his current and prospective needs accommodated even if he is an incidental, rather than the main, customer. He has to be interested in opportunities for achieving greater coordination and comparability of basic information. He should be aware of potentially useful sources of manpower information in federal programs devised originally for other purposes. Worthy of special attention are the many new federally supported operations on the local level that involve considerable expenditures for information collection. To influence these data-generating processes, which seem, or may be, uncoordinated or even haphazard, could be a rewarding activity.

Where his data needs cut across agency operations, the challenge to the manpower analyst is a difficult one. Like the laboratory scientist, he has to formulate his requirements explicitly and early enough. He has to anticipate the character of the information storage and retrieval systems, the planning and design of which are a more complex and lengthy undertaking than may at first be assumed. Successful systems have to take account not only of the supply of information but also of possible analytical uses. In the construction of such systems, decisions must be made that cannot be readily reversed. The design of systems thus poses major technical problems, entailing questions of concept and taxonomy which are less likely to be answered to the satisfaction of the various data users that do not participate actively in the planning stage. The manpower analyst should try to avoid having his information base reshaped or preshaped without due attention to his real needs.

Last, but not least, those currently engaged in manpower analysis have a heavy responsibility for the long-range evolution of their discipline, including the character of fundamental research. The future impacts of the establishment of a satisfactory statistical data system bene-fiting from new information storage and retrieval technologies can hardly be exaggerated. Major advances also bring new temptations and dangers, and gains in current operations achieved through adequate tactical de-cisions need not effectively serve future needs and may even handicap future initiatives. For problems that require highly ingenious solutions, no substitute has yet been found for the individual researcher's own contribution. Here the main challenge still rests with him, but he should not be unduly hampered; and, more positively, his analytical power can be prodigiously magnified by the ready availability of appropriate data. Tools are only as helpful as the user's ability to employ them, and dependence on this ability and on other special qualities of the man-power analyst must increase rapidly in any progression from routine description toward deeper and more fundamental research. Thus, new systems must be appraised not only in terms of conventional manpower analysis but also in terms of the highly conjectural and experimental uses of data for original answers to existing research problems and for the identification and handling of promising new problems. The best approach toward satisfying the first requisite, alas, is not necessarily the best also for the second.

Those now engaged in manpower research should, while assisting in construction of the emergent information system, keep in mind also the potentials of the system for answering questions not yet asked and for suggesting problems that will be more meaningful tomorrow. In view of the expected life-span of new facilities, technologies, and systems, in-cluding the hardware and the organizational complements, future re-quirements deserve careful consideration now. In manpower research, equal opportunity for solution of current and future problems has to be achieved and maintained.

16

AN INTEGRATED APPROACH TO
MANPOWER AND ECONOMIC DEVELOPMENT

HAROLD L. SHEPPARD

MORE THAN "ECONOMICS"

None of the separate social sciences provides comprehensive explanations of the phenomena it chooses to study. Accordingly, many pertinent factors and conditions typically tend to be neglected in analyses of what is popularly described as "economic behavior" and "economic data" relating to manpower and growth. Such phenomena as employment and growth surely involve more than "economic" factors, more than those factors which intellectual tradition or professional custom often accepts as adequate for explanation and analysis—e.g., supply and demand, fiscal and monetary conditions, income, prices and wages, etc.

Acknowledgment of certain additional variables is frequently made, even if obliquely, by students of individual disciplines. In the field of labor economics and in studies of unemployment, for example, demographic considerations have always had to be taken into account, too—e.g., skill levels and age groupings.

But new, emerging problems now call for a more systematic—perhaps even a more formal—integration of "sociological" and "psychological" variables into conventional analytical and programmatic approaches to manpower and economic development in the United States. The present paper is addressed to this important matter of enlarging the framework of inquiry and interpretation.

The recognition that economic phenomena such as employment levels and economic development involve more thàn the usually chronicled or measured factors, is, of course, not a new one. The literature is replete with well-known examples of scholarly works that disclose and document the relevance of so-called noneconomic factors in the domain conventionally considered the jurisdiction of economists. One outstanding example is Max Weber's classical study of *The Protestant Ethic and the Spirit of Capitalism,* which emphasizes the influence of religious thought and movements as vital to the "spirit of capitalism." Another is Emile Durkheim's study of the division of labor, which questions the usefulness of the notion of individualized contractual relations in explanations of the economies of his time.[1] The list of major scholarly contributors is long, and includes Veblen, Löwe, and Sombart, among the many luminaries.

Less "classical" examples of recent decades also merit notice. One is the analysis of interindustry propensities of workers to strike made by Clark Kerr and Abraham Siegel. These two economists were led by their international data to construct a sociological theory of strikes centering around the notions of "isolated mass" and "integrated individuals."[2] In another international time-series study of strikes, Arthur Ross and Donald Irwin also gave a sociological interpretation to their findings.[3]

THE CASE OF ECONOMIC DEVELOPMENT

The literature on the economies of less-developed societies gives much attention to noneconomic dimensions, but the same cannot be said for the vast majority of studies of the American economy. While social-psychological *causes* (or *conditions,* in the language of indeterminacy) are readily recognized in the literature on overseas economic development,[4] they are conspicuously neglected in studies of current inter-regional differences within the United States itself.

The most obvious explanation for the disparity of treatment may be that even the untrained observer can easily discern social and cultural traits in societies other than his own. The real challenge is to discover whether the historical changes and regional (or intergroup) variations in one's own society—especially in the economic sphere—may also be attributable, in part, to the equally real social, psychological, and cultural differences *within* that society.

Observers are quick to notice that even when capital is made available in underdeveloped societies—for example, through the construction of a factory—the mere existence of the factory does not automatically generate the necessary labor supply.

[1] *On the Division of Labor in Society* (Glencoe, Ill.: Free Press Publishers, 1947; 1st English ed., 1933).

[2] "The Inter-Industry Propensity to Strike," in Kornhauser, Dublin, and Ross (eds.), *Industrial Conflict* (New York: McGraw-Hill, 1954).

[3] "Strike Experience in Five Countries, 1927–1947," *Industrial and Labor Relations Review,* April, 1951.

[4] Cf. Neil Smelser, *The Sociology of Economic Life* (Englewood Cliffs, N.J.: Prentice-Hall, 1963). This brief volume is an excellent summary of the literature of economics, sociology, and psychology, and the actual and potential inter-relationships of these disciplines.

Sufficient numbers of workers are not promptly available for regular employment in a radically new social and physical environment, under new forms of authority, and under new reward systems. The "commitment to work" as we know it in our urban industrial-commercial society requires major transformations in the social-psychological and cultural patterns of individuals and their families. The ease with which such transformations are carried out is not a given or constant phenomenon.[5]

May not the same be true within our own society? Some evidence suggests an affirmative answer. Administrators of current programs, such as those under the Manpower Development and Training Act, and the Neighborhood Youth Corps as a component of the Economic Opportunity Act (the "war on poverty" legislation), regardless of how they themselves may conceptualize their tasks, have found that large parts of their time and funds are being devoted to "work-conditioning" projects. Most of their trainees are recent migrants from rural areas (or the children of such migrants), and they have special adjustment problems that must be acknowledged and managed.

In similar fashion, study after study has noted the need of an "entrepreneurial and managerial spirit" among the actual and potential elites of given underdeveloped societies. Indeed, studies of Italy and France, for example, have pointed to the role of the orientation of businessmen, even in highly developed economies.[6] Starting with Max Weber, we are now aware of the social factors that appear to encourage or inhibit the development of entrepreneurial orientations and talents, even in the evolution of western society. Again, may we not properly surmise that population and regional variations in such a variable also exist within contemporary America?

An analysis of 1950–60 data points to the practical importance of both the question and the answer. In the urban areas of the United States characterized by substantial and chronic unemployment (the "depressed areas"), the absolute numbers of managers and proprietors declined

[5] Cf. Wilbert E. Moore, *Industrialization and Labor* (Ithaca, N.Y.: Cornell University Press, 1951), esp. pp. 24–34; and Moore and A. S. Feldman (eds.), *Labor Commitment and Social Change in Developing Areas* (New York: Social Science Research Council, 1960).

[6] For example, see David Landes, "French Business and the Businessman" and John Sawyer, "Strains in the Social Structure of Modern France," in E. E. Earle (ed.), *Modern France* (Princeton, N.J.: Princeton University Press, 1952); Henry W. Ehrmann, *Organized Business in France* (Princeton, N.J.: Princeton University Press, 1957); Frederick Harbison and Eugene Burgess, "Modern Management in Western Europe," *American Journal of Sociology*, July, 1954; F. Harbison, "Entrepreneurial Organization as a Factor in Economic Development," *Quarterly Journal of Economics*, August, 1956; and Kerr, Dunlop, Harbison, and Myers, *Industrialism and Industrial Man* (Cambridge: Harvard University Press, 1960).

between 1950 and 1960 by nearly 10 percent, on the average, while in the viable urban areas the numbers had increased by more than 18 percent.[7] Such a difference, of course, is a result primarily of deterioration in the economic conditions of the depressed areas and of the maintenance or improvement of economic conditions in the more viable areas. But, given a depletion of entrepreneurial resources in depressed areas, does this deficiency serve as a *continuing* condition for the economic retardation of such areas, especially when new *objective* opportunities for economic growth appear (such as new liberal credit from government agencies—state and federal—and a *national* rise in aggregate demand and gross national product)? Indeed, administrators in the Small Business Administration, the Area Redevelopment Administration (succeeded by the Economic Development Administration), and the Office of Economic Opportunity have been sponsoring projects to "beef up" the managerial know-how of persons in disadvantaged areas and population strata (notably among Negroes). To some extent, then, they have recognized needs to compensate for outstanding deficiencies in entrepreneurial resources.

THE PSYCHOLOGICAL COMPONENT

In this connection, we should also mention the theoretical and practical contributions of David McClelland, a Harvard University psychologist, regarding the role of psychological factors in economic change and growth. His most comprehensive work, *The Achieving Society* (Princeton: Van Nostrand Co., 1961), explains his major theory of "achievement motivation," how this motivation is empirically determined, and the relationship of motivation to economic growth and entrepreneurial characteristics. His data include historical as well as intra- and intersociety comparisons. Briefly, his essential argument is that the factor of "achievement motivation" (the tendency and impetus to succeed and to excel, as measured by thematic apperception tests, rather than agree-disagree statements) is indispensable in any scientific effort to explain intersociety and intergroup differences in entrepreneurical characteristics and levels of economic growth.

McClelland's data show, for example, that persons of lower-class origins who have experienced upward social mobility have higher scores of achievement motivation (and of "achievement values," a related measure) than do nonmobile lower-class persons *and* persons born into

[7] From an unpublished analysis by H. L. Sheppard, Sheridan Maitland, and Frank Atelsek.

upper-class families. Occupational choice is also related to degree of achievement motivation; that is, the greater the difficulty of achieving success in the occupation chosen, the higher the motivation. Business managers have higher achievement motivation scores than do professionals. Societies of high economic levels, furthermore, are characterized by a high proportion of achievement-oriented persons.

In recent years, considerable interest has arisen in the cooperation of social scientists from many disciplines in efforts to deal with multidisciplinary problems. To some extent, for example, psychologists and economists are now working together on common subjects dealing with manpower problems. Though this situation is not to be found as a general case, it does represent a major departure from the tradition of separateness of the disciplines. Other examples will be cited to show the growing awareness of the potentials of research efforts which encompass multidisciplinary efforts.

As early as 1951, the psychologist, George Katona, pointed out disapprovingly that "some economists treat expectations about all relevant trends as given quantities." He warned that, even when expectations are recognized as neither given nor constant, some scholars "abandon the concept and proceed with their analysis without recourse to expectations." He took Keynes to task for evading the phenomenon of expectation in economic behavior after having admitted, for example, that "expectations as to future yield of capital goods" are crucial in investment decisions. He also questioned Boulding's reason for evading them as constantly changing and "hopelessly unpredictable." Katona contended that the alleged unpredictability of expectations did "not justify their disregard in economic analysis."[8] In real situations, policy-makers and administrators cannot safely rely on Keynes' comforting conclusion (actually an assumption) that expectations are "likely to average out for the community as a whole," that there is "too much uncertainty for it to exert much influence."

Expectations are not only relevant to the study of economic behavior: they can also be studied systematically and used effectively in quantitative inquiries. For this assertion, we rely on the experience of Katona, in his studies on consumer behavior. According to his work, "the as-

---

[8] George Katona, "Expectations and Decisions in Economic Behavior," in Daniel Lerner and Harold D. Lasswell (eds.), *The Policy Sciences* (Stanford: Stanford University Press, 1951), pp. 219ff. Quotations from Keynes are cited by Katona from *The General Theory of Employment, Interest, and Money,* pp. 95, 315, 317. Katona goes on to indicate that some economists, however, such as J. A. Schumpeter and A. G. Hart, have been critical of the tendency to treat expectations as given and/or unpredictable.

sumption that psychological factors need to be studied in economics in connection only with expectations is far too narrow."

If the domain of psychology is the study of human behavior, why cannot it be used specifically in the study of the behavior of business-men, workers, and government officials dealing with economic problems?

Katona's view that *external events* (such as changes in money supply or income, price changes, etc.) are not the sole conditions of behavior is certainly relevant to the manpower field. He wrote that:

> psychology recognizes that human beings do not react to stimuli as automata. It is not enough to know about the objective circumstances in which people behave differently. People's attitudes, motives, and frames of reference shape their perception of the environment and their be-havior. In order to understand economic behavior, subjective variables must also be studied.[8a]

These sentences should encourage the extension of the psychological approach to research in the manpower field.

In the study of manpower problems, "subjective variables" must indeed be included in our analyses. Attitudes, the definition of situations, motives, and frames of reference are not identical for different individuals, groups, or societies, nor are they constant in time. Furthermore, while they may often be correctly viewed as *effects* (or "dependent variables") of external conditions, they may also possess or acquire a functional autonomy and act as *causes* (or "independent variables") in the economic realm. Contemporary research in the area of unemployment problems rarely is carried out with this possibility in mind. More frequently, social and the psychological concomitants are studied only as possible results of such problems.

Whether we are dealing with manpower or other types of investigations, "subjective" variables are amenable to statistical inquiry and analysis. On this point, Katona is again encouraging:

> Fact-finding through economic surveys is not, however, restricted to compiling statistics on unemployment, or the distribution of income, assets and expenditures. From the point of view of survey methodology there is not much difference between finding out about employment status or income, and about the subjective feeling of well-being or dis-tress, or expectations of future income. Both types of data are obtain-able in an unbiased and reliable way, they are quantifiable and con-tribute to the description of the situation as it exists at a given time. Both types of data are subject to sampling and reporting errors, and if

[8a] *Ibid.*, p. 221.

there is a difference between them then it is that interviewing directed toward collecting attitudinal data is simpler than that directed toward collecting financial statistics.[9]

In an essay on the "Non-Economic Assumptions of John Maynard Keynes," the economist Robert Lekachman dealt with the need to identify additional factors influencing consumption, and to cope with population subgroupings.[10] He specifically refers to the value of surveys such as those by George Katona, and makes some other pertinent observations: "Thus, into the last home of rationality in economic affairs, Keynes introduced two interlopers, convention and emotion . . . but it is scarcely a satisfactory theory of the investment process. . . . The work that economists have done in investment theory is excessively vague as a guide to empirical investigations. . . . Relevant concepts are more likely to be found in psychology or sociology."[11]

Unfortunately, the statement that "relevant concepts are more likely to be found in psychology or sociology" is typical of many discussions about the role of noneconomic factors in economic phenomena. If, to explain (and/or predict) economic behavior and trends more adequately, *other* types of social sciences have to be called into play, who is to do the extra work and perform the synthesis? Who *is* systematically taking up the challenge to provide (or do research on) the "relevant concepts"? Lekachman's comment suggests, as a minimum, that a more effective technique has to be found for the coordinated application of all the relevant social sciences to large, complicated problems. Like economics, it is clear that psychology and sociology too must be moved in the direction of closer social science collaboration. Perhaps a new integrated social science is called for.

---

[9] George Katona, "The Function of Survey Research in Economics," in Mirra Komarowsky (ed.), *Common Frontiers of the Social Sciences* (Glencoe, Ill.: Free Press Publishers, 1957), p. 360.

[10] Komarowsky (ed.), *Common Frontiers of the Social Sciences,* p. 350.

[11] *Ibid.,* pp. 349–50. In the same volume, p. 380, William S. Vickrey, in a chapter entitled, "Keynesian Theory and Empirical Inquiry; A Note of Micro- and Macroeconomics," states: "Since the relationship of income to consumption postulated by Keynes is mediated by attitudinal factors, studies of attitudes toward saving and spending should improve the accuracy of prediction. . . . Insofar as changes in attitudes precede changes in behavior—to isolate relevant attitudes and to recognize changes in them would in itself improve prediction. *Attitudes are not in general capable of being studied by aggregative methods, and microeconomic methods must be employed*" (italics not in original). Microeconomic methods in this case would require the use by economists of attitudinal questions and responses —not merely disaggregated statistics on income, savings, consumption, investment, and employment.

LABOR MARKETS, MOBILITY, AND JOB-SEEKING BEHAVIOR

Much remains to be understood about the actual workings of labor markets, and here the need for an integrated social science approach is most urgent. How else can we learn about the specific dynamics in the interaction between employers and job-seekers? About the differences between national, regional, and local markets for separate occupations? About labor mobility (interoccupational, as well as geographical)?

It could be argued effectively that our current theories (and thus our policies) concerning such questions depend too much on simplistic models resting on a variety of unfounded (or changing) assumptions.

A widely accepted notion, regarding geographic mobility, for example, is that an adequate solution to area unemployment is automatically provided by large-scale migration to centers of economic opportunity. (There is even a corollary to this proposition relating to the mobility of capital: that enterprises will be attracted to areas of high unemployment because of the availability of cheap labor and thus contribute to the solution of area unemployment.) While large numbers of persons in depressed areas do leave for other areas presumed to contain job opportunities, there is no evidence that unemployment rates in the areas left behind are thereby lowered. Even after two decades of outmigration from sixteen urban depressed areas, the average rate of unemployment in these areas (in 1960) remained at about 8 percent.[12] Migration out of depressed areas is not necessarily a solution to the problems of *areas and regions,* even if it does become a solution to the problems of *individuals* who migrate to presumed centers of economic opportunity.

Moreover, the expectation that sufficient numbers of unemployed and low-income persons will automatically move in response to opportunities elsewhere is an assumption only. This expectation may be too high for rural as well as urban men and women. "Perfect" mobility would require a number of conditions,[13] including: (1) legal exit and entry rights from and to areas; (2) universal awareness of opportunities elsewhere; (3) a desire to improve employment and income status, even at

[12] Sheppard, Maitland, and Atelsek, unpublished analysis, cited earlier.

[13] These points are taken largely from Wilbert E. Moore, *Industrial Relations and the Social Order* (New York: Macmillan, 1951), pp. 462–72. Lest the reader believe that the first condition applies only to migration from one country to another, it should be noted that in 1935 and 1936, California attempted to reduce the number of migrants, such as drought victims, from entering that state. Los Angeles policemen stopped migrants at the Arizona border during 1936. Cf. *Hearings of the House of Representatives Select Committee Investigating National Defense Migration,* 1942, Pt. 26 (discussed by Moore, p. 465). Current resident requirements in states and municipalities concerning, for example, welfare eligibility may also be construed as efforts to restrain free geographical mobility.

the cost of (4) leaving family, friends, and property, if any; (5) absence of discrimination and prejudice in the new area; (6) willingness to move to, and live in, a new social environment; (7) means of transportation to the new area; (8) occupational interchangeability.

A recent empirical study by the Upjohn Institute is an interdisciplinary effort to understand, in greater depth than is usually attempted, a major topic of labor economics, the job-seeking behavior of unemployed blue-collar workers.[14] A major purpose of this research was to determine whether some selected social-psychological factors could be fruitfully applied—in addition to the usual variables of age and skill, and, in some cases, instead of these variables—to advance existing knowledge and opinion concerning *job-seeking behavior* and *job-finding success* among blue-collar workers. These social-psychological factors included (1) *achievement motivation,* (2) *achievement values,* (3) *job-interview anxiety,* (4) *job-finding expectations,* and (5) *self-identification,* pertaining to age. Only the first three will be discussed here, but they should suffice to indicate the potentials of an integrated approach to manpower problems.

The first factor has already been discussed above, in connection with David McClelland's contributions to the study of economic behavior. The second, achievement values (derived from studies by Bernard Rosen, a sociologist) seeks to measure degree of activism (versus passivism), orientation toward the future, and individualism as elements in the economic or occupational mobility of individuals. Unlike achievement motivation, it is measured by responses to agree-disagree statements (for example: "Planning only makes a person unhappy since your plans hardly ever work out anyway."). Job-interview anxiety, the third factor, refers to the fears that workers may have when confronted with the prospects of an interview for a job by an employer or his representative (for example: "Before being interviewed for a job, do you worry very much? A fair amount? Hardly worry? Not worry at all?").

The intricate interaction between the characteristics of unemployed blue-collar workers and the nature of the labor market (or local economy) requires attention. The latter has been studied extensively and intensively by economists, as a phenomenon *sui generis.* In similar fashion, a restricted number of characteristics of employed versus unemployed workers has been examined. But these characteristics should include more than age, schooling, and skills (not to mention race and

---

[14] Harold L. Sheppard and A. Harvey Belitsky, *The Job Hunt: Job-Seeking Behavior of Unemployed Workers in a Local Economy* (Baltimore: The Johns Hopkins Press, 1966).

sex): Job-seeking behavior patterns and social-psychological tendencies should also be added to this list.

Job-seeking behavior is affected by many factors, and consists of many components. One is the expectation of call-back to previous employers. Another is one's image of the labor market (for example, estimates of job-finding success). How soon does the unemployed worker begin his job search? What kinds of job-search techniques are used? How many companies are checked for job-finding? Does the worker restrict his "shopping list" of potential employers? What is his *method* of checking with such companies? Does he concentrate on companies he believes to be looking for new employees? Or does he check from company to company without prior hearsay information about possible openings? All such questions are pertinent to an analysis of the job-seeking process and its outcome.

An important point is that *job-seeking behavior* is not the same as *job-finding success*. Such success is a joint function of the worker's job-seeking behavior and the employer's demands (including skill, age, and racial and sex preferences). This is one way of expressing the reciprocal relationship between economic and social-psychological variables.

The Upjohn study has incorporated the above social-psychological factors as useful, explanatory concepts of the job-seeking behavior of unemployed workers. This job-seeking behavior, as already suggested, has a significant bearing on degree of job-finding success. The relationship between the social-psychological factors and job-finding success was accordingly analyzed, and it was found meaningful for a variety of subgroups in the sample. When such a relationship was not found (for example, among high school graduates), *length of unemployment* prior to reemployment was found, nevertheless, to be related to such factors as achievement motivation and achievement values.

As an example of the interaction between economic and social-psychological variables, the researchers found that to a far greater extent than workers *not* expecting to be called back to old jobs, the workers who *did* expect (and actually received) a call-back chose not to look at all for new jobs when laid off; the "nonlookers" in the second group were characterized by lower achievement motivation than the "lookers." That is, despite the relative absence of economic pressures to find a new job (because they accurately expected a call-back), a certain number of workers nevertheless chose to seek a new job. With respect to achievement motivation, such workers were different from those with similar call-back expectations but who did not look at all. On the other hand, among those workers not reemployed at old jobs, the lookers and non-lookers were not different from each other with respect to this and other social-psychological characteristics: the economic necessity to find a new job was strong enough to obscure any social-psychological differences. But such differences were found to be related to *how soon* the lookers in the group not reemployed at old jobs actually started their job search after being laid off. That is, achievement motivation did not affect the decision to look for a new job among workers not called back to old jobs, but it *did* apparently affect the *timing* for starting their job search.

Even the *ways* in which new-job finders found their new jobs were found to be related to social-psychological factors. For example, none of the workers characterized both by high achievement motivation *and* achievement values obtained their new jobs through the state employment service, as compared to one-sixth of all other workers finding new jobs. It was also found that more workers with high achievement motivation *and* low job-interview anxiety tended to find their new jobs through direct application at the company hiring gates than did other workers. Workers with the very opposite traits (low motivation *and* high anxiety) tended to find their new jobs through the state employment service more than did other workers. The fact that one-half of all the new-job finders obtaining jobs through the employment service had low motivation and high anxiety—in sharp contrast to less than one-fifth of all other new-job finders—points to the important role played by this public agency in the job-seeking problems of unemployed workers. Persons with certain social-psychological characteristics often require some type of institutional intermediary between themselves and the ultimate employer.

Finally, it should be noted that, in the analysis of the ways in which new-job finders actually found their jobs, the variables of age and skill had no explanatory value. This finding is an example of the proposition that social-psychological variables may frequently provide *alternative,* and not *supplementary,* explanations of economic phenomena.

As for the relationship of job-finding success and social-psychological variables, the Upjohn study found that: (1) workers with high motivation *and* high values—regardless of age or skill level—had a significantly higher rate of success than all other workers; (2) among skilled and semiskilled workers only, those with high motivation *and* low anxiety had the highest rate of success, while workers with low motivation and high anxiety had the lowest rate; (3) among older workers (39 years and above) only, those with low values and high anxiety had a lower rate of success than all other older workers.

As for geographic mobility, the Upjohn research disclosed first of all that little, if any, relationship existed between reemployment status and past geographic mobility. Workers still unemployed when interviewed had been just as mobile in the past as other workers in the sample. When asked if they would take better jobs even if it required being away from their families, or having to move 1,000 miles from home, the still-unemployed workers said "Yes" much more frequently than did the other workers. Further analysis revealed that 16 percent of the male sample would not be willing to move 1,000 miles, nor even *less* than 1,000 miles, *and* would not move even if their moving and new home-buying expenses were provided. This "hard-core immobile" group (in contrast to the group saying in the first place that they would move 1,000 miles for a better job) tended to be much lower in achievement motivation. In other words, even when all the economic costs of moving for a better job are eliminated, workers with low achievement motivation would tend more to refuse such opportunities than would those with high motivation.

INTERDISCIPLINARY APPROACH

These illustrations should confirm the value of including social-psychological variables in unemployment and labor market studies. Furthermore, such an interdisciplinary endeavor cannot depend on a strict division of labor between economists and sociologists or psychologists. Economists have to integrate the concepts and variables of the other social scientists into their traditional approaches, and sociologists and psychologists interested in the same phenomena have to do likewise.

Each social science, of course, has a reason to view its own subject matter as primarily a set of abstractions logically developed from *selected* facets (or "data") of the total reality. Each has an established charter for pursuing the construction of mutually exclusive (and closed, non-eclectic) "theoretical systems." As long as the "users" of such neatly departmentalized conceptual schemes recognize that they and their fellow conceptualizers are making excursions into the realm of "as if," no harm really follows.

But when individuals and organizations (public and private) are seeking solutions to, and making decisions pertaining to, employment and economic and manpower development, they have to be aware that "pure" noneclectic theories of economics, psychology, and sociology used separately alongside each other (or used singly to the neglect of the others) can result in practical failures and in inaccurate predictions. The practical pursuit of such ideals as "rational utilization of manpower," "expansion of employment and economic opportunities," and "mobility in response to opportunities," requires a synthesis or distillation of pertinent ideas and approaches characterizing the various existing social sciences.

266

Interdisciplinary endeavors on the analytical level are more likely to be successful when relevant concepts and variables drawn from the several disciplines are at the command of one individual. This is one of the major implications of the development of a formal "manpower social science." Similarly, the practical planning and application phases of programs to meet the challenges of unemployment and manpower development are more likely to prove successful when administrators who sense the need for such a "manpower social science" are responsible for policy and program implementation. Greater alertness to the interdisciplinary aspects of real manpower situations and problems should, in any case, help to remedy the deficient supply of well-rounded practitioners.

17

PRODUCTIVITY MEASURES AND FORECASTS FOR EMPLOYMENT AND STABILIZATION POLICY

IRVING H. SIEGEL

THE STORY IN BRIEF

This paper explores certain aspects of the meaning, measurement, supply, quality, and use of productivity statistics in the light of policy requirements concerning employment and wage-price stabilization in our evolving economy. It touches on some of the many conceptual, technical, and practical problems that merit wider attention in our changing environment. Such problems must be appreciated by public and private policy-makers and by program administrators as well as by the constructors and various users of productivity measures.

Two points should be made first about the economic context of this paper:

1. The strong interpretation of the Employment Act of 1946 in recent years has already conferred new importance on labor-productivity time series, including forecasts.

2. The recent trend toward strong interpretation is likely to become confirmed as our "mixed" economy continues to shade into a "monitored" one.

With respect to interpretation of the Employment Act, a reminder is needed that the language is heavily qualified and may therefore be read (as it has been by different Economic Advisers to the President) with varying emphasis. The tortuous Teutonic sentence that comprises the Act's Declaration of Policy (Section 2) does provide a federal charter for directing public and private policy toward fuller employment with reasonably stable prices; but the law assumes no unconditional obligation, sets no priorities, and gives no unhedged pledge of jobs. Just before the familiar terminal words, "maximum employment, production, and purchasing power," we find the infinitive "to promote"—rather than, say, "to guarantee." Furthermore, although the law is frequently miscalled the "Full Employment Act," the adjective "full" is nowhere used, and no criterion for "maximum" is offered.

The second of the two points refers to the emerging economic order. In the future, we may expect federal prestige, laws, regulations, and market power to be marshaled still more systematically for the exertion of "countervailing" force. More positive, though selective, use will be made of governmental tools, with due but elastic regard for our democratic traditions, to induce "responsible" private behavior in a widening range of productive activities and business situations.

The discussion that follows suggests several ways in which the productivity information base might be strengthened to assist the future formulation and execution of employment and stabilization policy:

1. Improvement, as opportunities permit, in the scope and quality of the corpus of productivity information for individual industries, industry combinations, and larger economic sectors.

2. Support of further research into stubborn problems of concept and meaning—including test computations, where feasible, to disclose the direction and magnitude of the difference between (a) preferred measures and (b) the available or derivable ones that have to be used as substitutes.

3. Promotion of the design, construction, and testing of algebraically consistent index numbers that are especially suitable for joint analysis of changes in productivity and other economic variables, such as wages and prices.

4. Encouragement of: (a) experimentation with productivity forecasting, since explicit outlook estimates are often much more appropriate than routine extensions of past trends; and (b) related research efforts to anticipate the nature, extent, and implications of technological and other important changes.

5. Maintenance, insofar as practicable, of "flexible" governmental and public attitudes toward "official" productivity statistics and measurement techniques that cannot qualify as definitive.

6. Stimulation of further company interest in the construction of measures, trends, and forecasts of productivity as well as other variables relating to company operations.

7. Extension, at modest cost in comparison to obtainable benefits, of the education of policy-makers, administrators, analysts, the press, and the general public with respect to the character and limitations of available and normally derivable productivity statistics.

This statement of needs neither overlooks nor is intended to disparage past accomplishments in the labor-productivity field; and it does not mean that data outside the immediate realm of productivity measurement are less deserving of continual attention. The lifetime of the Employment Act has indeed been a period of great progress in economic statistics; but productivity work has not been especially favored and its various prunings have hardly been intended to assure robustness. The realm of productivity measurement is aided in some degree, on the other hand, when improvements are made in other statistics that are utilizable in pertinent indirect methods of estimation (e.g., price deflation). But it could be aided much more if significant improvements were made along other lines, as indicated in the preceding seven statements.

THE PRODUCTIVITY NEXUS

The developing need for more and better labor-productivity tools for policy is clearly reflected in the Employment Act. Productivity, in the present context, means the ratio of production to employment (man-hours or persons, unweighted or weighted in some appropriate way); and these are two of the three variables mentioned in the concluding phrase of the Declaration of Policy, already cited. Productivity also enters into the practical definition of "purchasing power," as the promulgation of explicit "wage-price guideposts" in the 1962 *Economic Report of the President* illustrates. Finally, productivity forecasts have a place in the discharge of the presidential responsibility to report annually the "current and foreseeable trends in the levels of employment, production, and purchasing power" (Section 3).

At this point, a necessary distinction between "verbal" and "literal" algebra should be noted. The mere cancellation of words in such identities as "production = employment × productivity" or "wages = unit labor cost × employment × productivity" is not a sufficient criterion for the construction of suitably matched index numbers. Ideally, compatibility in a more "literal" sense—in the detailed data, formulas, and weights—is also required. Since these more exacting requirements can rarely be met, however, it is desirable, at least, to appreciate their nature and the risks involved in substituting an available and seemingly equivalent measure for a preferable but unavailable one.

Though commonly neglected, the distinction between "verbal" and "literal" algebra in index-number measurement is not a technical trifle. Policy-makers, administrators, and specialists in nonproductivity fields, even those who consider themselves "practical," ought to know or care that algebraic operations help to determine the meaning and appropriateness of alternative productivity measures, that different plausible sets of operations may lead to significantly different productivity numbers, that different numbers may counsel different decisions, that absence and ignorance of the most suitable alternative productivity measure may foreclose consideration and choice of the most warranted course of action. "Practical" people cannot really afford to rely on the mere names of series, on symbols, and on form, and to show indifference to content.[1]

UNEVEN RECOGNITION OF NEEDS; UNEVEN PROSPECTS OF REMEDY

As our mixed economy progressively becomes a monitored one, in which the federal government exercises a more positive and a wider coordinating role, the creation of more and better productivity statistics and outlook estimates will very probably proceed at a rate that is far less than satisfactory. The expansion in supply and the advance of quality may be much too limited for the demands placed on the national data base. The popularity of macro-economic series-watching already tends to favor certain broad aggregates and general economic indicators over detailed measures. Easy reliance on these comprehensive measures leads to neglect of their conceptual and technical flaws and their incomplete appropriateness to many of the uses to which they are put. Their apparent adequacy diverts attention from requirements for other pertinent and detailed series, especially building blocks. Indeed, a preoccupation with aggregates and a complacent widespread acceptance of "verbal" algebra may make it appear that buildings no longer have to be built by experts, or with bricks or similar elemental materials, and that, therefore, little need exists for the creation and improvement of such materials and for the careful drafting of specifications and blueprints.

Inattention to the basic shortage of productivity building blocks is easy to document (although some of the more experienced students of economic affairs do occasionally file pointed reminders). It is remarkable that only a few scattered references were made to labor productivity by the individuals, organizations, and users of statistics canvassed in 1965

---

[1] For further discussion of "verbal" and "literal" algebra, see three items by Irving H. Siegel: *Concepts and Measurement of Production and Productivity* (Washington: U.S. Bureau of Labor Statistics, 1952); "On the Design of Consistent Output and Indexes for Productivity Measurement," in *Output, Input, and Productivity Measurement* (Princeton, N.J.: Princeton University Press, 1961), pp. 23–41; and "Systems of Algebraically Consistent Index Numbers," *1965 Proceedings of the Business and Economic Section, American Statistical Association,* pp. 368–72.

by the Joint Economic Committee for views on improvements required in the federal information base.[2] The 1967 Budget, furthermore, shows a trivial increase in expenditures for "salaries and expenses" of the Bureau of Labor Statistics for 1966 over 1965 and for 1967 over 1966 "for improved statistics and statistical research on employment and unemployment, wages, prices, and productivity." [3] A related newspaper item reports a proposed "boost" from 30 to 35 or 37 in the number of industries covered by separate productivity indexes of the Bureau.[4] Practically no reference was made to statistical needs with respect to productivity in the papers presented at the symposium celebrating the twentieth anniversary of the Employment Act in February, 1966.

Whatever is added to the existing stock of productivity information by federal agencies (including, incidentally, the industry data of the Bureau of the Census) will be most welcome, but the gains will very likely be much too small and come much too late to satisfy any purist. The nature, scope, and rate of progress affecting published industry and sector statistics will doubtless be restricted, as in the past, by technical difficulties of concept and measurement (as in the service industries), by proper differences of opinion among experts as to priorities, by the costs (in time, money, and scarce statistical manpower) of data compilation for new series (especially for making algebraically consistent measures for particular analyses), and by the proliferation of competing demands for available funds. Private organizations, such as the National Bureau of Economic Research, will presumably add to the supply of historical series, but their contribution can hardly prove decisive in view of the growth and diversity of foreseeable needs.

Plentiful opportunities for theoretical, analytical, managerial, and educational advances will be afforded by the challenges of policy to the confined data base. The construction of test measures and projections, the elaboration of econometric models, and the empirical study of production functions could yield some productivity-information bonuses. Additional companies, furthermore, may find sufficient reason to prepare indexes of production, labor input, productivity, and unit labor costs as guides for internal operations and planning, but these indexes will most probably not be published.[5] Individual government agencies will

[2] U.S., Congress, Joint Economic Committee, *Improved Statistics for Economic Growth,* July, 1965.

[3] *The Budget of the United States Government: Fiscal Year Ending June 30, 1967,* p. 299.

[4] *Wall Street Journal,* February 1, 1966.

[5] See, for example, J. W. Kendrick and Daniel Creamer, *Measuring Company Productivity* ("Studies in Business Economics," No. 89; New York: National Industrial Conference Board, 1965).

surely expand their measurement programs for managerial purposes too.[6] The stage will be set for a continuing project that merits governmental acceptance on cost-benefit grounds—enhancement of the sophistication of the various classes of users, the press, and the general public with regard to the character, applicability, and pitfalls of available productivity statistics and with regard to the properties of more suitable special-purpose measures (including forecasts).

The Employment Act has served as a focus for orderly efforts to improve the statistics needed for coordinating public and private policy in the interest of economic expansion with reasonable price stability. In the 1940's and 1950's, "gaps" in productivity and other statistical areas were widely advertised—for example, by the Joint Economic Committee in cooperation with the Bureau of the Budget.[7] In the 1958 *Economic Report of the President,* prepared when the federal economic role was far less activist, a special appendix dealt with problems of productivity measurement. In the 1962 *Report,* which promulgated the wage-price guideposts as informational rather than directive, the limitations of productivity statistics again were frankly addressed. In subsequent *Reports,* as the guideposts acquired doctrinal force, the caveats became muted despite their continuing applicability to available statistical gauges. A mellow retrospective chapter in the 1966 *Report,* reviewing the first two decades of the Act, points to notable improvements, especially in the timely processing of an increasing number of widely used "economic indicators"; but it also notes that "our data are not completely satisfactory" and cites productivity and fringe benefits among the areas "where there are important gaps and weaknesses," remediable "only by expansion of our statistical programs."

In 1962, a Presidential Commission reported on productivity and other statistical needs expressed to it by the Council of Economic Advisers and other organizations and individuals. An explicit interest in industry series was registered by the Council: "its analyses of . . . economic developments would be greatly aided by better statistics on employment and hours for major industrial sectors, which could be used in conjunction with gross national product and other output estimates to determine shifts in productivity." The Council also "indicated that one of its most urgent statistical needs is for better data on hours worked in all major sectors of the economy as a prerequisite for early and

[6] U.S., Bureau of the Budget, *Measuring Productivity of Federal Government Organizations,* 1964; and its *War on Waste,* December 31, 1964.

[7] *Statistical Gaps,* a Committee Print, was issued in 1948. Also noteworthy are the Joint Economic Committee's *Hearings on Economic Statistics,* 1954, and *Hearings on Employment and Unemployment Statistics,* 1955.

reliable estimates of productivity changes." [8] In the long run, it is to be hoped, even immediate statistical requirements of the Council may be partially accommodated!

In 1965, while the Council still had its old needs for productivity information, it acquired an additional context in which to restate them. A Council member, addressing the Federal Statistics Users Conference at the end of October, noted that "rough, global figures" had proved adequate for public economic policy relating to reduction of the gap between actual and potential employment. Successful reduction, however, rationalized a shift of primary interest to specific spheres in which "we need to strengthen our knowledge substantially"—productivity, as well as prices (domestic and export), capacity, job vacancies, and fringe benefits.[9]

THE GROWING FEDERAL ROLE

What are the pertinent features of the evolving environment in which productivity is assuming new significance, regardless of the state and adequacy of the information at hand? A trend toward a "monitored" economy, even in "peacetime," is indicated by recent domestic events, and also by earlier developments in Great Britain and Western Continental Europe.[10] Emergence of a new pattern, a new "style," is discernible—although detours, inconsistencies, and reversals are also to be expected in the transition from a "mixed" economy, as competitive forces and as the flux of international affairs continue to register their effects.

Two characteristics may be said to differentiate the monitored economy from the mixed economy. In the latter, the central government already demands a sizable share of the national product and already has a wide assortment of powers relating to taxes, money and credit, resource development, welfare, and markets. Thus, it already possesses a capability of influencing private economic decisions significantly and selectively. More important, through impact on both aggregate demand and the supply of critical resources, it can also influence the general tempo of economic activity and the total volume of employment. The

---

[8] President's Committee to Appraise Employment and Unemployment Statistics, *Measuring Employment and Unemployment*, 1962, pp. 39 and 94.

[9] See reference to remarks of Otto Eckstein in *The American Statistician,* December, 1965, p. 2.

[10] See the various essays in B. G. Hickman (ed.), *Quantitative Planning of Economic Policy* (Washington: Brookings Institution, 1965); and M. W. Edelman and R. W. Fleming, *The Politics of Wage-Price Decisions: A Four-Country Analysis* (Urbana, Ill.: University of Illinois Press, 1965).

monitored economy is distinguished, first, by the use of government prestige and power (in our case, through the presidential office) to define a comprehensive master objective or small cluster of dominant "national goals," to set "targets" relating thereto, and to pursue these aims with deliberativeness (*primarily* by the manipulation of "instrumental variables" and by "exhortation" of the private sector). The second distinguishing characteristic is the governmental disposition to achieve the collaboration deemed essential to the "national interest" or the "public interest" by going *beyond* general exhortation to threats, sanctions, and the mobilization of public sentiment against recalcitrant private groups.

In the monitored economy, formal detailed "planning" is not attempted for society, although quantitative and other simplified forecasting "models" may be used as aids in public and private policy design. Heavy stress continues to be placed there on private initiative and money incentives, and wide latitude remains for freedom of economic choice and action. The national output retains its dominant consumer orientation, at least in "peacetime." Indeed, if the monitored economy is successful in sustaining growth, an extra welfare bonus becomes available to the population through more complete and more continual access to goods and services produced in greater abundance.

While traditional cultural values are strained in the monitored economy, the spine of dominant ideology could remain intact. The changes would tend to be regarded as rational or necessary modifications in the rules of the game in response to new challenges. On the whole, the people may seem, like Macbeth following the dagger, to be marshaled where they were already going. The targets indicate general directions, rather than personal quotas, and gains in material welfare could go far to compensate for any felt deprivation in the realm of intangibles. Projections that are judged desirable are expected to derive a self-fulfilling impetus from the responses of the private sector, and corrective private responses are expected to be induced by the announcement of national prospects regarded as objectionable. In addition, government has to "plan" its own complements to such private responses, which may not be deemed sufficient for attainment of established national targets.

The roots of the emerging U.S. version of the monitored economy are ramified and deep, traceable without exaggeration back to the Constitutional Convention—long before our system even became recognized as "mixed." If specific historical tributaries are to be singled out, first importance must be assigned to the experience and to the threat of wars and recessions—emergencies that fundamentally jeopardize personal and national security, that accordingly provide occasion for the enactment and exercise of extraordinary federal powers, and that also tend to focus and fix federal leadership in the Presidency.[11]

EMPLOYMENT ACT AS INTEGRATING FRAMEWORK

The Employment Act of 1946, passed in an atmosphere of concern that the economic sluggishness of the 1930's might return after World War II, provides a handy and "logical" matrix for coordinating federal policies with each other and with those of lower levels of government and the private sector. The turgid single sentence that constitutes the Declaration of Policy is nowadays being interpreted, as already noted, as a charter for strong federal monitorial action rather than as a negotiated baseline of bipartisan unanimity. A reconciliation of the Employment Act and the older Federal Reserve Act, which provides another, but less comprehensive, approach to the same sorts of national goals, remains to be effected in the future. A contribution to this rapprochement is offered at the end of this paper.

One of the major recent strides toward a monitored economy within the framework of the Employment Act involves the adoption and policing of guidelines for relating wages to productivity and restraining prices. Introduced in the 1962 *Economic Report of the President,* the "guideposts" have since been energetically enforced to frustrate industry intentions to raise steel, copper, and aluminum prices. Government intervention has included threats to use "monopsonistic" market power and to release materials stockpiled for military emergency. Redistribution or withholding of federal contracts has been threatened in other instances—for example, in an effort to restrain construction wages— and federal intercession helped to undo cigarette price increases in 1966.

In 1964, furthermore, fiscal policy was used boldly to expand total economic demand and thereby reduce unemployment. A drastic tax reduction that had been wistfully contemplated for many years was daringly executed at the President's request by an agreeable Congress.

---

[11] In recent years, congressional hearings and the reports of such groups as the President's Commission on National Goals, the Committee for Economic Development's Commission on Money and Credit, the Rockefeller Brothers Fund, the American Assembly, and the National Planning Association have helped to modify professional, business, and public attitudes concerning master objectives and the potentials for government-private cooperation. Earlier contributions have been made, of course, by the *Economic Reports of the President*—and also by the widely advertised concepts of "partnership" and "shared responsibility" of the Eisenhower era, which are forerunners of the current "creative federalism." Precedents were provided before World War II in the reports of the Temporary National Economic Committee and of such New Deal agencies as the National Resources Committee and the Works Progress Administration.

Growth was spurred as the potential economic energy previously wound into the progressive rate structure became quickly converted into the kinetic energy of private spending. The popularity of this tax cut and the President's own prestige facilitated subordination of "market" decisions by industry leaders to the Executive's interpretation of the national interest.

To add concreteness to our discussion, we refer to various passages in the preface to the 1965 *Economic Report of the President*. For our purpose, it does not matter that some of the assertions are, and must remain, arguable, despite the wide advertisement of a "new economics." The Employment Act is interpreted there as a "mandate" for pursuit of "full employment" and certain other supporting objectives: "rapid growth, price stability, and equilibrium in our balance of payments." The consistency of these goals, even of their "mutually reinforcing" character, given "proper policies," is considered to have been proved by experience. The President also stated that he regards "the goal of over-all price stability as fully implied in the language of the Employment Act."

Lauding "the imagination, prudence, and skill of our businessmen, workers, investors, farmers, and consumers" for their fundamental contributions to "our basically private economy," the President observed that an important ingredient had been added since 1960 "to invigorate private efforts." This ingredient is positive government policy, which provides "the vital margin of difference" for "steady, but noninflationary, growth." Indeed, 1964 marked "the first time our Nation cut taxes for the declared purpose of speeding the advance of the private economy toward 'maximum employment, production, and purchasing power.' " The President pledged new efforts to eradicate joblessness in accord with his interpretation of the Act: *"The promise in the Employment Act of job opportunities for all those able and wanting to work has not yet been fulfilled.* We cannot rest until it is."

With respect to wages and prices, the President appealed to "the sense of public responsibility of our labor leaders and our industrial leaders to do their full part." He commended the wage and price guideposts to these leaders and to the public. He cautioned that he would "maintain a close watch," would "draw public attention to private actions which threaten the public interest," and would ask "for special, detailed analysis of price or wage increases in key sectors of the economy."

With respect to job opportunities, the President placed prime reliance on "fiscal and monetary measures," but he also recognized certain structural problems that would have to be met in other ways. In addition to referring to proposals for manpower training and for strengthening the U.S. Employment Service, he noted that an "active manpower policy" is being developed "to reduce human costs, raise productivity, and make possible full employment without inflation."

FORECASTING PRODUCTIVITY AND TECHNOLOGY

The hazards of forecasting changes in productivity and technology will add to the frustrations already encountered in historical measurement as federal policy demands a wider variety of explicit estimates of the future. The follies committed in academic as well as journalistic discussions of the prospective impacts of, say, research and development activity and of "automation" cannot modify the government's increasing requirement for better appraisals and they need not assure significant or rapid improvement in techniques or in judgment. Earlier public and private efforts to forecast technological change and its implications (e.g., by the National Resources Committee and the Twentieth Century Fund) as well as more recent efforts (e.g., by the Bureau of Labor Statistics) do suggest useful study approaches. Among other things, they alert us to the importance of distinguishing stages that have different economic significance: invention, engineering development, innovation, and widespread acceptance. Even within the last of these phases, which may seem relatively well defined, a valuable lesson may be learned through reflection on the persisting and extending economic significance of an "old" invention such as the automobile in a period so rich in "new" inventions. Clichés such as the "accelerating pace of technological advance" obviously require fine-grain scrutiny in the interest of formulating relevant policy.

Since productivity outlook depends on technological and other contingencies, it may always seem foolhardy to attempt more than a "conservative" extrapolation or minor modification of past trends. Planning for action, public and private, tends to discount talk about an "accelerating pace," especially if errors of overcommitment of resources are penalized more heavily than errors of undercommitment. But experimentation with explicit—detailed and time-specific—productivity forecasting is surely desirable. Furthermore, since implicit forecasts of productivity are being generated whenever forecasts are made in studies that focus specifically and explicitly on related variables, the productivity implications should be recognized. Such implicit productivity forecasts merit explicit formulation for comparison with, or for replacement of, figures derived in some other manner.

Whatever the vocabulary one prefers, it is desirable to differentiate two kinds of forecasting and two subclasses within each.[12] These distinctions acquire new importance with the enlargement of governmental interest in employment levels and price-wage relationships. One major forecast category refers to outlook statements made by an objective or neutral outsider—an observer who does not try to affect what he anticipates. The second category refers to outlook statements that immediately involve the forecaster or his principal as an actor—statements that are intended to be fulfilled through the exertion of direct or indirect influence. Within the first main class, two varieties should be differentiated: *prediction* (or *prophecy*), which refers to unequivocal statements about what *will* happen; and *projection,* which refers to conditional (if–then) statements about the future, to the implications of various assumptions that need not be (or may not prove to be) correct. Within the second major category, we distinguish two subdivisions: *programming,* relating to statements that the forecaster or his principal attempts to validate through manipulation of variables under direct control, through use of resources and powers under command; and *propaganda,* relating to statements to be fulfilled through influence on other decision-makers by communication of information or opinion.

If a policy-maker has complete control over relevant variables and the environment, all varieties of forecast are equivalent; and, if he can, therefore, make reliable predictions or prophecies, these cease to be of interest to him and no longer need to be made. In the more usual case, projections, preferably more than one alternative, are devised; and the persons or organizations having an interest in applications and outcomes pursue the one deemed "best" or most likely of realization through programming and propaganda. It is clear that, for the advancement of national goals, public and private decision-makers engage in projection, programming, and propaganda activities. The federal role of "higher-system" monitor depends in some degree on the prestige and credibility of official forecasts. Interactions and dynamic effects that are induced by federal programming and propaganda should ideally encourage fulfillment of desirable forecasts (those in the "national interest") and inhibit or counter forecasts of events deemed objectionable.

Interest in forecasting has increased greatly in recent years, but it favors the broad economic indicators (e.g., national price indexes) and such aggregates as the gross national product and its major components.

[12] See Irving H. Siegel, "Technological Change and Long-Run Forecasting," *Journal of Business,* July, 1953, pp. 141–56. This paper was prepared in the course of a study made under the auspices of the Twentieth Century Fund.

The shorter run seems to attract special attention, and there is an unwarranted tendency to interpret past good estimates as evidence of the improvement of forecasting art without reference to the specific circumstances involved and to the many past failures. The review of forecasting performance, however, is a wholesome activity that is becoming more evident. On the other hand, distinctions like those noted above among varieties of forecasts are still far from fully appreciated.[13]

Productivity forecasting in particular seems to be a weak and neglected art—certainly in comparison to the art of estimating the future population and labor force, which are also important factors in the manpower-requirements outlook. Perhaps, because the average annual increase in output per man-hour computed for, say, the private sector is numerically small, the task seems easy and the consequences of error seem minor.[14]

Let us look briefly at some approaches to productivity forecasting. *Econometric forecasts* are hard to make because productivity need not be significantly related in given periods to, say, investment in plant and equipment, the growth or supply of educated manpower, or expenditures for research and development. Even production and employment do not move together in the short run, and the long-run divergence is not stable from industry to industry.[15] *"Naïve" forecasts,* which assume the persistence of an observed past rate of productivity increase, also lack realism. *Judgmental forecasts* naturally differ according to the knowledge, intuition, competence, and temperament of the students making them. Recent experience with forecasts of the employment implications of "automation," to which we have already referred, should warn us how erratic judgment may be when not tempered by an appreciation of

[13] On this paragraph, see, for example, Victor Zarnowitz, "How Accurate Are the Forecasts?," *Challenge,* January–February, 1966, pp. 20ff.; statement of G. H. Orcutt in *Improved Statistics for Economic Growth,* pp. 102–5; George Jaszi, Lawrence Grose, and Maurice Liebenberg, *Forecasting with Judgmental and Econometric Models: A Case Study* (Washington: U.S. Department of Commerce, May, 1965); D. B. Suits, "An Econometric Forecast of the Outlook for 1965," *1964 Proceedings of the Business and Economic Statistics Section, American Statistical Association,* pp. 18–21; A. M. Okun, "A Review of Some Economic Forecasts for 1955–57," *Journal of Business,* July, 1959, pp. 199–211; P. A. Samuelson, "Economic Forecasting and National Policy," in *The Employment Act: Past and Future* (Washington: National Planning Association, 1946), pp. 130–34; and *Business Week,* January 15, 1966, pp. 19–20.

[14] See remarks by Samuelson, "Economic Forecasting and National Policy," p. 133.

[15] Siegel, "Technological Change and Long-Run Forecasting"; an unsigned article on "Productivity: Key to Price Stability," *Challenge,* January–February, 1966, pp. 24–25; and various papers included in *Manpower Implications of Automation* (Washington: U.S. Department of Labor, December, 1964).

history, an interest in statistical and other evidence, a sensitivity to the difference between technical feasibility and economic practicality, and a concern for the eternal distinction between scholarship and journalism.

PRODUCTIVITY FACTOR IN EMPLOYMENT AND PRODUCTION OUTLOOK

The more deeply one is involved in forecasting manpower and output prospects, the more troublesome becomes the problem of choosing appropriate productivity factors. Naïve forecasts are often made; for example, the figure for the last year or the average for a recent period is commonly accepted. But a seemingly conservative approach need not lead to realistic results, since annual productivity change is not smooth, and an occasional decline may be experienced. Furthermore, even past multiyear averages vary according to the length and the character of the period selected. Close students of productivity are reluctant to forecast accelerations in the annual rate of increase [16] or are content with only small upward adjustments in the rate—despite strong contrary propaganda aimed at influencing public policy.

This is an appropriate place at which to state that our society courts needless dangers through (1) neglect of the gaps and the more easily remediable defects in productivity information, (2) only patchy support of nonjournalistic research into the nature and implications of technological currents and prospects, and (3) inadequate attention to needs for general education on these matters for the responsible exercise of the functions of citizenship. Government manpower policy could be forced massively in the wrong direction in the absence of sufficient and more or less objective information for distinguishing between a new era and a new error. A worthy objective of public instruction is to endow "the people" (including bureaucrats) with enough "sophistication" to detect the gist of a message embedded in noise even before, say, a National Commission on Technology, Automation, and Technological Progress comes into being, deliberates, and prepares a report. The difficulty of achievement does not diminish the importance of dedication to such an objective, especially in a democracy.

[16] In *Measurement of Technological Change* (Washington: U.S. Department of Labor, July 1965), Solomon Fabricant, the leading student of U.S. productivity, stated that there is no "good basis for supposing acceleration, in recent years, in the rate of technological change" (p. 23). Fabricant prefers to estimate such change by means of a productivity index for capital and labor combined, although he also cautions against belief that "there is or ever will be a single simple measure." (Formulas for productivity referring to *all* economic inputs combined were presented by Siegel in *Concepts and Measurement of Production and Productivity*.)

Informed students and practitioners recognize and acknowledge many limitations in techniques and data that bedevil manpower forecasting. The 1965 *Manpower Report of the President,* for example, observes (p. 52) that "projecting future manpower requirements is inherently a difficult and hazardous undertaking, in view of the endless variety of technological, economic, political, and other events which may affect these requirements." An outstanding productivity authority, having had occasion recently to note the existence of aggregate productivity measures based on two sets of labor-input data (i.e., "establishment" and "labor force" figures) that do not always agree, further observed: "For some purposes, . . . the difference is a bit of a nuisance, and this is one of the sources of our problems, the fact that we don't have really very good basic statistics even on employment and hours of work." [17]

For at least three reasons, it would be desirable to project manpower requirements industry by industry (ideally, within an input-output framework) and then aggregate the results, but this approach can be pursued only part of the way. Detailed forecasting would permit averaging of the errors that arise in component estimation; allow finer examination of the prospects of particular categories of workers and of specific occupations; and preclude intrusion of an algebraic factor that occasionally distorts aggregate productivity magnitudes when these are derived directly. The authority cited above comments thus on the paucity of industry productivity series:

> Nobody is preparing current statistics on productivity by individual industries covering a substantial number of industries. I do not know why there should be such a lack of vital statistics. We need to know more than just the average, or the figures for just a few highly aggregated industrial groups. We need to have some idea of the spread among different industries.[18]

Aggregate productivity estimates are frequently used in forecasting "growth," which is commonly represented by gross national product or private-sector output expressed in supposedly "constant" prices. The productivity figures are applied to labor projections in this case. In the 1965 *Economic Report of the President,* it is observed (p. 92) that the rapid rise of productivity during the long expansion "is typical of a period of improving utilization rates" and "does not provide clear evidence that the long-term trend of productivity growth has changed." On the other hand, sustained expansion favors higher rates of investment and the introduction of advanced production processes, and these

---

[17] Fabricant, *Measurement of Technological Change,* p. 17.
[18] *Ibid.,* p. 21.

changes, according to the *Report,* should contribute to a "gradual" rise in the productivity trend although the net quantitative impact "defies careful measurement."

The occasional anomalous divergence of an aggregate productivity measure from the figures for components is only one of the many impediments to accurate forecasting. It is also a source of confusion in the administration of wage-price policy, as will be noted again later. Thus, it is possible for a measured rise (fall) of productivity in the private sector as a whole to exceed (be less than) the indicated productivity gains for the farm and nonfarm components of the sector. Moreover, an observed anomaly of this sort may disappear upon revision of the output statistics *after* it has been "explained"! The "effect of intersector manpower shifts," as this type of distortion [19] is designated in the 1963 *Manpower Report of the President* (p. 72), is normally positive and hence welcomed as a source of national productivity gain. But it can also be a source of puzzlement (and mischief), especially if it is not shown as a separate "effect." Algebraic bonuses, alas, cannot be distributed twice in the form of pay.

PRODUCTIVITY FACTOR IN WAGE-PRICE POLICY

Government efforts to establish personal, puritanical "inner checks" on wages and prices once thought to be determined by market forces add to the burden on existing productivity series and on forecasting techniques. The difficulties surrounding establishment and administration of guides for "responsible" wage and price decisions have frequently been discussed by students fearing an evolution into coercion of an initially voluntary system before its eventual collapse. Some of the critics of "jawbone" controls have become keenly aware of conundrums of productivity measurement and interpretation that impede reasonable determination and fair and sound application of guideposts.

As early as 1958, the President and the Council cautioned in the *Economic Report* that "wage increases that go beyond prospective productivity gains are inconsistent with a stable price level." The word "prospective" indicated that outlook is more relevant than trend; that any trend estimate employed in price-wage deliberations is actually to be regarded as a "naïve" forecast. The statement as a whole has a more

---

[19] The same kind of phenomenon can occur in the computation of single-industry productivity measures from industry-wide output and labor series, the only data normally available. Unfortunately, the absence of company or plant data precludes avoidance—or analysis—of this possible distortion in productivity estimation for industries.

satisfactory tone, furthermore, than the guidepost version included in the 1965 *Report,* which seems to insist "that the percentage increase in total employee compensation per man-hour be equal to the national trend rate of increase in output per man-hour." This kind of statement may gratuitously encourage emergence of a new questionable concept—a guaranteed annual wage increment equivalent to the guidepost productivity percentage. Widespread expectation of such an annual rise, reinforced by an annual increase for federal workers in conformity with guideposts relating to the private sector,[20] could easily undermine a national policy of quasi-voluntary restraint. The language of the 1966 *Report,* comparable to that of the 1965 *Report,* also seems less satisfactory than the wording of the 1958 statement cited above.

Another feature of the 1958 *Report* is the general stress on improvement of federal statistics, including productivity. In a special appendix on productivity, temporary and minor discouragement was given to the emerging cause of guideline specification—by the inclusion of (1) two sets of productivity measures for the private economy and its two major components and (2) an extensive account of "problems of measurement and meaning." Among the problems mentioned were: the theoretical multiplicity of plausible productivity measures, the dependence of meaning on the data and methods actually used, the danger that an aggregate productivity measure may lie outside the range of the measures for components, the frequent need to substitute "gross" output data for desired "net," the nebulosity of output indicators that have to be derived by means of vaguely relevant deflators (as in the case of the service industries and research activity), the multiplicity of conceivable labor-input concepts, and the nonequivalence of labor series for hours remunerated and hours worked.

The 1962 *Economic Report of the President,* which explicitly advanced the guidepost concept "as a *guide* rather than as a *rule* for appraising . . . behavior," acknowledged existence of measurement problems and of difficulties of choice among alternative indexes that may disagree. It noted that year-to-year fluctuations in productivity change complicate the selection of a trend, and that the part of change reflecting variation in capacity utilization should be isolated from trend. It also made the important point that, when comprehensive productivity measures are used as "benchmarks" for wage adjustment, allowance has to

[20] A statement made in a National Planning Association publication, *Looking Ahead,* February, 1966, p. 7, ignores the inflationary potential (both direct and indirect) of annual increases for federal workers in accordance with private-sector expectations: "The guidelines gain in persuasiveness when the Federal government adheres to them with respect to Federal workers."

be made for the changes they reflect in occupational composition and in grades.

In 1965, a former chairman of the Council of Economic Advisers made reference to many inadequacies of the statistics in his strongly critical commentary on the guideposts.[21] He felt that the price criterion would require every company to know its own industry's productivity trend in relation to aggregate experience. The present and prospective condition of the public information base, however, rules out such comparisons:

> The productivity indexes now being published, besides being often out of date, lump together a great variety of products. In time, more detailed and more current indexes of productivity will doubtless be constructed, but there are limits to what is statistically feasible. Even if measures of this type become available for each of a thousand or ten thousand industries, much confusion or perplexity will still remain.

Among the additional "puzzles," he too refers to the danger that the wage guidepost may suggest general entitlement to a wage increase already "granted" in part through payments reflecting an increase in average skill composition of the work force.

Another informed student, answering an inquiry of the Joint Economic Committee in 1965, pointed to a timeliness gap in the reporting of data on fringe benefits, requested an increase in the number of industries represented by individual productivity indexes, and called for comparable coverage of the hourly earnings and productivity measures. "It would then be possible," he observed, "to estimate unit labor costs for a larger number of industries and, hence, . . . to identify the extent to which cost pressures develop because of higher labor costs and conversely." [22]

SUGGESTIONS ON GUIDELINES

We conclude this essay with four suggestions, the first of which is to consider afresh the theoretical and statistical requirements of an ideal guidelines system. An improved system should be available for later "peacetime" periods in which guidepost monitoring may seem appropriate and in which "policy escalation" to formal wage and price control is unwanted. Important insights for improvement would be afforded by a patient test of the numerical differences between (1) available pertinent

[21] A. F. Burns, "Wages and Prices by Formula?," *Harvard Business Review,* March–April, 1965, pp. 55–64.

[22] Jules Backman, in U.S., Congress, Joint Economic Committee, *Improved Statistics for Economic Growth,* pp. 2–3.

indexes that merely satisfy the verbal algebra and (2) *ad hoc* indicators for the same variables constructed according to the principles of literal algebraic consistency. A productivity measure derived from aggregate information for an industry, a combination, or a large sector need not be arithmetically equivalent to a productivity index designed for use in conjunction with others for wages and prices. Comparisons should also be sought, of course, for alternative wage and price measures.

The second suggestion is to consider the use of explicit productivity forecasts (preferably "predictions") in wage-price guidelines when future quasi-voluntary efforts may again seem warranted. Availability of *both annual and longer-term forecasts* would be desirable, with the *more conservative* of the two figures serving as the preferred guide for decisions in a particular year. These figures, however, should be the *same* as, or *compatible* with, those used or implied in estimation of the gross national product, its major components, and other key variables in the *Economic Report of the President.*

Third, "real" wages deserve attention as well as "nominal" wages in the definition of any future guidepost policy. Unfortunately, wholesale prices seem to be of much more interest than consumer prices in the discussion of inflationary prospects. If consumer prices were introduced into the stabilization criterion (for adjustment of the nonfringe component of wages), greater official notice would have to be given to, say, the type of long-term inflation that has actually been occurring in the services. Persistently rising prices of services (which account nowadays for much of the average employee's budget) stimulate new wage demands, handicap cooperative union leaders, and typically lie beyond the reach of federal monopsony power. Of course, cost-of-living adjustments could not reasonably be superadded to those based on productivity when consumer prices rise significantly—if equity *and* inflation control are to be pursued jointly.

Finally, the wage guidepost should be restated in an algebraically equivalent form that is simpler and has certain clear analytical and administrative advantages. It does not seem to be generally appreciated that the usual criterion for assuring control of unit labor cost is the same as the following guide: *that the percentage increase in payrolls should not exceed the percentage increase in volume of output.* (If the second of the suggestions made in the preceding paragraphs were adopted, the word "prospective" should be introduced before "percentage increase in the volume of output.")

This restatement makes it easier to understand what to do in the face of intersectoral shifts, changes in skill and occupational mix of the work force, and persistent increases in living costs.[23] Furthermore, it dramatizes the adjacency of the domains of the Federal Reserve Act and the Employment Act of 1946, for monetary policy too emphasizes the role of prospective increases in output. According to the traditional formula for restraining inflation, "the growth of the money supply must be held to a rate that approximately corresponds to the expected rate of growth in real output of goods and services." [24] A common border is thus identified between the informal guidepost approach and the conventional approach deemed more appropriate to containment of diffused and increasing inflationary pressures—the classic "demand-pull" situation.

[23] The criterion might also be adjusted to refer to "real" payrolls—to give another, more explicit meaning to the concept of maximum "purchasing power" embodied in the Employment Act.

[24] "Guidelines Won't Do It Alone," *Business Week,* January 15, 1966, p. 148.

INDEX

INDEX

Crusade for Opportunity in Syracuse,
22–23, 75–76
Cultural deprivation: effects of, 4

Daley, Richard J., 76
Dana Corporation, 145
Data center, federal, 245–47
Defense Department, 232, 238, 239
Delaware:
labor force attachment of claimants
in, 134
reserve funds for unemployment in-
surance, 115, 117, 121
Denver Opportunity School, 186
Department of Agriculture, 58
Department of Commerce, 232
Department of Defense, 232, 238, 239
Department of Health, Education, and
Welfare, 12, 16, 46, 47, 48, 59
Department of Labor, 12, 16, 17, 59,
109, 127, 143n, 149, 190, 193n,
232
Dependents' allowances under unem-
ployment insurance, 101
Detroit:
multi-employer plan in, 146
unemployment benefits in, 151
unemployment studies in, 103
Development of manpower: training
programs for, 3–28
District of Columbia:
anti-poverty war in, 56
labor force attachment of claimants
in, 134
reserve funds for unemployment insurance, 114, 116, 120
Dominick, Peter H., 71
Douglas Aircraft Company, 144, 147
Dropouts from high school, 7
potential, aid to, 164–67
Dunn, Edgar S., 209n, 245, 247
Durkheim, Emile, 255

Economic activity:
federal role in, 272, 275–77
and manpower, 255–58
monitored economy, 275–77
wage-price policy, 40, 269–88
Economic change and community welfare, 201–13
ability to compete, 201–2
conditions for maintaining sound
economies, 202–3
Erie economy, 204–9, 235
exploiting obvious opportunities, 210
human resources development, 211

manpower projections, 212
public programs, 211
training programs, 212–13
Economic Development Administration, 36, 232, 258
Economic Opportunity Act, 3, 5, 6, 35,
36, 39, 43–60, 68, 84, 203, 211,
229, 257
amendments to, 71
Community Action Program, 35, 44,
51–57, 68, 69, 73–77
difficulties with, 58–60
funds allocated for, 45
groups of programs in, 44
Job Corps, 16, 17, 35, 37, 39, 44,
48–51, 59, 69
loan programs, 57–58
neighborhood youth corps, 44, 45–
47
rural loans, 44, 58
small business loans, 44, 57–8
summary of, 44
work experience program, 44, 47–48
Education:
college preparatory courses, 160–61
community colleges, 178–79
dropouts from high school, 7
Elementary and Secondary Education Act, 35, 166
and employment opportunities, 84
federal role in, 12
goals of, 41
Higher Education Act, 44, 179
industry participation in, 181–99
occupational education in Kalamazoo
County, 159–79
potential dropouts, 164–67
preparation for unskilled jobs, 162–
64
preparatory courses for technical
education, 161
trade courses for skilled jobs, 162
and war on poverty, 216
See also Vocational education
Education Office, 12, 17, 181, 195, 196,
198, 232
Election of representatives of the poor,
55–56, 75
Electrical Workers Union, 144
Employment:
job-bidding systems, 171
job-seeking behavior, 262–66
labor force attachment of claimants
for benefits, 126–36
productivity factor in, 282–84
protection for, 142

291

public employment service. *See* United States Employment Service
workings of labor markets, 262–66
Employment Act of 1946, 32, 42, 82, 229, 269–71, 274, 288
as integrating framework, 277–79
"Employment-Bound Youth," 164, 175
Employment Service Act, 86
See also United States Employment Service
Erie County, Pennsylvania, 201–13, 235
Erie Manufacturers Association, 206, 207
Europe:
government economic role, 275
labor force in, 37–38
manpower policy in, 31
Expediter team approach, federal, 16

Family planning projects, 52
Family status: and labor force attachment of claimants for benefits, 129–31
Farmers Home Administration, 58
Federal Data Center, 246–47
Federal government:
and community action, 64–67, 73–77, 203, 211, 222–24
coordination of programs, 15–17
and economic activity, 275–77
expenditures of, and Gross National Product, 66
functional organizations in, 12–13
manpower programs of, 3–28
network of federal relationships, 61–68
and poverty programs, 61–78
and state agencies, 68–73
Federal Reserve Act, 277, 288
Federal Statistics Users Conference, 275
Federalization of employment service, 86
Financing of state unemployment insurance, 118, 120
Fisher Body Division of General Motors, 170, 173
Florida:
labor force attachment of claimants in, 134
reserve funds for unemployment insurance, 114, 116, 120
unemployment insurance in, 94
Ford Motor Company, 147
Forecasting productivity and technology, 279–82

Frelinghuysen, Peter, 70
Functional organization in government, 12–13

General Electric, 205
General Motors, 170, 173
Geographical factors:
and benefit plans, 151
and employment, 262–66
Georgia:
labor force attachment of claimants in, 134
reserve funds for unemployment insurance, 114, 116, 120
unemployment insurance in, 104
vocational education center in, 177
G. I. Bill of Rights, 42, 229
Glass Workers Union, 151
Government: *See* Federal government; Communities; States
Governors and poverty programs, 69–72
Governors' Conference, 65, 71, 249
Great Britain: government economic role, 275
Gross National Product: federal expenditures, 66
Group conferences for community improvement, 216–18, 221

Hartford poverty election, 75
Hawaii:
labor force attachment of claimants in, 134
manpower authority in, 18
reserve funds for unemployment insurance, 115, 117, 121
Head Start programs, 4, 35, 52, 60
in New York City, 78
Health, Education and Welfare Department, 12, 16, 46, 47, 48, 59
Health insurance plans, 149
High schools. *See* Education
Higher Education Facilities Act, 44, 179
Hoover, Herbert, 81
Hormel wage plan, 142
Hughes Aircraft Company, 146
Human Investment Act, 212
Humphrey, Hubert, 76

Idaho:
labor force attachment of claimants in, 134
reserve funds for unemployment in-

state differences in, 133–34
See also Employment
Landrum, Phil, 74
Lanier, Jess, 71
Lansing conference, 221
Legislation:
  for employment policies, 34–35, 81–82
  for extended unemployment benefits, 139–40
  See also specific measures
Leiserson, William M., 81
Lekachman, Robert, 261
Loan programs in Economic Opportunity Act, 57–58
Local government. *See* Communities
Los Angeles:
  apprentice program in, 190
  community action in, 55
  supplemental unemployment benefits in, 146, 152
  Trade-Technical College, 186
  Watts incident, 16
Louisiana:
  Brewery Workers of New Orleans, 148
  labor force attachment of claimants in, 134
  reserve funds for unemployment insurance, 115, 117, 121

Maine: labor force attachment of claimants in, 134
Manpower Development and Training Act, 3, 5, 6, 10, 34, 35, 36, 41, 178, 185, 191n, 193n, 194, 208, 211, 212, 213, 220, 257
Manpower policy:
  and community activity, 18–20, 211–12
  coordination of programs, 15–20
  development of, 33–35, 82–84
  and economic development, 255–58
  evaluating developments in, 36–37
  federal programs, 3–28, 61–78
  future pattern of education, 4–5
  historical perspective of, 32
  integrated approach to organization, 24–27
  interdisciplinary approach to, 266–67
  international perspectives on, 30–32
  job-seeking behavior, 262–66
  neighborhood center approach, 21–24
  objectives of, 8–12, 29–30
  problem of priorities, 6–8

productivity measures and forecasts, 269–88
and public employment service, 81–88
realistic expectations, 27–28
research strategy for, 88, 229–40
state level organization, 17–18
unfinished business of, 37–42
See also Economic Opportunity Act; Employment
Marshall, Alfred, 230
Maryland:
  community conference in Baltimore, 221
  labor force attachment of claimants in, 134
  reserve funds for unemployment insurance, 115, 117, 121
Massachusetts: labor force attachment of claimants in, 134
Mayors:
  community action programs, 74–77
  U.S. Conference of, 64, 69, 74, 76
McClelland, David, 258, 263
Michigan:
  advisory committees from industry in, 181
  community colleges in, 178
  community conference in Lansing, 221
  labor force attachment of claimants in, 134
  multi-employer plan in Detroit, 146
  occupational education in Kalamazoo County, 159–79
  unemployment benefits in Detroit, 151
  unemployment studies in Detroit, 103
Michigan University, 103
Migrant workers, 262
Miller, Richard, 244n
Minneapolis meeting: National Governors Conference, 249
Minnesota:
  area vocational schools in, 177
  labor force attachment of claimants in, 134
  meeting in Minneapolis, 249
  St. Paul project, 19
Mississippi:
  labor force attachment of claimants in, 134
  reserve funds for unemployment insurance, 115, 117, 121

Dimensions of Manpower Policy:
Programs and Research

Edited by Sar A. Levitan and Irving H. Siegel

designer: Gerard A. Valerio
typesetter: Monotype Composition Co.
typeface: Times Roman
printer: Universal Lithographers
paper: Perkins & Squier GM
binder: Moore and Co., Inc.
cover material: Columbia Lynnbrook